THE JOURNALS OF A
VICTORIAN TRAVELLER

THE JOURNALS OF A
VICTORIAN
TRAVELLER

FROM THE JOURNALS OF JULIA ERRINGTON BIDDULPH,
1844-1933

MARTIN LAURIE

The Book Guild Ltd

First published in Great Britain in 2020 by
The Book Guild Ltd
9 Priory Business Park
Wistow Road, Kibworth
Leicestershire, LE8 0RX
Freephone: 0800 999 2982
www.bookguild.co.uk
Email: info@bookguild.co.uk
Twitter: @bookguild

Copyright © 2020 Martin Laurie

The right of Martin Laurie to be identified as the author of this
work has been asserted by him in accordance with the
Copyright, Design and Patents Act 1988.

All rights reserved. No part of this publication may be
reproduced, transmitted, or stored in a retrieval system, in any form or by any means,
without permission in writing from the publisher, nor be otherwise circulated in
any form of binding or cover other than that in which it is published and without
a similar condition being imposed on the subsequent purchaser.

Typeset in 12pt Adobe Jenson Pro

Printed and bound in the UK by TJ International, Padstow, Cornwall

ISBN 978-1913208-554

British Library Cataloguing in Publication Data.
A catalogue record for this book is available from the British Library.

For Catherine and my family.

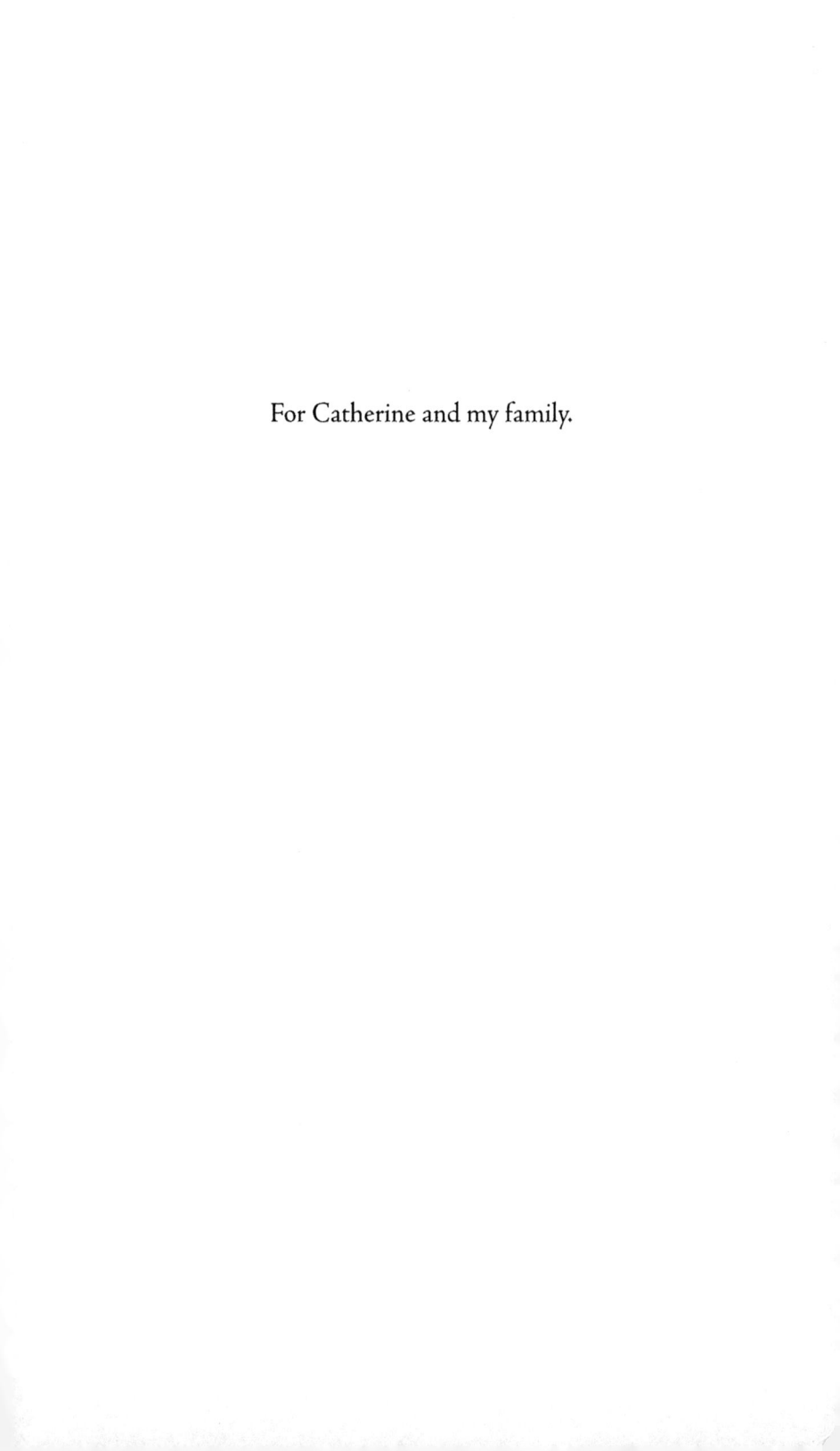

Introduction

These journals, written by Julia Errington Biddulph, are lucky survivors; they were picked out of the ruins of my great-grandmother's house in Canterbury the morning after Hitler's Baedeker raid on the city during the night of 31st May to 1st June 1942.

The Baedeker raids, sometimes known as the Baedeker Blitz, took place between April and June 1942, and were named after the famous guidebooks published by Karl Baedeker. Baedeker's guide to Great Britain was used by the Luftwaffe when choosing targets for their bombing raids on historic cities, namely Bath, Exeter, Norwich, York and Canterbury.

The journals tell the story of Julia's travels during the last two decades of the nineteenth century.

Julia Errington Martin was born in London on 22nd March 1844, the younger daughter of Inspector General Sir James Ranald Martin (1796–1874) and his wife, Jane Maria (née Paton). One of thirteen children, she had nine brothers and three sisters. Her youngest sister, Amy, would later become my great-great-grandmother. Her family had long-standing connections with India.

Julia's father had qualified as a surgeon at the age of eighteen, and in 1814 became a member of the Royal College of Surgeons. He first went to India in 1817 as Assistant Surgeon to the Honourable East India Company in Bengal. In 1821, he was appointed Surgeon to the Bodyguard of the Governor-General, the Marquess of Hastings. He was to remain in India for twenty-five years, holding many senior medical positions, eventually returning to practise in London in 1840, four years before Julia was born.

Julia Martin made her first visit to India in 1864. She was twenty years old and by her own account not at all keen to go. I do not know why she went or was sent to India at this young age, but it is probable that she went as companion to Emily Lawrence, the daughter of Sir John and Lady Lawrence. Sir John had recently been appointed viceroy. Julia travelled out with Emily and Lady Lawrence.

Julia travelled many thousands of miles across the oceans of the world during her lifetime; she was never a good sailor and suffered dreadfully from seasickness.

Julia Martin left England on Friday 21st October 1864 an anxious and rather frightened young lady; her journal for this period is in a very tattered state and a good deal of it is missing. I have transcribed as much of it as I can, because it is an important part of Julia's story and quite possibly the cause of her future travels.

Chapter I

1864

FRIDAY OCTOBER 21ST 1864.
This day I left home and England. Mamma, Frank, Robert and myself came straight to Paris. Rather a miserable day for me but I shall hope for the best.

Memo: I intend to come home to England as soon as I can.

[*As Julia does not mention their surnames it is not possible to say who Frank and Robert were. Frank, who was a soldier, travelled to India on the same ship as Julia. It is possible that Robert was one of Julia's brothers, Robert Paton Martin.*]

SATURDAY.
We had a very jolly breakfast and arranged all our plans for the day. We all went to the Louvre where we spent some hours. I was charmed with everything. Murillo's pictures and Raphael's Madonnas were enchanting. In the afternoon Mamma went to the Countess Monte St Angelo.

I, Robert & Frank went again to the Louvre where I saw the sculpture. The Venus of Milo is the thing to be seen there.

Then we went to Notre Dame the most majestic Church I have yet to see – splendid. Then I purchased some eyeglasses and some books – Martin Chuzzlewit [*Charles Dickens, 1844*] and The Last Days of Pompeii [*Edward Bulwer-Lytton, 1834*]. Then we came home and chatted with Mr Macdonald and I thought of home and felt very much inclined to cry. Robert and Frank gave me a splendid photograph book. We spent the evening with the Macdonalds [*Julia's cousins, then living in Paris*].

SUNDAY OCT. 23ᴿᴰ
A wet day, the morning tolerably fair so we went to Church somewhere in the Madeline direction.

Princess Cariati came to see us with her children whilst we had breakfast. We lunched in the Rue [de] Rivoli at a famous confectioner's. In the afternoon I got a letter from Amy [*Julia's youngest sister*], which nearly made me cry and as I was in Robert and Frank's room I had to gulp down my tears. We all went then to the Bois de Boulogne (lovely) then to the Chapel Orleans where I was much interested. We finished up with the Madeline, which is a splendid Grecian Temple. We came home and found Mr M. ill. We had a chatty little dinner altogether.

MONDAY OCT 24ᵀᴴ
Robert gave me Ether at breakfast [*ether was sometimes used by the Victorians as a sedative or calmer*], after which we all started to the station. Mamma and I left for Lyons at 11 o'clock. Robert told me in his wildest moment he thinks of going to India, in which case he would come and see me. We arrived at Lyons at half past 10 in [the] evening, dreadfully tired. Leila and the Maréchal [*marshal*] met us. He is very good and kind. I wrote a note to Amy. A wet day.

[*Maréchal François Certain Canrobert, Marshal of France, 1809–1895. Canrobert married Leila Flora MacDonald, great-granddaughter of the Jacobite heroine Flora MacDonald. Leila was Julia's cousin.*]

TUESDAY OCT 25TH
A wet day, though the morning was fine and I saw Mount Blanc and the Alps. I saw the horses, took a short walk with Leila, was very entertained with one Madame Berger with fuzzy hair, chatted much [and] was cheered about my prospects in India.

WEDNESDAY OCT 26TH
Another wet day. Mamma and I came to Marseilles, the hotel full. The King of Belgium here [and] the hotel magnificent. I wrote to Papa and could hardly help crying over it. I wrote to Leila, frightfully tired and weary.

THURSDAY OCT 27TH
My last day with my own dear Mother for some little time I fear but please God we shall meet again. We walked about Marseilles and bought a box to hold my dresses.

A coiffeur came in the morning and made Mamma pay a good deal for soap etc. Frank arrived about 12 o'clock, he lost all his valuables but after much search he found his register bag but not his sword and coat.

We three dined together. In the evening Mamma went to see Lady Lawrence. I was a good deal stared at in the streets and came to the conclusion it was my monstrously high hat (which Amy calls a brigand's hat), which attracted observation. Marseilles was in a commotion owing to a visit from the Emperor of the French, who is on his way to Nice. There are many questionings as to what the Crowned Heads are going to do there.

FRIDAY OCT 28TH
Miserable day – I left my own dear Mother – got on board the Baroda and was sick all day. Miss Emily Lawrence was in my cabin.

SUNDAY OCT 30TH
Sick all day. Heard the service from my berth. At night we came to Malta. I then got up and remained on deck till past twelve at night. I saw Malta, but dimly. Frank wrote to Mamma and he went ashore and posted the letter.

THURSDAY NOV 3RD
We reached Alexandria about 7 o'clock in the morning. Frank and I had 10 minutes' conversation, I have seen much less of him than I hoped to do. The Consul came on board and arranged all for Lady Lawrence. We came to Cairo by a special train and in the Pasha's own carriage – a magnificent saloon of damask, crimson and white. We lunched à l'Orient on the banks of the Nile at a small station. We got to Cairo about four o'clock or so; we had a distant view of the Pyramids.

We got rooms at Shepheard's Hotel on the ground floor. In the evening we took a delicious drive through a long avenue. I took a warm bath and saw a monster of an insect, which did not enhance the pleasures of the bath at all.

FRIDAY NOV 4TH
After breakfast today we went to see a magnificent Mosque, it was made of exquisite marble and the proportions were wonderfully fine. We drove through a great many of the streets of Cairo, such quaint figures met one at every turn; one could not make the most of one's eyes. The shops were very curious, the people dirty to a degree; dirt and the picturesque certainly here go together. The poor children were mostly covered with

flies. The soldiers look so very young here; there seems an immense body of them. I bought an umbrella and a fan. After luncheon we went out again in the same state. We saw two Palaces and some gardens out of Cairo, where they gave us heaps of lovely flowers; we all got tired to death.

[*Julia travelled from Cairo to Suez by train across the desert. The Suez Canal would not open for another five years in November 1869.*]

SATURDAY NOV 5TH

We left Cairo at 11.30 by especial train and reached Suez about 3 o'clock. We lunched at the hotel and then came on board the Feroge [*sic*]. The desert was interesting in its utter dreary bleakness and desolation. The Feroge was much roomier than we anticipated and to my joy I have a cabin to myself.

[*For the next eight days between Suez and Aden, Julia suffered from seasickness and heat. They passed the Straights of Bab el Mandeb on Sunday, 13th November and reached Aden the next day, Monday, 14th November.*]

MONDAY 14TH NOV.

Arrived at Aden, we went on shore at 6 o'clock in the morning. Col. Merewether and Mrs Woollcombe received us at the Residency [*Colonel, later Major-General Sir William Lockyer Merewether, 1825–1880, British Resident at Aden, 1863–1867*]. Col. Woollcombe also was there but as his wife always takes the prominent parts in the reception etc. I need say nothing about him, except that he appeared a good-natured creature enough. We had breakfast at half past ten. It was a long weary day for we had to play company nearly all day. In the evening we went to see the Tanks [*reservoirs*], which were very curious and there were some tremendous tunnels in the mountains through which we drove. We saw the 95th

Regt. march into camp. At dinner we had Capt. Burnes, Mr Goodfellow, and Mr Falconer of the 95th – a stupid dinner. Miss Macpherson slept with me, but very little sleep I got as she was continually getting out of bed. Once she washed her feet and at other times she imagined she heard a fox in her room etc.

TUESDAY.
We played at a game called the Moorish Fort all the morning. In the afternoon we went to see the shooting at the Battery and in the afternoon, or rather the evening, for it was six o'clock, we again re-embarked.

[They left Aden early the next morning, Wednesday, 16th November. Julia notes that nothing interesting occurred during the next nine days. They played quoits on deck, had a heavy storm of rain one night and the captain read a service on Sunday morning. She had also recovered somewhat from her seasickness.]

SATURDAY 26TH NOV.
Frightfully hot. I am nearly deaf with one ear I suppose I have caught cold at night. I have liked this part of the voyage from Aden to Galle [*Ceylon*] (which we hope to reach on Monday) better than I could have imagined it possible to like a week on board a steamer. The heat is great during the day but the nights are delicious.

SUNDAY NOVEMBER 27TH
All day expecting to have our coals finished. At 12 at night they were all expended, we then had to burn all the spares and ropes that could be obtained and this just cost 150£s [*sic*] to Government; however it was necessary to keep up the fires. We ladies all slept in the Captain's cabin.

MONDAY NOV 28TH
We saw land early this morning, but no one knew what land. Some naked natives in the most original of boats pointed out the direction of Galle [*Ceylon*] to us. At 2 o'clock we got into the harbour and about three we found ourselves safe in Queen's House. The heat was fearful all day. In [the] evening we went out driving. Miss Emily Lawrence and I drove in a sort of dogcart with Miss Bailey behind; the drive was lovely. The natives here are not oppressed with too much clothing. Capt. Barnes came to dinner in gorgeous apparel, epaulettes etc. and Mr Lettes (the doctor on board the "Feroge") actually talked – wonders will never cease. Miss Macpherson, Miss Bailey and I shared a room.

TUESDAY NOV 29TH
We spent the morning in bartering with the natives, the afternoon in trying to keep ourselves cool and in the evening we drove out to a missionary school. Mr Kennedy and Mr Tawney went out riding, such brutes of horses! Mr Langley was thrown just opposite Queen's House.

WEDNESDAY NOV 30TH
Re-embarked at three o'clock in the afternoon.

WEDNESDAY DEC 6TH
Sir John Lawrence came on board about six o'clock in the evening. We were lying in Diamond harbour longing to get to Calcutta. We had telegraphed twice and we hoped that the Celerity would have arrived and taken us off to Calcutta – no such luck though. At six o'clock we had given up all hopes of seeing the Celerity that day, when Mr Tawney, Miss Lawrence and I spied a green light in the distance, it came nearer and nearer and at last a ship made its appearance; at

last they called out, "The Viceroy is on board." Sir John dined with us, we did not get our dinner till long past eight and we were famished. We slept on deck and I was chilled, I thought I should have been ill; the cold was frightful, so damp. Mr Feddes never opened his mouth once at dinner except to eat, he was alarmed at the Viceroy I suppose, and Capt. Barnes was very subdued.

[*It had taken one day short of seven weeks to reach Calcutta since leaving England on that miserable October day.*]

THURSDAY 7TH

At last we are in Calcutta. We went on board the Celerity at six in the morning, breakfasted on board and got fresh bread and butter to our intense joy; it really seemed homelike to look at butter again. We landed at Budge Budge [*on the Hooghly River*]. Dr Hathaway escorted me to Mr Grote's. At Budge Budge (absurd name) the horses would not start. Miss Macpherson and I jumped out once and were on the point of returning to the Steamer when the horses started, so we rushed over, jumped into the carriage and they went on all right. Dr Hathaway talked incessantly, he told me all sorts of stories about Clara and Therese but I believe he is not always to be believed.

Lottie Grote met me most kindly and cordially. She said her father was at Government House expecting me there. Lottie is very nice looking with pretty coloured hair and a neat little figure. We played at croquet all the afternoon; Frank and Mr Grote joined us early in the afternoon and a Miss Tickle and a Mr Princep played with us. John also came, he plays croquet vilely – he is so grey but he looks very good-looking with his grey hair. Clara and he dined in the evening – Clara is discontented with John, rather nags at him and displays no affection towards him whatsoever. Clara is nicely dressed but she does her hair so badly.

Frank I was delighted to see again, there is something peculiarly winning about him; I think he is looking very well.

ALIPORE FRIDAY DEC 8TH

I lunched with John and Clara. Paid some visits with John and was taken for his wife by a Col. Lane. I saw Therese; she was looking very well. Miss Turner is a fine looking girl, but bad style. I went shopping in the afternoon; I bought myself a waistband and buckle.

Lottie picked me up in the evening for a drive on the Course, I saw all the elite of Calcutta driving and riding; I was not particularly struck with anybody. However at dinner – how odd it is, the gentlemen rising with the ladies in the dining room; it is the French custom, I think it is a bore.

I got English letters yesterday from Papa, Mamma and Amy, oh how I miss them all, no words can describe. I have no one to tell all my little gossip to, oh dear when shall I get back to England? I received an invitation to a dinner at Government House on Thursday 15th and also Lady Lawrence requested me to come and see them tomorrow.

SATURDAY DEC 9TH.

I spent the morning, or rather the day, at Government House. I was so very kindly received; the Lawrence girls took me all over the house, such a splendid ballroom.

SATURDAY DEC 23RD.

I have not been able to write a regular journal so now I must give a recapitulation of my doings.

On Monday the 11th I dined with the Turners. I wore my white silk dress and some natural roses in my hair. I went down to dinner with Frank and so I had a jolly time of it at the actual dinner, for Frank and I are great chums; but John I do find so jungely [sic], and Clara is really dreadful, she slights John on every occasion.

TUESDAY DEC 26TH.

I went to see the Lawrences again, Frank and I drove together and Major Vicars met me at Government House and took me upstairs. I found them all well but they had lost their lace pocket-handkerchiefs and were in rather trouble about it. I missed Mr Tawney as he arrived at Alipore about the same time as I got to Government House. I went to Wilson's Hotel afterwards and picked up Frank. In the evening Frank and I drove on the Course and Lottie and her father rode together.

On Wednesday I had luncheon with the Macphersons, Mary Macpherson looked much brighter than I ever saw her before; she sang and was quite brisk. There were heaps of people at the luncheon. First there was a curry, which burnt my mouth fearfully, and finally I tasted a cocoanut [sic] ice, which nearly, very nearly, made me sick. After luncheon Mr Macpherson, Miss M's brother, came and conversed with me, a most free and easy young man who said, "Oh! Gemini" to everything I said. Lottie called for me in the carriage; she and her father rode again, and Frank and I first walked round to the hockey-ground where the gentlemen were playing at hockey on horseback [polo]; a really very pretty sight, and then we drove on the Course again. On Thursday I went to Garden Reach to see Miss Barratt who was looking very fat and jolly. In the afternoon Lottie and I fought Frank and Mr Tom Lewin at croquet and we got beaten twice.

In the evening there was the Government House dinner. I wore white silk and Lottie white tarlatan trimmed with blue. At the entrance of the drawing room Mr Kennedy came forward and gave Lottie his arm and Capt. Tenpey took me,

Lady L and Sir John shook hands with me and I sat down by Miss Emily, so then I felt all right; about sixty people were assembled.

Between the drawing room and the dining hall is a curtain, this was suddenly drawn aside and we all marched in. Lady Lawrence and Sir Mark Trevelyan following Sir John and Lady T. [*more likely Sir Charles Trevelyan KCB (later 1st Baronet) 1807–1886. Trevelyan was a colonial administrator and had been Governor of Madras from 1859–1860. He was Sir John Lawrence's Finance Minister 1862–1865*]. I went with Dr Francis and I sat next to Capt. Randall one of the aides-de-camp; he is such a nice little man, a friend of Cunliffe's [*Julia's brother*] and he knows Papa. Also he is a Berkshire man so we got on together swimmingly. Frank sat opposite me with a Mrs Mackenzie, a deaf authoress with a wonderful turban-like headdress. Mr Grote, Mr Beynion, Miss Lawrence, Major Vicars etc. sat all round about, so I felt quite at home. Major Vicars and Capt. Randall tried to persuade me to stay in Calcutta for the Government House Ball and reception, so we exchanged a good deal of chaff and badinage on the subject. After dinner several people came up to talk to me; Mr Kennedy, Capt. Beynion, Mr Tawney, Mr Grant, Capt. Randall and Major Vicars. Capt. Tenpey took me into the second drawing room where Miss Lawrence and I had a chat then we all dispersed. The Lawrences asked me to come and say goodbye the next day, which I promised to do. Mr Kennedy asked me to account for any late proceedings and asked what were the reports he heard about me at mess? I suppose this is again something about Mr Church, or perhaps it is because Frank and I have been a good deal together. Getting into the carriage I shook hands with Major Vicars and was forgetting to shake hands with Mr K. He pretended to be very much hurt; I like Mr K very much.

On Friday morning I drove to Government House and bade farewell to the Lawrences. I was so sorry to say goodbye to them they have been so very kind to me and said they should hope to see me again and they were very sorry I was not going to stay in Calcutta any longer; they asked me to stay to luncheon but I could not. I gave Miss Emily Lawrence a lesson in hairdressing and then I returned to Alipore. After luncheon, Lottie, I and Frank had several games of croquet; we beat Frank each time, dear old Frank!

After dinner at eight o'clock Mr Grote, Lottie, Frank and I started for the station. Frank came across the river with me; but Lottie and Mr Grote bid goodbye to me in the steamer, I was so sorry to leave them. Col. Turner, Therese, Miss Turner, Col. Barnes and John were all fussing about, Clara was weeping, Frank and I embraced at parting and I felt as if my last link to England had broken for the time being. I knew I should be all right as soon as I got with Mary and Simon [*Julia's brother and sister-in-law; Simon Martin was serving as a judge at Ghazipur, Uttar Pradesh*]; but I found my journey so horrible. Clara cried all the first night, we had sleeping compartments with hammocks, but I could not sleep; I was so cold. We travelled all night and all Saturday arriving at Mrs Kennedy's at Benares [*Varanasi, Uttar Pradesh*], on Sunday morning at 2 o'clock.

We crossed the Ganges by a bridge of boats. Mrs Kennedy came to meet us after we had sat down to something to eat, such a dear old lady! Clara slept with me. We made our appearance in the drawing room just before luncheon. The inmates of the house were the aforesaid old lady, Capt. Kennedy her son, a bearded man, rather jolly but noisy, and her daughter Mrs Pratt.

[*Julia was on her way to stay with her brother Simon Martin at Ghazipur, which is downstream on the Ganges from Varanasi.*

Here this journal ends; it has been badly damaged and the rest of the contents lost.]

I do not know how long Julia remained in India on this, her first visit to the country where she would spend so much of her later life. She was living in London again by 1871 at her father's house in Upper Brook Street.

Chapter II

Julia married Colonel John Biddulph (1840–1921) at St Paul's Knightsbridge on 13th April 1882; she was thirty-eight, surprisingly old for the time, and her husband was forty-two. I do not know when or where she first met her husband, though I cannot help but wonder if the 'John' that she refers to whilst in Calcutta all those years ago – and who she thought was being so badly treated by the said 'Clara' – was in fact John Biddulph; it would seem that she had taken quite a fancy to him! John Biddulph would have undoubtedly been in India at the time as a serving soldier.

John Biddulph was born in London on 25th July 1840, the son of Robert and Elizabeth Biddulph of Eaton Place, London and Ledbury, Herefordshire.

John had first gone to India at the age of eighteen when he joined the Bengal Cavalry and served during the Oudh campaign of 1858.

On 1st November 1858, the Crown took over the government of India from the East India Company, which then ceased to exist. Consequently, the army in India had to be reorganised and new regiments formed from the remains of the old native regiments. On 17th August 1861, John Biddulph became a lieutenant in the newly designated 19th Hussars.

From 1872 to 1877, John Biddulph served as aide-de-camp to the Viceroy Lord Northbrook. He was given special duty as a member of the mission to Yarkand 1873–74 and employed on a secret mission to Gilgit in 1876. As Major Biddulph, he was the first British Agent at Gilgit. It was here that he wrote *Tribes of the Hindoo Koosh*. He remained on special duty in Gilgit from 1877–81.

Following their marriage in 1882 and until 1895, John Biddulph served as Political Agent or Resident in various Indian princely states, including Tonk, Ajmer, Gwalior and Baroda. He also served as a Boundary Settlement Officer at various times between 1885 and 1888.

The British Resident or Political Agent was a senior official of the British Administration who lived at the 'Resedency' in the principal town or capital of the said princely state. The Resident liaised with local monarchs, Nizams, maharajas, sultans, nawabs, etc. to aid British indirect rule; they would conduct diplomatic functions, intervene in succession disputes, boundary disputes and the rule of law.

John Biddulph was the author of several books:

- *The Tribes of the Hindoo Koosh* (1880)
- *The Nineteenth and Their Times* (1899)
- *Stringer Lawrence, the Father of the Indian Army* (1901)
- *The Pirates of Malabar, and an Englishwoman in India Two Hundred Years Ago* (1907)
- *Dupleix* (1910)

He was also a keen naturalist and collected many specimens of birds and mammals, some of which he sent to the British Museum. He discovered an unknown species of *Podoces*, which was named after him by Allan Octavian Hume as '*Podoces*' Biddulphi (*Podoces* is a ground jay or ground chough, from the crow family found in central Asia).

Biddulph was an avid collector of many other things, including ancient weapons and armour, and Indian coins. John Biddulph left his collection of Indian arms and armour to the Victoria and Albert Museum.

Julia and John Biddulph returned to England when John retired, and from 1901, they lived at Grey Court, Ham, Surrey (now demolished) until John's death in 1921. Julia then moved to Castle Street, Canterbury, where she lived until her death in 1933 at the age of eighty-nine. They had no children.

Julia Biddulph saw a great many changes during her long life. I have a letter that she wrote to my grandfather in 1928, just after his father had died, which shows just how aware she was of these changes; she was eighty-four when she wrote it.

August 7th 1928

I do not think life generally will slow down in the coming years. Though in your life I hope this year with so much that is sad and exhausting will not be repeated.

In the future I think the pace will be even faster for the World in general. The equality of the sexes, the nearness of what used to be distant countries, the demands on the brains and energies of human beings, the competition, the appetite for novelty and the longer life that exists, do not make for slow going. But I do believe that Wars will cease in time. If War is to be a mere matter of scientific poison, surly men will decline to enter War.

> Women do not now contemplate having large families in any rank in life, and in every way life has changed in detail. I often think of your little son being "mad on motors" at 2 years old, probably his little son at 2 will have aerodromes instead of stables, and his grandfather will lament.
>
> The present weather is delicious.
> With love,
> Your affectionate Aunt, Julia Biddulph

It is very 'lamentable' that her prediction, 'Wars will cease in time', has not materialised, though the rest of her letter rings quite true.

The Biddulphs had returned to London from India sometime in 1884. John had taken some leave, or 'furlough' as he called it, while he waited for a new appointment in India. They had decided to take a holiday on the Nile in much the same way as people do today. Julia is now forty-one and has been married for nearly three years; she is a confident, mature, middle-aged woman, which shows in her writing compared to that of the timid twenty-year-old who sailed for India in 1864. The year 1885 was an interesting time to be in Egypt.

In her journals Julia usually refers to her husband as 'J.B.'. I have transcribed her journals exactly as she wrote them, adding explanatory notes where possible. The world was a very different place 140 years ago and some of the events that Julia witnessed and recorded would hardly seem possible today, let alone acceptable. These journals are not intended to cause offence to anybody.

Julia spends a good deal of time sketching during her travels; I get the impression that she was quite an accomplished artist. Sadly if any of her sketchbooks were in the house in

Canterbury on that fateful night in 1942 they were destroyed. Some of her sketches may survive somewhere; I am sure she will have given many away during her long life, but who knows?

Chapter III

Egypt, 1885

TUESDAY JANUARY 20TH 1885
Crossed the channel in a cold wet fog at 10 pm having some difficulty in getting into Calais harbour owing to the very thick fog.

Had some curious fellow passengers from Calais to Marseilles; an elderly lady who existed on one lemon all the night and day, her stuttering son in vain trying to urge her to try something more substantial. And a fussy old English woman who was endeavouring to drive everybody mad because she was going to Geneva. Declaring that she had lost her purse and her keys and when everybody was in full pursuit, tranquilly remarking they were on the seat of the carriage; then trying to get out at every station, and arranging her multitudinous baskets and bags so as to injure everybody's elbows and toes.

MARSEILLES JANUARY 22ND
Left at 12 o'clock in the S.S. Sindh.

JANUARY 24TH

Arrived at Naples and spent 2 pleasant hours there, visiting the aquarium. On board the Sindh [are] some pleasant English & Americans, and an "Assorti" of foreigners. First and foremost the sister of the present Khedive [*title of the Ottoman Viceroy of Egypt from 1867–1914, Mohammed Tewfik Pasha, Khedive from 1879–1892*], a large lady with a quantity of fair hair who was travelling under the protection of a French or Mexican millionaire, the happy owner of an immense stomach and a perpetual grin.

SUNDAY JANUARY 25TH

Horribly rough, getting worse towards evening; ending in a regular first class storm.

MONDAY

Rough and very unpleasant but storm subsiding, everybody presenting a care worn appearance, very few presenting any appearance at all.

TUESDAY JANUARY 27TH.

Crawled on deck.

JANUARY 28TH

Arrived at Alexandria and put up at the Abbat [*Hotel*]. The Princess and her Mexican adorer adorned the head of the table d'hôte. The lady indulging in great mirth and her aide-de-camp trying to appear in high spirits though still carrying the traces of the storm on her countenance, the poor woman having suffered fearfully on board the Sindh.

We took a drive before dinner and went out of the Rosetta Gate to come upon a little village of Arab tents looking so out of place among the houses.

[*The Biddulphs had arrived in Egypt on 28th January 1885; the very same day that Brigadier-General Sir Herbert Stewart's relief column reached Khartoum during the Nile Expedition to relieve General Gordon. In fact Stewart had been mortally wounded on 19th January and his command handed to Sir Charles Wilson, who arrived only to find that the town had fallen to the Mahdists, and that Gordon was already dead. Gordon had been killed on 16th January (Major-General Charles Gordon, 1833–1885). Although the Biddulphs had arrived in Egypt during the height of the Sudan Campaign (1881–1889), it would seem that the war had little effect on the tourist industry.*]

JANUARY 29TH

We went on a long drive after breakfast and visited some gardens belonging to a Greek Merchant; formerly the Khedive's property. In the garden were a motley crew of statues, a plaster Neptune and some marble representations of Columbus, Nelson and several thin looking ladies, who might be Venuses or Dianas, but if so they had long suffered from famine judging by their very thin limbs & distressed countenances, perhaps they were intended for cholera and hunger.

In the garden were the remains of a Greek temple or catacomb completely underwater and covered with lovely maidenhair fern. J.B. was carried on a gardener's back to inspect the altar, which had a serpent carved on it. A heap of bones were lying in one corner.

When J.B. returned, the Dragoman [*interpreter and guide*] grandly offered me a mount on the gardener's back.

Saw some curious snake like creeper, which the Dragoman said was supposed to be a cure for leprosy if rubbed on the skin.

We were also much struck by the lovely bougainvillea which grew all over the house in two colours, the usual red lilac colour and a bright orange red, the two colours growing together.

When we returned [we] found M. & R. Martin just arrived by the Brindisi Steamer and looking battered after a very rough disagreeable voyage. We all did justice to luncheon. By the by, on board the Sindh we were introduced to an old friend under a new name, 'Oeufs à la Mirroir' was on the menu one day – fried eggs being the result.

After luncheon we started off to see some of the disabled forts and had only just time to scamper through two before leaving by the 6 o'clock Express for Cairo.

[M & R Martin: Richard and Mary Martin. Richard Martin (created 1st Baronet 1905) was Liberal MP for Tewkesbury until the seat was abolished under the Reform Act of 1885. He later became Liberal Unionist MP for Droitwich, Worcestershire. His wife, Mary, was born a Biddulph and was a cousin of John Biddulph.]

JANUARY 30TH
Cairo.

We arrived on Thursday night to find rain and mud triumphing in Cairo, but this morning fortunately only the mud survived. London mud is a poor thing compared to Cairo mud, which is decidedly a thing of substance.

After luncheon we drove to a Mosque on the old Cairo road to see and hear the howling Dervishes, a very curious sight, the devotees shouting and gasping and waving backwards and forwards, flinging their hair over their faces.

Having done the Dervishes we attended a small race meeting where most of Cairo society was assembled and where we met the Barings.

[Sir Evelyn and Lady Baring, Baring was Consul General in Egypt, 1883–1907. Baring and John Biddulph had met in India during the 1870s while Baring was serving as private secretary to his cousin, the Viceroy Lord Northbrook and Biddulph was on Northbrook's staff. Baring was later created 1st Earl of Cromer 1901.]

The menagerie race between a turkey and a monkey was very amusing, the monkey coming in at a gallop at last. At the last race of the sort, Lord C. Beresford ran an Ibis or Paddy bird, which he had been training most carefully. Unfortunately wishing to get a good start, he hit the bird such a whack that the astonished creature buried his head so far into the sand he couldn't extricate it again, but it remained anchored. The egg race was very well ridden, two riders keeping their eggs in the ladles until the end, making a dead heat of it.

[Lord Charles Beresford, Royal Navy, 1846–1919, 2nd son of the Marquess of Waterford, he was later admiral and created 1st Baron Beresford. Lord Charles served on General Wolseley's staff during the Nile Campaign and commanded the Naval Brigade on the Nile.]

JANUARY 31ST

We made a very early start of it, getting off about ½ past 9 in the morning and visiting the Boulak Museum, besides taking a long drive through the streets before luncheon.

A wooden figure of a Sheikh quite 4,000 years old interested us all immensely; the figure being so wonderfully life like and so wonderfully perfect. The mummies, jewellery, bronzes etc., were all very interesting and so excellently arranged. We also visited a Mosque before luncheon, the Hassanein.

After luncheon we made a long and tiring expedition to the Citadel, 1360 A.D., Sultan Hassan's Mosque, the Well of Joseph, the Tombs of the Caliphs etc., coming home in pouring rain with no desire to continue our Mosque hunting.

The view from the Citadel is very fine, the town lying below one, the Pyramids standing out boldly, and beyond, far away, the green Delta, with Pyramids again to the left.

The old 31st [*Regiment of Foot*] were occupying the Palace in the Citadel and apparently had the best quarters in Cairo.

Sultan Hassan's Mosque is the finest in Cairo, tumbling to pieces though, with great cracks in the walls. It was made out of the blocks of stone or casing stones of the Pyramids. The Mosque in the Citadel is far more modern and made of alabaster mostly, or rather faced with it. The finest thing is the court where the worshippers perform their ablutions, with the long corridors almost like cloisters running round the court. The coloured windows inside the Mosque are horrible, such vulgar staring colours.

We had a very rough drive over sand to get to the Tombs of the Caliphs. J.B. and R. & M. having to get out of their carriage once while a broken trace was being repaired, & another time we all had to get out of our carriages while they were heaved over some stones in an archway.

We then drove through miles of tombstones. A mad, monotonous drive, and we were not at all rewarded by the beauty of the Tombs when we arrived. Crowds of dirty little girls screeched at us for "Baksheesh".

We all put on the customary slippers on entering the tomb when the old custodian suddenly discovered it was not necessary for ladies, so M & I gladly got rid of the horrid things.

We dined with the Barings and met several people who are at Shepheard's [*Shepheard's Hotel, Cairo*]. The Barings' house is quite lovely; the walls completely covered with Indian stuffs. In one room all the lamps with crimson shades, in the next blue, giving the effect of red & blue rooms. We had an excellent dinner and enjoyed the evening very much.

FEB 1ST SUNDAY

I went to Church with Mary, Richard, Mr Lucas etc. and we had a long sermon without much point, the subject being the labourer worthy of his hire; in which the clergyman quite lost himself and said nobody had the right to complain of their promotion as everybody must be in their right places. Providence guiding the authorities that be.

After luncheon we drove to the Coptic Church which is exceedingly interesting, with a most lovely carved wooden screen and some very fine ivory inlaid work; then the Greek Church and on to the Nilometer.

There I refused to do anymore sight seeing, so went for a long drive down the Shoobra Road and saw the Khedive and his two little sons, and had tea with Lady Baring afterwards.

[*The Nilometer, built 1,000 years ago (AD 861) on the southern tip of Rhoda Island, used to measure the water levels of the River Nile.*]

FEBRUARY 2ND

We spent the morning in the Bazaars and shoved about in a very unsavoury crowd. The carpet bazaar was very amusing, but the picturesque saddlebags smelt so fearfully that no amount of beauty could cover the defect. I came away from a morning's shopping with one spoon made of horn and mother o' pearl.

For the afternoon we drove to Heliopolis to the Virgin's tree (which the Virgin was supposed to rest under before entering Egypt) and then to the Ostrich farm, which was most interesting.

There were 300 ostriches in the farm, the owner Mr Otto Wetter, said he made a profit of 12£s [sic] yearly on every ostrich and hoped soon to have 1000. The incubation (which is artificial) room was very attractive. The eggs take from 37 to 49 days to hatch, and a few days before hatching the eggs are lightly chipped with a hammer, which is supposed to help the chick. The birds do not lay till they are three years old but their feathers are valuable before that age. An old cock bird in good plumage yields 30£s [sic] worth of good feathers a year, and Mr Wetter said the old birds were extremely pugnacious and attack everybody who goes near them. It takes ten men to hold down a bird while he is being plucked.

FEBRUARY 3RD

We left about 11.30 for the Pyramids with the Lucases and had a charming cool drive. Before starting J.B. and I drove up to the Citadel to enquire for Colonel Taylor in a thick white fog, which was extremely chilling, but when the fog cleared the day was delicious.

On nearing the Pyramids I felt disappointed as they look so much larger when quite far away in the distance, than they do in proportion as one approaches, until one is quite under them, and then indeed one does realise their size.

I felt no great desire to mount the Great Pyramid after seeing Mrs Lucas pulled and pushed up some way, then she became giddy and had to return. Every Arab accompanying her staring in her face offering her water, one especially asking tenderly how she felt as he said he was the doctor; most of them offering her antiquities and all without exception asking for "baksheesh".

I scrambled up to the gateway and sat there and looked across at distant Cairo, with the great plain of green between us. Only one of our party scrambled to the top, and when he returned we had luncheon. And then Mrs Lucas mounted her donkey, "Ginger Bob" while I got on "American George" and rode to the Temple of the Sphinx and passed a great Tomb with a Sarcophagus at the bottom called Campbell's Tomb. The enormous blocks of granite in the Temple were most wonderful, the cornerstones especially, all fitting with marvellous niceness. The Sphinx has become so familiar to everyone long before one sees it and yet I don't think I at all realised it till it was actually before me, it seems somehow a sort of living thing compared to the Pyramids. I suppose the Pyramids were built so far away on the edge of the desert as the land round the towns had become valuable and was all secured for cultivation, and then when the sand was found to drift so, and cover all objects so quickly, and Kings were anxious to have a lasting memorial of their greatness, they were obliged to build something of a great height, and so designed the Pyramidal form for their tomb.

FEBRUARY 5TH

Went up to the Citadel with J.B. early in the morning and saw the Canadian voyagers there. They were shown all the sights of Cairo, having tea at the Pyramids. A queer looking lot, a good many of them half bred Indians. I believe they have struck work and have not been a great success.

[*The Canadian Voyageurs, or Nile Voyageurs as they were known at the time, were Canadian boatmen and lumbermen, many of them Indians, who had been employed at the request of General Sir Garnet Wolseley to operate the boats on Wolseley's Nile Expedition to relieve Gordon at Khartoum. Wolseley chose the Voyageurs after his experiences in Canada during the Red River rebellion of 1870, when he had led the expedition against the Métis leader Louis Reil at Fort Garry, Manitoba. The request for the Voyageurs was telegrammed from the British Colonial Office to Lord Lansdowne, the Governor-General of Canada on 21st August 1884, to engage 300 good Voyageurs from Caugnawaga, Saint Regis and Manitoba, as steersmen in the boats for the Nile Expedition. The Voyageurs arrived in Egypt in October 1884 and remained for six months. Their contract ended on 9th March 1885 and although higher wages were offered to encourage them to stay longer, many decided to return to*

Canada for the spring logging season. The Voyageurs whom Julia saw in Cairo would have been en route to Alexandria to begin their journey home. Contrary to Julia's belief that the Voyageurs had not been a great success, Wolseley's expedition would have been very difficult without them; their experience in handling and navigating the small, heavily laden boats up and downstream and through the Nile cataracts was unique and professional; it was also backbreaking work. The Voyageurs were thanked and praised by both Wolseley and the British Government.

General (later Field Marshal) Sir Garnet Wolseley led the Nile Expedition to relieve Gordon at Khartoum. Wolseley was created Baron Wolseley in 1882 and in September 1885 he was created 1st Viscount Wolseley; his statue stands on Horse Guards Parade, London.]

After luncheon I went to the Jeseerah [*Gezirah*] Palace with the Lucases, and was much struck by the vile taste inside the Palace. Splendid rooms furnished from Paris with the most glaring colours. One room was apple green and yellow satin, the large centre ottoman being half green & half yellow. The bathroom was most gorgeous being all blue satin, ceiling & walls; while the large ballroom & reception rooms had the walls distempered and whitewashed only.

Just as I was starting for the Barings I was told by Colonel Schwale that Khartoum had fallen, the dismay and horror on everybody's face in the hall at Shepheard's Hotel told the tale even before Colonel Schwale told me.

Khartoum had fallen on the 26th, Sir Charles Wilson getting up to its walls found no British flag flying and was obliged to retreat under heavy fire; he and his party on two steamers were then wrecked; and steamers had gone to their assistance.

I found E.B. [*Sir Evelyn Baring*] looking sadly worn and tired, Sir E.B. had received the news early in the morning, but Lord Wolseley had stressed that it should not be made public for 24 hours. It was telegraphed home, and came back public property. We all were very down hearted and nothing else was talked of during dinner.

I went to the Opera afterwards, leaving J.B. to pack and write at home.

"La Perichole," and the Ballet was most inferior with hideous costumes. Several fat, middle aged women being dressed as a sort [of] Robin Hood, with a large gap between their boots and knickerbockers, and others in thick stiff short skirts bordered with velvet.

FEBRUARY 6TH FRIDAY

We left Shepheard's at 7.30 in the morning to catch the early train for Assioot [*Asyut*]. The Railway station was very amusing; English soldiers, Egyptian ladies, French and German travellers, and a wedding party provided with bouquets and bonnet boxes to stock a small store. About ½ past 10 we picked up R. & M. who had been to the Fayum [*the Faiyum Oasis, south of Cairo and west of the Nile*].

We passed a good many interesting places, the Pyramid of Maydoom [*Meydum*], and the miles of bean fields struck one very much after the small ones at home. We passed quantities of sugar cane and Soya Mills in all the larger towns.

A lovely sunset with such a beautiful glow on the hills, and then half an hour of darkness before we got into Assioot, the dust had been most affecting all day, and the dust and heat combined had well nigh tired us out.

The confusion at the Assioot Railway Station was great. J.B. and I rode on donkeys to the steamer, I protesting all the time against the Egyptian saddle – my first experience of this uncomfortable seat. And the night being so dark I could see nothing, made me very thankful when the lights of the steamer showed and I jumped off much quicker than I got on.

An inspection of our very small cabin did not make me thankful, there being hardly room to turn round in, though I managed at once to upset the water can and gave J.B. an opportunity of doing housemaid and restoring our tiny apartment to order. Everybody ran about with bags and bundles for the final half hour and then we sat down to a terribly nasty dinner, after which we sat on deck in rather a melancholy manner while the soldiers were sorted out and put in a pen for the night. And sundry good Mohammedans wrapped themselves up into bundles and went to sleep, and then were kicked up and everybody seemed generally to be in the wrong place, till I found myself in bed which I discovered to be exactly the right place and ended my first day's journey up the Nile.

FEBRUARY 7ᵀᴴ

A lovely day, we all sat on the deck of the steamer and watched the many birds, Herons, Ibis, Ducks, Sheldrakes, Vultures, Spoonbills, Plover etc. The Nile boats with their two graceful sails, the tombs in the sides of the hills, the quaint little mud villages; one especially amused us looking like a clump of little castles, all the little huts having castellated tops made of mud. Richard and I sketched several little bits of the Nile, the Nile boats etc., and amused ourselves very much.

We passed several big towns, Soohag [*Sohag*] and Ekhmeem [*Akhmim*] being the largest. We watched an immense number of people making a canal and I was delighted to think I had seen a Corvee [*free feudal labour*] while I pointed out an old man with a stick as the Sheikh of the village to Mary, who at once accepted the fact, as I did, that of the Corvee.

The evening was most lovely as we got to Ekhmeem [*Akhmim*] and we were looking back upon a lovely stretch of the river with the sunset glow on the hills.

The people were still very busy, and building was going on close to the banks; the men throwing up the bricks to the workmen on the roof of the houses who caught them most neatly every time without fail.

We stopped at Gingeh for the night, getting there about 8.30 and J.B. went on board another steamer that was stopping there for the night, and found the Colvins on board; they were returning to Cairo after a very pleasant visit to Thebes. They came back with J.B. and had a long chat about many things, especially the voyage on board the "Kaiser-i-Hind" [*SS Kaiser-i-Hind, a P&O steamer, built 1878*]. Of course they had not heard the bad news about Khartoum and were very anxious to hear all the particulars of the telegram.

FEBRUARY 8TH SUNDAY

Sketched again and had a little service after breakfast with a sermon from an American Missionary, in which he introduced a great many anecdotes about Washington; but no doubt it interested the soldiers who were very nice and attentive.

We have a party of 5 or 6 Engineers going up to Assouan [*Aswan*], and a Commissariat Officer taking white umbrellas up to Lord Wolseley and the soldiers. [*Lord Wolseley had ordered 1,000 white umbrellas to keep the sun off the Camel Corps, which then became known as the 'Nile Circus'.*]

We passed Tarrivoust and Richard went ashore there to send a telegram; there seemed a flourishing trade in water jars judging by the large quantities lying on the banks of the river. Tarrivoust was once famous for its breed of horses and sheep dogs.

We got to Keneh just before dinner and found it too late to go on shore or see anything but we were much agitated all dinnertime between our efforts to get some dinner and see the lovely sunset. At last the sunset won and we sat outside and watched the afterglow with intense satisfaction; such a lovely orange colour fading into the grey river very slowly.

Richard lighted a candle and put it into a little box; Colonel Crozier scrambling into a boat to start it, the little light sailed away (or rather floated) down the river keeping on burning for quite five minutes and at last disappeared in a small flare, the box having caught light.

Everybody but myself lighted their cigarettes; coffee was brought to us and we thoroughly enjoyed the lovely restful scene, hardly a sound to be heard, except a very short bark from a dog that we thought must come from the superior breed mentioned by Murray, it was so different from the usual Egyptian dog's shrill voice [*J Murray*, Handbook for Travellers in Egypt, *1874*].

FEBRUARY 9TH

Arrived at Luxor in the morning and stayed for a few minutes only to land some passengers, among them the Missionary and his wife and a terrible man who we called always the "Dom Palm" as he never would allow anybody any peace, but was always pointing out Dom Palms, or regretting that somebody or other had arrived on deck two minutes too late and so missed a Dom Palm [*the doum palm is a tree native to North Africa, also known as the gingerbread tree; it has edible fruit and its leaves are used in basket making*].

We had quite a hurricane of wind and the awning had to be taken down so there was no sketching to be done.

Immediately after dinner everybody hurried off to see a Temple at Esuch [sic] where we stopped about ½ past 6. J.B. and I walked about the deck until they returned saying the Temple was well worth seeing. So then we started off, an Arab at once pulling me up the sandbank and we followed a guide with a lantern, passing through a quaint market place until we came to the gates of the Temple. Some boys with rope and lanterns which they lighted, then showed us down some steps and we found ourselves in a magnificent Temple with immense columns, all covered with hieroglyphics.

The decorations on the walls are lovely, with sharply cut figures of men with beasts' heads, and every inch almost covered with writings and figures cut deeply into the stone. We returned to the steamer with a small crowd showing us the way with lanterns, one little boy being most active, a mite of about 7 years old skipping about here and there.

While we were having tea an English officer came in and talked over the Khartoum news; he had been buying camels and was quite ignorant of our disasters. He told us that in Aboo [*Abu*] Klea, the first fight (Metemmeh) lately, they had lost 500 camels as they had made a barricade of the animals [*the Battle of Abu Klea, 17th January 1885; the column advanced to the town of Metemmeh on 19th January*], and were now very much crippled for want of camels, the price of camels seems to have doubled since the war began. The officer (Capt. Lovatt) saying he had bought the best Egyptian camels for the Egyptian Camel Corps at 9 Napoleons each, and now he paid 15 ½ sovereigns apiece, and for very inferior animals.

FEBRUARY 10TH TUESDAY

We got up early as the steamer stopped at Edfoo [*Edfu*] for three hours in the morning that we might see the great Temple. The Temple is seen from some distance, the towers of the Propylon [*monumental gateway*] standing out against the sky. It is a most beautiful Temple, and we were all fascinated with the figures carved on the walls [of] a long gallery going round the Temple, every inch covered with figures of Gods & Kings etc. and all sorts of interesting scenes, boats especially, one being manned with birds.

We mounted to the top and looked down upon the village; the pigeon towers, the little Mosque, and a long stretch of green corn with the desert beyond. We found the cartouche of the two kings by whom the Temple was begun & completed. Richard and I tried to make a sketch of the gateway and then we had to hurry back to the steamer.

The steamer stopped again for half an hour at the quarries where most of the stone was cut for the Temples; but there was not much to be seen in so short a time.

FEBRUARY 11TH WEDNESDAY
Arrived at Assouan [*Aswan*] early in the morning, having been roused up at sunrise by everybody buzzing about in eager expectation. It is very pretty coming into Assouan with the banks so green, and dark rocks scattered about.

Elephantine Island was dotted all over with white tents and the Dahabiehs [*type of Nile boat*] were full of soldiers and there was a great feeling of soldiers everywhere. We moored alongside of a Dahabieh full of Engineers; it is used as a telegraph office.

We walked through the Bazaars before going to the train that was to take us to Philae, and were offered ostrich feathers, Moses baskets, and "Madame Nubias"; the latter are fringes of strips of leather ornamented with a few shells, the only costume worn by the ladies of Nubia. The said fringes are steeped in castor oil and the greater the coquette, the stronger the castor oil.

Then we went up to the station where we fell in with Capt. Yorke who travelled with us to Philae. At Philae we saw some of the Egyptian army who were going to the Front, and were much struck with their sturdy looks and smart appearance.

We crossed over to the Temples in a small boat and visited the Pharaoh's Bed & the Temple, it is beautifully situated and there is a capital view of the Cataract from the top of one of the towers of the Propylon. The walls are covered with figures and hieroglyphics. Isis giving birth to Horus, and kings slaying a lot of captives in a bunch and many other scenes, but the figures have been sadly mutilated and the rubbish about is annoying, as well as the dust and the children begging for Baksheesh.

After luncheon in Pharaoh's Bed and a further inspection of the Temple, we went down in a big boat to the Cataract, which I thought much more interesting than the Temple. Several natives swam through the big gate of the Cataract for our benefit, one man on a log, and the others without anything. The Cataract swimmers then became vociferous for Baksheesh and we returned to our boat leaving Richard to play with the shouting blacks.

We found we had an hour and a half to spare before the train left, but fortunately Colonel Hallam Parr [*Sir Henry Hallam Parr 1847–1914, Adjutant-General and second in command of the Egyptian Army, 1885*] did the Good Samaritan and gave us tea on board his Dahabieh; it was delightful to sit in the cool little room after a real baking all day long.

Capt. Yorke came back with us in the train and afterwards dined with us and we had a long talk about the war.

The little French lady accompanied us everywhere on our day's expedition; I have never described this queer little woman who is travelling quite alone and is full of intelligence & activity. She is dressed in the very shabbiest manner, with a short grey dress, shoes down at the heel, wearing no bonnet and carrying no parasol; but speaks English & Italian, has travelled all over Algeria, Spain & Italy, asks for no help from anybody and enjoys herself immensely apparently.

It was very lovely looking at the Philae Temple standing out against the sun setting as we came home in the train, with the palm trees all round; but one's interest is much divided between all the military life and the antiquities. I think the English occupation gives great zest to one's interest & enjoyment of Egypt.

We heard today among other snaps of gossip that Lord Wolseley's private mailbag had gone astray for the second time and he had been telegraphing furiously for it. I suppose it will be returned as the first one was, when all the useful information to the Mahdi has been extracted.

[Muhammad Ahmad bin Abd Allah, 1844–1885, had proclaimed himself the Mahdi in 1881. The Mahdi was played by Laurence Olivier in the 1966 film Khartoum, while Charlton Heston played Gordon.]

They say the French are exceedingly troublesome at the Front. The news of the fall of Khartoum was received on Friday evening the 6th at Assouan [Aswan] just before dinner, and it was being discussed freely before the servants, when another telegram arrived saying the news was to be kept secret, rather late in the day. Sir Charles Wilson appears to have behaved with great gallantry in this last affair.

[Major-General Sir Charles Wilson KCB KCMG, 1836–1905. Wilson took command of the Desert Column after Sir Herbert Stewart was mortally wounded; he reached Khartoum on 28th January 1885 to find that the Mahdists had seized the town and the inhabitants slaughtered, including General Gordon. Here the handwriting changes to that of Julia's husband, Colonel John Biddulph.]

Owing to a curious want of foresight the troops in Assouan have till now been encamped on Elephantine Island, and the stores & sick on the mainland. The fall of Khartoum and possibility of other troubles arising from local disaffection has brought home to the military mind the mistake of this and the troops are now being shifted to the mainland, while the hospital & stores are being transferred to the island.

To the rear of Assouan covering the plain on the desert side a small mud redoubt has been constructed. The two towers at the angles were formally windmills erected 85 years ago to grind corn for the French troops; the tops have been knocked off & they now make good flanking towers for our men. It is queer to find ourselves treading on the Frenchman's heels in this way.

In the Temple of Isis at Philae is a tablet with the names of the Commandants & Staff under Desaix [*General Louis Charles Antoine Desaix, 1768–1800*] who came here, "in pursuit of the Mameluks after the occupation of Egypt & Battle of the Pyramids under Genl. Bonaparte". Above is painted in carefully formed letters, "Une page d'histoire ne doit pas être salie" [*A page of history should not be sullied/soiled*] as if a more pretentious inscription had been first intended. In another place the Longitude (East of Paris) and Latitude, are carefully chiselled & this was probably the first time they had been precisely ascertained.

Everything is dated "the 7th year of the Republic". Mois Ventose [*the sixth month of the French Revolutionary Calendar, 19th February to 20th March*], which corresponds to 1799. In the Edfoo [*Edfu*] Temple where officers and men of the 21st Chasseurs have inscribed their names, the date 1799 only is employed.

A great quantity of railway rolling stock has arrived. It was originally built for us at the Cape; [it] is of a different gauge from the Assouan railway so it is therefore useless, & even if it could be used, is not required. This is a specimen of the way in which money is wasted in war times. The length of the Cataract itself is 4 miles; the rail round it is about seven. The Cataract itself hardly deserves the name, it is rather a series of rapids with innumerable black rocks irregularly scattered along the whole distance; the channels are narrow and winding & require a pilot. The fall is only 7 or 8 feet in the whole distance.

[*Julia Biddulph:*]

FEBRUARY 12ᵀᴴ

The dreadful bad news arrived at Assouan of poor General Earle's death [*Major General William Earle CB, 1833–1885, killed at the battle of Kirbekan, 10ᵗʰ February 1885; his statue by Charles Bell stands outside St George's Hall, Liverpool*]. It was telegraphed that he was killed while leading his troops; the other wing also lost their leader Lt. Col. Eyre [*Lieutenant Colonel Philip Eyre, 1ˢᵗ South Staffordshire Regiment*]. Our side had a complete success, 7 men & 2 Egyptians only were killed, but several officers fell & Colonel Wauchpole of the Black Watch was severely wounded [*the British losses were nearer sixty and the Mahdists some 2,000*].

Elephantine Island is very green and pretty, but there is nothing much to see on the Island. The people are Nubians and the women were very anxious to sell us their ornaments and some very dirty baskets. The Bazaars at Assouan have not many attractive objects for sale; baskets, beads, Nubian women's apron fringes, horns, and such like things. The Nubian women's attire are manufactured expressly for Europeans to buy, it is difficult to get a real "Madame Nubia". [*Madame Nubia is a type of decorated fringe or skirt worn by young women; it is made from many strips of platted leather.*]

We left Assouan about ½ past 3 in the afternoon. Two officers came on board, Colonel Gordon, 93ʳᵈ and a Canadian officer. Om-Khombo was our halting place for the night.

FEBRUARY 13ᵀᴴ

Left the steamer at Luxor about 6 p.m. At Edfoo [*Edfu*] Capt. Lovatt came on board and told us many things about the Egyptian Army. He said General Baker's army [*Valentine Baker, 1827–1887, 'Baker Pasha'. The Battle of El Teb, 4ᵗʰ*

February 1884] was composed of men who were caught from the fields and who had no notion of handling firearms or even defending themselves in any way. They were simple Fellaheen and in terror at the idea of going to the Soudan, which they regard as their Siberia. Some of them were given Remington Rifles, but many of them had no weapons at all, not even a stick. They were taught no formation, or maintaining any military order and were more like a flock of sheep than an army of soldiers. General Baker was hurried off with these poor fellows and then they were attacked; he and his brilliant staff were so far off from them that by the time he got up to his own army it was destroyed, and he & his Staff had to cut their way through the masses of murdered men and the murderers.

Once in Cairo, Capt. Lovatt took these poor men out for rifle practice; they had only Remingtons and Capt. Lovatt took one from one of the men, lay down and fired at the target, making a Bull's-eye the first time; the next shot was a flare, his eyelashes and eyebrows gone, and he saw nothing for half an hour, the rifle having burst. This happened to ten men in a short time till Capt. Lovatt lost all patience and brought the men home, refusing to go out with them again, the rifles being so dangerous.

Colonel Gordon dined with us at the table d'hôte at the Luxor hotel.

FEBRUARY 14TH

We left early for the Tombs of the Kings starting about 8.30. Colonel Crozier told us at breakfast that when he gave his coat to be brushed, one man put it on while another brushed it.

I got on No: 1 donkey, a most lively moke with a powerful voice and high action. I led the way as he would allow no other donkey to pass him & whenever he saw anybody in front, he raised his voice tremendously. The little girls who ran by our side carrying water on their heads were pretty; one little girl especially, Fatima by name, had a sweet little face.

We had to cross the river before we got onto our donkeys, and again had to get into a boat to cross a canal. Donkeys, water carriers, donkey boys, guides and ourselves all crammed into a very dirty old boat. Fortunately my noble steed was game to carry me into the water, to & from the boat, but the other ladies had to be carried.

We first visited the temple of Koomeh or Gooma [*Guma*], which did not take us very long to see, dedicated to the memory of Ramasses I by Settie [*Seti*] & finished by Ramasses II, now in very bad repair. We were not happy till we had made out outlines of the Ethiopian Ox and Capricorn mentioned by Murray; having done that we mounted our donkeys again and had a good hour's ride to the Tombs of the Kings. A hot ride too, the road winding between hot bare hills without an atom of vegetation to be seen anywhere.

No: 2 the Tomb of Settie I [*Seti I*] called Belzoni's Tomb [*Giovanni Belzoni, 1788–1823, discovered the Tomb of Seti I*] and No: 6 the Tomb of Ramasses IX, were the three we saw, and I believe the best to be seen. The colouring in Belzoni's Tomb is most wonderfully fresh and the figures that were drawn only, and not finished were very interesting, the outlines so bold and clear. In No: 6 the animals, ducks, bees & beetles took our fancy, and I took a portrait of a Bee.

FEBRUARY 15TH SUNDAY

Capt. Lovatt invited us to see his camels that he had been buying for the Front. They were all collected at the Consul's house a little out of the town and were very small weak looking animals, most of them unfit for much work, several of them ill and all very thin. The highest price had been given for these animals 15£s [*sic*], as they are now so much in demand. I mounted the Consul's own particular camel but found it decidedly uncomfortable. Coffee and cigarettes of course were handed round.

Luxor Temple is so full of dirt & debris that one cannot comfortably enjoy it, but it is very fine and the obelisk is splendid, the finest we have seen yet. It will take a long time to clear out all the rubbish from the Temple and excavate the colossal figures at the entrance. Meanwhile the children throwing the dirt and earth down the bank of the river renders sightseeing a perfect misery.

Several Dahabiehs and steamers have come in; General Baker and his party from Assiout [*Asyut*], Lord Abinger and Col. and Mrs Maitland from Wady Halfa [*Wadi Halfa*] in the Khedive's yacht.

The accounts of poor Sir Herbert Stewart are bad; they say he is worse as they cannot extricate the ball [*Sir Herbert Stewart died of his wounds 16th February 1885*].

In the afternoon we went to Karnak; the Great Hall, the first gateway and the Obelisks are splendid. The Great Hall or Hall of the Pillars strikes one immensely and one enjoys lingering about in it looking at all the sculptures and staring up at the gigantic pillars. The rest of the huge ruins is such a mass of fallen pillars and stones that it is quite impossible to make out what the buildings were.

The Consul gave an evening party, to which Lord Abinger, the Maitlands, Mr Moore etc. came. Coffee & cigarettes and dancing girls, the latter are most repulsively ugly and dance without any grace whatever, their movements are most objectionable and the entertainment does not present a single pleasing feature. The music was terribly monotonous, 5 musicians played, one with a small stringed instrument and the others beat small drums with their hands.

FEBRUARY 16TH

J.B. and I went alone to Karnak and examined the sculptures on the north wall of the big Hall for some time. The scenes with the Kings fighting in their chariots, and the captives being dragged along in gangs are most spirited, and the different types of prisoners are so curious.

J.B. noticed the first sword he had seen depicted; a King slaying his enemy with a curious curved sword, something like a scimitar. Some of the captives are handcuffed in a strange manner; also we noticed a row of prisoners with cartouches on, evidently with their names written on them, they were all featured together and were, we supposed, men of rank from some distant country.

In the evening we dined with the British Consul and had an Arab dinner. We all sat down to a huge round brass tray on which were loaves of bread all round, a spoon apiece, and some salt. Soup was first brought in; we ladled out a spoonful each and then back went our spoons into the same bowl of soup till it was finished.

Our table consisted of the Maitlands, J.B., Mary Martin, Lord Abinger, Mr Moore and Capt. Lovatt, the son of the Consul and myself.

At the other table were R. Martin, Col. Crozier and others. After soup came a turkey, at which we all looked in dismay till Mr Moore plunged his fingers in and pulled out a great string, and then the Consul's son did ditto and handed us bits of the meat in his fingers. After the turkey we had a dish of bits of chicken liver and meat; then a dish of tomatoes farcie, sausages, spinach, tomatoes again, beans, mutton, potatoes, rice pudding jelly, savoury rice and stewed apricots. Some of the vegetables were really nice, especially the tomatoes, but in most dishes grease and garlic were the prevailing taste & the consul's fingers were the crowning horror of the entertainment.

He sat between me, and Lord Abinger, and kept pulling out pieces of sausage and other delicacies for our benefit, which I found quite impossible to accept. We came back to the hotel quite hungry but Col. Crozier was simply rampant and said nothing would induce him to dine à la Arab if he had known all the horrible flavours he would have to consume.

FEBRUARY 17TH TUESDAY

Another long day of ancient monuments. We crossed the Nile and went to No: 35 Tomb, Dayh el Bahree [*Deir el-Bahri*], lunched at Dayh el Medeenah [*Deir el-Medina*] (this is not in the least interesting, nothing to see, quite a one horse Temple) then on to the Ramesseum & the Colossi.

We first went to Dayh el Bahree which is really very charming; the sculptures are so good and so well presented, we found some delightful monkeys among the sculptures, wonderfully life like, and the fish of all kinds, Cuttle fish, Turbots, Skate, Swordfish and many others are most beautifully modelled. No: 35 is interesting from all the domestic life of the Egyptians being depicted on the walls but the smell, heat & fleas were quite intolerable, particularly as one ran the chance of a shower of tallow down one's back from the candles which are fastened to the end of long bamboos and were carried about by the guides and ourselves, it being quite impossible to carry them straight.

[*In the margin of this page, John Biddulph has written:*] (No: 35 is the Tomb of a private individual & is interesting for the friezes depicting the life of wealthy Egyptians in old times. The friezes have been much injured by the torches of tourists & are now almost effaced in many places, but are all to be found in Sir G. Wilkinson's work.) [*Sir John Gardner Wilkinson, 1797–1875, known as the 'Father of British Egyptology'.*]

The Ramesseum is very fine and the sculptures on the walls of a great Battle with chariots, captives, infantry, drowning men etc. are most splendid. In one corner is a drowning chief being restored to life by being held upside down. The huge colossal figure (the largest in the world) is an enormous mass of granite. Only the head, arm and part of the body are left, but on this mass J.B. climbed and looked quite small sitting on the head. I noticed some turtles carved on the roof of the hall of the Ramesseum, I wonder if the Egyptians knew of the soup.

The Colossi stand out splendidly and must look very weird when the Nile rises and flows all round them. We tried a new place to cross the canal which here runs parallel to the Nile, instead of going all round as we had always done before. There was no boat to take us over so the Arabs stripped and carried most of the party over, with the exception of myself and Richard. No: 1 carried me, and Richard walked, having first caught his foot in some weeds and fallen right into the water; to see an English M.P. walking through the Nile arm in arm with 2 naked Arabs was rather quaint, but certainly not a dignified spectacle.

Colonel Crozier was carried over so forcibly that all the treasures he had been buying all day at the Tombs and Temples were crushed, and his misery was almost complete. His cup of misery was quite full when at the Hotel they gave him Brandy instead of Vermouth in his peg; and in the evening again lemonade being given him instead of soda water; the British lion was at last roused and he solemnly forswore Temples & Tombs for the rest of his days.

J.B. and I watched the Camels being embarked for the Front for about an hour; anything more maddening than the Camels' behaviour cannot be imagined. They ran backwards when wanted to go forwards, they lay down and had to be dragged in a sitting position over the gangway into the barge, grunting and struggling they fell overboard into the mud between the barge and the river bank and required a whole army to dig, pull and push for many hours before they were got out. Everybody shouted & banged everybody else with sticks and at last the sun went down, darkness came on, and everybody left off working and the Camels were left on the barge to think over their late outrageous behaviour for the night, there being no possibility of starting them off before next morning.

FEBRUARY 18ᵀᴴ WEDNESDAY

We went to Karnak in the afternoon where Capt. Lovatt joined us; J.B. showed us the Poem of Pentaur and the extradition treaty on the outside walls [*the Poem of Pentaur is an account written in hieratic of the victory of Ramesses II over the Hittite King Muwatalli II at the battle of Kadesh, 1274 BC*].

While I was upstairs painting there was an exciting scene downstairs; Richard having lost a pair of drawers, and possessing only 2 pairs he naturally was very excited on the subject. Taking everybody into his confidence he soon had the whole hotel in pursuit, [the] washerwoman very indignant declaring she had not got them, and waiters, proprietors, visitors, all joining in the explanations. At last Richard rushed upstairs as the washerwoman declared the only pair of "pantaloons" she had seen were the trousers he had on, and upstairs rushed washerwoman, waiters, proprietors, all crowding into Richard's room.

R started for Karnak in a frightful state of indignation vowing vengeance on everybody if the drawers were not found, and just as he had started the laundress flew up to the hotel holding up a pair of dirty drawers with a large hole in, wanting to pursue Richard to Karnak with them (not being able to overtake him she triumphantly carried the garment round & showed it to every soul in the hotel).

FEBRUARY 19TH THURSDAY

The hottest day we have had; we crossed over to Medinet Haboo [*Medinet Habu*] in the morning and were rather disappointed with it, being satiated with sculptures and pillars and tired of temples altogether. We found out the sculpture of the naval engagement, the only one to be found in Egypt, and J.B. was interested in the different kinds of helmets and shields depicted.

The game of draughts so often described is most difficult to see as it is on the third storey of a tower and one cannot climb up to examine it; so in fact one only sees the king seated with his hand out as if to put down a chessman or draught, and this from outside the walls.

Capt. Lovatt told us an amusing story at breakfast one day, a small boy was asked his age and gave the smart answer "Mother says I am seven, but from the fun I've had I should be a hundred."

The corridor or hall with pillars one side of the great Temple is very beautiful at Medinet Haboo, all the colouring can be traced on the pillars and the ceiling must have been such a lovely blue.

FEBRUARY 20TH

Our last day in Luxor. We strolled over to the Belgian Consul after breakfast and looked over his antiques. He has a great quantity and proposes to keep one table full of imitations only, but I am afraid is not too careful of mistakes. Richard & Col. Crozier bought some scarabae, which were declared to be bad imitations by Mons. Maspero [*Monsieur Maspero, Gaston Maspero, 1846–1916, the French Egyptologist*].

The scarabae are so cleverly imitated though that it is almost impossible for the ordinary buyer to discover or detect them.

We were shown several curious things by Mons. Maspero, among them an ancient bed; which was exactly like the "charpoy" used in India, and now in use in Egypt. Some pottery, mummies, and bows and arrows, also two Boomerangs which were used by the Egyptians when they hunted animals and are exactly the same as are now used by the natives in Australia.

Mons M. said the Egyptians used flints or stone a great deal as instruments. He mentioned a curious thing; he wanted to cut some granite and only being able to get Arab workmen, they brought their own tools and went to work their own way. They brought about 100 iron pointed chisels and hammered them into the granite, one after the other getting its point broken and being replaced with another. There was a special forge at work to re-point them.

In talking of the figures, he said some little time ago they discovered a sculptor's workshop and in this atelier were several figures only half finished. That is to say the body and legs & arms would be finished, but not the head or face, or front of the body where they would generally put inscriptions or hieroglyphics. So that he concluded the ancient Egyptians kept the figures ready so for sale, and then when an order was given, the head and face were copied from that of the customer and the figure was complete.

He also told us of an old Arab who was in his employ, who still shaved himself with a flint razor, though his sons had long been accustomed to use steel. The stone razor caused inflammation which had to be allayed by green leaves, so whenever the old man shaved his head he had to wear a bandage of green leaves round his head, but he could not be persuaded to use any other kind of razor.

[*In John Biddulph's handwriting:*]

He also showed us two mace heads of stone used in war as depicted on the sculptures; these are the first that have been found.

In talking of manufactured antiques he said that 80 per cent of the scarabs offered for sale are forgeries and some are so cleverly executed that even the savants themselves are at times puzzled to distinguish them.

On purchasing a scarab the first thing to do is to read the hieroglyphic, the clumsy forgers use three or four hieroglyphical signs at random so that no word or words can be formed of them; the cleverer rogues have now learned to copy hieroglyphics exactly from genuine scarabs. If this test is satisfactorily passed then the sharpness and precision of the cutting must be examined. In a genuine scarab of glass or hard stone such as granite or amethyst, the engraving will appear very precisely cut, but with edges & surface worn by age; this peculiar appearance cannot be artificially imparted. If in a softer material imitation is easier and particular attention must be paid to the clearness and correct drawing of the original engraving. If this test also appears to be satisfactory then the orifice bored through the scarab from end to end must be examined.

In old scarabs, however hard the material, the edges of the orifice are worn and rounded by the metal ring on which they were set, in forgeries the edges will appear sharp as when newly cut. The forgers have not yet learned to supply this defect but doubtless they soon will.

Besides scarabs everything else is imitated, some of the forgeries being works of art in themselves.

The only articles that are not forged are the alabaster articles found in tombs. The guides themselves who generally have good things amongst heaps of rubbish do not know the real value of the things they offer for sale, and are as likely as not to ask less relatively for the more valuable things. In this way M. Maspero pronounced a scarab I had purchased to be far more valuable than another I had also bought with it, but for which the smaller price was asked, both being genuine.

[*Julia Biddulph:*]

FEBRUARY 21ST

The steamer left for Luxor at ½ past 4 in the morning and stopped at Keneh where we arrived at about 9 o'clock that we might see Denderah [*Dendera*]. J.B. was suffering so from rheumatism and cold in his eye, that he could not go with us, and Mary was afraid of the long ride on an Egyptian saddle.

A frightful scrimmage took place with the donkey boys when we landed, Richard broke his stick, and the noise was quite deafening. We finally got away with two men in front to show us the way, and an idiot or deaf and dumb boy running by our side. At the temple several others joined us, guides, guardians etc. and the everlasting scarabs were shown as usual.

Denderah is about 20 minutes ride from the landing place, and is more like Esnah [*Esna*] than anything else we have seen. A most magnificent hall is the principal feature with massive pillars. The capitals formed by 4 women's heads with draperies, and the walls covered with fine sculptures. The ceiling is in wonderful preservation and the signs of the Zodiac are to be seen on it; not that we discovered the scarabae mentioned in Murray, in place of the scorpion or crab.

We found Cleopatra and her son on the outside walls, but Cleopatra's features are being rapidly destroyed by bees, who swarm everywhere. Bats make the inside of the Temple almost unbearable and bees plague one outside.

We found two curious ceilings in two small Temples on the roof, which puzzled us much. A woman's arms encircled one side, while her legs were round the other side and her head in the centre, her body apparently being all of a twist. She is mentioned in Miss Edward's [*Amelia Edwards, 1831–1892, novelist and Egyptologist*] book as Nut, and is supposed to be embracing the vault of the heavens.

We stopped at Gingeh about 9 o'clock for the night. Richard went on board our old steamer the Boutak, which was also stopping there for the night, but got no news from the two or three officers on board, with the exception that our troops had left Metemmeh, evacuated it for Aboo Klea [*Abu Klea*].

FEBRUARY 22ND
[*John Biddulph's handwriting:*]

Among other things described to us by M. Maspero he told us of the ingenious contrivance used by the Ancient Egyptians for lowering the huge granite sarcophagi into the deep mummy pits in which they are so often found. Their plan was to fill the pit up to the level of the surrounding surface with fine sand; on this the sarcophagus was placed. The sand was then scooped away on the four sides & taken out, like water finding its own level the sand under the sarcophagus filled up the scooped out hollows, and in this way the huge masses gradually sank to the bottom of the pit into its proper position.

[*Julia Biddulph:*]

We got into Assioot [*Asyut*] about 4.30 and walked up to the hotel to see if the rooms were possible for the night. Finding them very dirty & uncomfortable, we decided to sleep in the steamer, but to dine at the hotel where several officers were messed.

J.B. met Colonel White of the 92nd [*later Field Marshal Sir George Stuart White VC, 1835–1912. His statue by*

John Tweed stands in Portland Place, London] at dinner, he was going up to the Front with Sir Owen Lanyon [*Colonel Sir William Owen Lanyon KCMG CB, 1842–1887*], they started the morning we left for Cairo in the "Queen Victoria" the ambulance steamer. They all spoke of the great difficulties that were sure to be met with now that Khartoum was gone, and Sir Owen Lanyon especially seemed to dread inaction for the troops during the summer and said so many would fall sick, and so many would die when the excitement of fighting was withdrawn, that he thought it would be better to fight through the heat of the summer than lay by for the autumn campaign. Colonel White too seemed to think that Lord Wolseley would be called home for a short time in the summer to consult with the authorities.

The evening finished with a wedding party, the bride being escorted home to her husband under a pink canopy with a band of music.

FEBRUARY 23RD

We left our steamer without regret though we had the privilege of eating "pain riche à discrétion" [*rich bread at discretion*] according to the printed rules in the salon; but the dirt & general discomfort of the steamer made us heartily glad to turn our backs upon it. The railway journey is a very tiring dusty one from Assioot to Cairo, there are no refreshment rooms at the stations, and one has to picnic in the midst of heaps of dust in one's carriage; every now & then a creature comes into the carriage and with a small broom raises a fearful dust storm by way of making one comfortable.

FEBRUARY 24TH

Richard & Mary left in the evening for Alexandria, after a rush up the Great Pyramid in the morning. J.B. & I went to the theatre to the Barings' box and saw "Madame Boniface" a decided improvement on "Perichole" which I saw before.

Prince Hassan [*Prince Hassan of Egypt, brother of the Khedive*] came into the box and talked about his preparations for the Soudan, which seemed to include racehorses and greyhounds.

J.B. had an interesting talk with General Stephenson [*General Sir Frederick Stephenson KGCB, 1821–1911, Commander-in-Chief, British Army, of occupation Cairo*] and heard of poor General Gordon's last letter dated the 14th December and received here by his friend Colonel Watson today; it was almost verbatim as follows, "The game here is up, it is now the 14th of December and in another ten days or possibly a little later, there must be a catastrophe, it is a pity that our people did not make their movements known earlier, however this is all spilt milk." The letter ended by giving goodbye to him and to other friends, and giving directions for the payment of debts due by Gordon.

FEBRUARY 25TH

We spent a very pleasant hour at the Boulak Museum before luncheon and had a good look at the mummies and especially at the mummy case of the great Ramesses. After luncheon I drove with Lady Baring and visited the hospital at the Citadel.

Sister Cannell showed us all the wards except the fever one in which a poor man was very ill indeed. The room for ophthalmic cases struck me as excellent with a blue soft light caused by blinds, and screens of deep blue, the whole room being darkened to a subdued cool blue colour. Most of the men who could move had gone out for a little smoke. The hospital is really a large Palace with marble floors everywhere, so easy to keep clean and sweet. A large number of men with

6 officers had arrived the day before from the Front, and the wards were nearly full.

FEBRUARY 26ᵀᴴ THURSDAY
General Graham and his staff arrived in the afternoon. Sir George Greaves, Colonel Warren & Capt. Rochfort among them [*General Sir George Greaves GCB KCMG, 1831–1922, Chief of Staff to General Sir Gerald Graham VC GCB GCMG, 1831–1899*].

J.B. had a chat with Sir George on the subject of his getting to the Soudan, or to Suakin, and also spoke to Colonel Warren about it. Capt. Rochfort dined with us and Suakin was the general topic with everybody.

[*John Biddulph's regiment, the 19ᵗʰ Hussars, was at the front; it had fought at Tel-el-Kebir on 13ᵗʰ September 1882 and with the Suakin Force, commanded by General Graham. The regiment had also fought in the Battle of Abu Klea on 17ᵗʰ January 1885, one of the regiment's battle honours. The battle of Abu Klea is the battle referred to in the second verse of the acclaimed poem by Sir Henry Newbolt, Vitai Lampada:*

> The sand of the Desert is sodden red, –
> Red with the wreck of a square that broke; –
> The Gatling's jammed and the Colonel's dead,
> And the regiment blind with dust and smoke.
> The river of death has brimmed his banks,
> And England's far, and Honour a name,
> But the voice of a schoolboy rallies the ranks:
> 'Play up! play up! and play the game!'

John Biddulph saw an opportunity of joining General Graham's staff and spending some time at the front. He was due to return to India later in the year but was still waiting to hear about his new *appointment from the Indian Government; he was a colonel and no doubt relished the chance to return to military duty.*]

FEBRUARY 27TH

General Graham consented to J.B. joining his Staff if the Indian Govt. agreed so he telegraphed to the India Office and also to Michael [*Michael Biddulph MP, J.B.'s brother, Member of Parliament for Herefordshire, and later created 1st Baron Biddulph, 1903*].

Mr Clementson and Mr Barry dined with us, Dr Barnet joining us, and afterwards we went to the Turkish Theatre.

A great number of boxes were prepared for the Khedive's harem and other ladies, with muslin curtains drawn across. There was very little plot apparently in the Turkish piece but of course we could only guess at it, as none of us understood the language. The audience roared over the jokes; the dresses were rather pretty, and the dancing not bad; the girls spoke with great vivacity too, and the whole thing was bright. We were satisfied with two acts, for the smell of garlic was overpowering. There were no ladies in the stalls, the Levantine element being in the ascendant.

FEBRUARY 28TH

We breakfasted with the Barings and met Sir George Greaves, Capt. Rochfort & Dr Barnet. I had a long drawing morning with Lady B. only interrupted by visitors now and then. Mrs Amos of the Slaves home called and was anxious Lady B. should go to Sakara [*Sakkara or Saqqara*] with her, riding a donkey from there to Cairo, saying a donkey embodied the poetry of motion!

Sir Evelyn was very depressed about everything, and then the telegram came in that the Govt. had won by a majority of 14 in the House of Commons (in the vote of censure) he said it was a defeat and he didn't care if the Govt. went out at once & himself with it; he was so disgusted with everything, nothing could be worse. I had a long talk with Sir G. Greaves about John getting to Suakin.

In the afternoon I called on the Vice-Reine [sic] [*the Khediva, wife of the Khedive*] with Lady Baring. The Princess is very stout, quite young, and has a fair complexion and dark eyes & hair; she has a nice expression and seemed anxious to please. The conversation turned entirely on children and the Turkish play. Some English ladies sent up their cards for presentation asking Lady B. to do the needful for them. They came in most ungracefully and sat down in a most awkward manner. When the customary cigars and coffee came round two of the ladies accepted the cigars and an old woman, Lady Ross, attempted to smoke hers, evidently the first time she had ever tried smoking. After some ineffectual puffing she laid the cigar down on the ashtray in despair. Some of the English ladies behave in a most extraordinary manner to the Vice-Reine, walking into her rooms without any introduction, not even choosing her reception day for doing so; she has complained to Lady Baring, very naturally.

A visit to the cricket ground finished up our day. The heat and noise at Shepheard's [hotel] was quite unbearable. After dinner we sat with Mrs Le Mesurier for some time. During dinner J.B. received a telegram from the India Office "Apply direct Government of India" this is very unsatisfactory and looks like refusal.

MARCH 1ST SUNDAY.

We went to the station to see Sir George Greaves and all the officers start for Suez by the 11.30 train en route to Suakin. Colonel Warren drove with us; the station was crowded with men but very few ladies appeared. Sir George had two nice little chestnut Arabs in the train. Everybody enquired if John was going on and seemed to think from the telegram his chances were small. On returning to Shepheard's he sent the following telegram, "General Graham applies for my services Suakin, with India consent, Military, Calcutta."

We spent an hour in the Arabian Museum after luncheon, it is poor as a museum but the lamps and lanterns and carved doors & windows are beautiful & interesting for their age. This carved work is rapidly disappearing in Cairo and the new work is not nearly so carefully finished. The glass lamps in the museum were made in Venice 5 or 6 hundred years ago, and the colours & designs are very fine.

Mr Moore also took us to see the library where there are some very fine manuscripts of the Koran, very beautifully illuminated. We saw the first book of the Koran that was written in Arabic character; before that the writing was all Kufic. A drive on the Shoobra road finished up our day.

2ND MARCH.

We drove to the Pyramids after luncheon and pottered about till sunset. It was very beautiful to see the Pyramids standing out against the deep orange sky; the afterglow threw them out so splendidly. One of the Arabs who lives at the Pyramids and the doctor of the village came and amused us with their chat and showed us their variety of antiques, consisting of old coins and bits of sorts. They complained of not finding a profitable living at the Pyramids and the doctor offered to go to the Soudan with J.B. as his servant. One of them mentioned that he had a very fine Dromedary for sale, a super excellent animal who only required a "little lunch" in the way of food.

We dined with the Dormers in the evening and met Colonel Arbuthnot, Major Hutton, Mr Dormer & Colonel Ardayle; the latter showed me some capital sketches of Egypt

& Palestine. The great amusement just now seems moonlight excursions to the Pyramids. On Sunday evening some of the people from here started off at ½ past 9 and did not get back till ½ past 2 in the morning.

3ʳᵈ MARCH TUESDAY
Strolled out in the morning for some small shoppings and bought a little portmanteau for 30 francs, also three pieces of tussaud for 100 francs. In the afternoon we had a visit from the Dormers who talk of going out to India in the winter. Afterwards we drove out to the tennis and sat with Lady Baring; she told us her husband had received a letter from poor General Gordon in which he was very angry with everybody for the way he had been treated. We dined with the Barings and went to the Opera after dinner; "Le Petit Duc" a bright, pretty little piece with several talking airs in it and a charming little scene in a Convent, the young ladies having a music lesson.

No telegram from Calcutta, so that J.B. has given up all hope of going to Suakin and has been arranging for us to leave Cairo for Cyprus.

4ᵀᴴ MARCH WEDNESDAY
I met Donny Stewart in the morning, he had been telegraphed for by Lord Wolseley and was going to join him at Korti. Donny was looking very delicate & said he had had a sunstroke but was getting all right.

The telegram from India saying Sir Peter Lumsden [*General Sir Peter Lumsden, 1829–1918*] had fallen back upon Kerat, and had advised the Afghans to withstand any advance of the Russians by force has been the chief topic of interest today.

J.B. paid General Graham a visit and had a long chat on Frontier politics etc. General Graham expressed his regret that John was not going with him to Suakin.

I said goodbye to Mrs Le Mesurier, who promised to get me some brass things and a Koran stand and send them either to England or Bombay to me. Poor old Le Mesurier is very seedy.

I rushed into Lady Baring to see the boys dressed up for their Fancy Ball, they looked such darlings, Rowland was in crimson and yellow satin, Wyndham in pale blue and yellow, two sweet little fools, their caps were particularly effective coming over their ears and they jingled all over with bells. Ethel [*Lady Baring*] herself looked most dreadfully ill with neuralgia in the head, she had only just left her bed and would be forced to return to it.

We left Cairo at 6 o'clock in the evening for Alexandria and had a huge bill to pay at Shepheard's at the last moment, just to take the edge off our regret at leaving Cairo.

MARCH 5TH
Abbat's Hotel Alexandria.

We met Cunliffe [*Colonel Cunliffe Martin CB, Julia's brother*] in the morning, he arrived quite early from Brindisi and we had an hour and a half's good chat with him & saw him start for Suez. Cunliffe was looking particularly well, and seemed in good spirits. [*Cunliffe would have been returning to India from leave, he commanded the Central India Horse.*]

We spent the afternoon driving about to the different shipping agents, visiting the Ras el Tin Fort and taking a drive beyond the Rosetta Gate. We decided to stay on in Alexandria till the direct steamer to Cyprus starts, which will probably be on Sunday morning.

MARCH 6TH
At 12 o'clock today John received a telegram from the F.O. Calcutta giving him permission to join the Suakin expedition pending arrangements about pay and leave.

MARCH 7TH
Cairo, Shepheard's Hotel.

We spent all day in uncertainty, as John had to find out exactly how he stood as to pay and prospects if he went to Suakin with General Graham. He had a talk with Genl. Graham at 9 o'clock and came back without any results as Lord Wolseley had been telegraphed to and his answer had not arrived. About ½ past 11 J.B. was sent for again, the answer from Lord Wolseley was, "Take Colonel Biddulph if India consents". General Graham could not take J.B. with him until the answer from India arrived settling the question as to J.B.'s political appointment in India being kept open, and this would entail further telegrams, delay and possible disappointment. The pay J.B. would receive at Suakin would be 29s [*shillings*] a day including everything; he would have to pay a servant £3.10.0 a month and the length of time he would be away on this campaign would be indefinite.

With great regret J.B. had to give up his hopes of going, as he could not afford the loss of pay and the possible loss of promotion in India. This is a very great disappointment.

We returned to Alexandria by the 6 o'clock train and found ourselves back again in our old room 23 in the Abbat Hotel.

I went to see Ethel Baring before leaving Cairo and found her very busy with Lord John Hay etc. [*Admiral Lord John Hay, 1827–1916, Commander-in-Chief Mediterranean Fleet*] staying in the house, and dinners etc. on hand. Lord John Hay is full of there being an immediate war with Russia and is planning war by fire & sword, bombardments, blockades etc., he thinks the Suakin affair will be a very long one; that Osman Digna [*Mahdist Commander*] will not fight when he hears of the large force sent out from England. Major Macdonald thinks Osman will fight, but with far more precaution than he did before as he has learnt by experience since last year. If we had followed him up last year he could easily have been smashed as he had literally only 100 followers, and those nearly all his own family; now he has a large number of men and is likely to make a good resistance. Major M. said the climate of Suakin was quite abominable, that the long time of inaction if it came, would be dreadfully weary in such a place; and that if John was subject to fever he very much doubted his standing it (the climate) but would almost certainly have fallen sick and been invalided.

[*John Biddulph:*]

The present outlook of affairs in Egypt is most discouraging. The Ministry have added blunder to blunder and our position today is more difficult and dangerous than it has been at any time during the last three years. The violence of party feeling in Parliament, the want of a definite policy, the clinging to office and attempts to reconcile their proceedings with the discordant views of different groups of their supporters on the part of the Cabinet, and the studied resolution to ignore unwelcome facts have led us step by step, deeper & deeper into a hopeless quagmire. We are now engaged in a desperate war with people with whom we have no original cause of quarrel in a country that is capable of swallowing up the combined armies of Europe. The only way open to escape from our present difficulties, & to retreat without further loss of credit from this desperate position we are now occupying, is to make use of the Turk [*Ottomans*] & bring him to restore order in the Soudan; this is the only solution of the difficulty, unwelcome as it may be in itself.

The occupation of Massowah [*Eritrea*] by Italy which is now taking place, will lead eventually to the subjugation of Abyssinia by the same power, but the Soudan question will be settled one way or the other long before the influence of Italy is felt there.

In a conversation with me some nights ago, Evelyn Baring took credit to himself for having been the author of the scheme of allowing Italy free action in this way; but unless we are to occupy Egypt permanently the only benefit I can see in the plan is the temporary one of detaching Italy from the European combination now directed by Bismarck against us. In Egypt itself the outlook is not much better; the people themselves who have benefited by our interference are hostile to us and their hostility is increasing daily.

The French stir up popular feeling against us, and the Greeks who are spread over the whole of Egypt from Alexandria to Khartoum, and who are themselves one of the greatest pests in the country, are most hostile to us. The land is excessively rich, so rich that its resources are practically inexhaustible; but this makes it a more desirable bone of contention for the powers of Europe, to all of whom its geographical position is of more or less political importance. The establishment of the Multiple Control that has practically been resolved on must lead to a conflict between the different powers at no distant date; and the Eastern Question has now a double kernel in Constantinople & Cairo.

E. Baring told me that when the expedition for Gordon's relief was being planned in Sept. last, he was anxious that the Suakin-Berber line [*the Suakin–Berber railway line*] should be acted on simultaneously with the line of the Nile; but Wolseley, on score of economy, determined to act on the single line only. How much might we have been spared now if the double line of operations had been insisted on?

Chapter IV

Return to England

MARCH 8ᵀᴴ SUNDAY
We embarked on board the S.S. "Ararat" and left Alexandria about 5 o'clock. A few hours before starting we found that the steamer was bound to stop at most of the ports down the Syrian coast instead of going straight to Cyprus.

MARCH 9ᵀᴴ MONDAY
Arrived at Jaffa just as it was getting dark, consequently saw nothing but a few shore lights.

MARCH 10ᵀᴴ TUESDAY
Left Jaffa early in the morning, the Captain finding there was no cargo to be had, and arrived at Haifa in the afternoon. The Captain went on shore without giving notice to any of the passengers, so they had no chance of doing so. We anchored within sight of Mt. Carmel, Acre being on the opposite side of the Bay and Mount Hermon showing up boldly against the sky, being covered with snow.

MARCH 11TH WEDNESDAY

John went on shore to Haifa in the morning, leaving me in a bed with a bad headache. He visited the Convent on Mount Carmel, getting the most fearful jolting in a box on wheels, which was the cab of Haifa. J.B. returned to luncheon and after establishing me comfortably on deck, went on shore again to call on Mr Laurence Oliphant; in a short time he returned saying Mrs Oliphant had kindly asked us to spend the night with them, so we put a few things together and met Mr Oliphant at the Haifa landing place.

[*Laurence Oliphant, 1829–1888. Oliphant was at times a politician, author, traveller, diplomat and 'Christian Mystic'; he and his wife, Alice, moved to Haifa in 1879 to oversee his plan for the Jewish colonisation of Palestine. His wife died in 1886 and he returned to England in 1887, never returning to Haifa. Oliphant died in 1888 and is buried in Twickenham Cemetery, London.*]

He drove us through the quaint little town with very narrow streets and most astonishing large stones on the road over which we bumped gaily. We passed through Haifa very quickly and after going through a lane with high hedges of cactus on each side, found ourselves in a little German colony where the Oliphants had bought a house and where they have been living for the last 2 years. Mrs Oliphant met us at the door and took us straight into the dining room where we found their other guests assembled; Dr & Mrs Martin, an American lady and the daughter of the Consul at Beyrout [*Beirut*]. Both Mr and Mrs Oliphant were delightfully kind and made us at home at once.

The establishment amused me very much, it consisted of an Egyptian servant and his wife, the latter had been taught to cook by Mrs Oliphant but being a very fat woman, the unaccustomed standing (for like all Egyptian women she had sat down all her life) made her legs swell so much that she was often obliged to rest for a week at a time. The cook's sister was the laundry maid and her big black baby, the toy of the household; a German girl from the Colony did the housemaid's work but slept out of the house. There was also a small Egyptian boy who did page and messenger and any other work that might be wanted.

The house was very comfortable, heaps of books of course, and all necessary comforts. The garden was not very advanced but the American lady was very busy gardening and while we were there a great supply of young orange and lemon trees, jessamine [*jasmine*], and other plants arrived from Beyrout which were to be planted at once. The great difficulty is the want of water and sinking a well costs from 40 to 70 £s [*sic*].

After dinner we had a long talk about Egypt and Syria, it seemed so strange to hear them talk of Nazareth and Jerusalem etc., as everyday sort of places within everybody's reach. Our bedroom windows looked straight across the bay to Mt Hermon.

MARCH 12TH THURSDAY.

We dawdled about in the morning hoping to get news as to when our steamer was to start, J.B. having sent a message to the Captain to ask him, but at last failing to get an answer and seeing the steam getting up on the "Ararat" we thought it best to say goodbye to our kind hosts and reluctantly returned to the steamer at 12 o'clock, only to find it did not start till 4 o'clock in the afternoon.

MARCH 13TH FRIDAY.

Beyrout [*Beirut*]. We spent most of the day at Beyrout while the ship was unloading cargo. Beyrout is a very bright lively town with large bazaars and quaint little open places in the middle of the bazaars, with always a well in the centre. The fruit and vegetables are quite a sight; such heaps of tomatoes, peas, cauliflowers, and native vegetables of all kinds; with mountains of oranges, lemons, limes, green almonds, melons & walnuts.

At every corner of a street were stalls of sweetmeats, or coffee trays or cook shops of some description; but the sweetmeat stalls were most abundant. The shops were full of Manchester goods [*goods or articles made in Manchester, especially cotton cloths, etc.*], but also of the silk things manufactured in Beyrout, some of them extremely pretty.

The women wear charming dresses of striped silk, but the Mohammedan women cover their faces with handkerchiefs made of thin gauze with flowers printed on it; this has a curious effect as one woman's nose seems to be bright purple, while her companion's is dark green, or pale pink, according to the colour of her handkerchief. J.B. felt strongly inclined to seize hold of their noses, and I must say it was a temptation. The Christian women wore white veils or cloths round their faces, which were of course uncovered. We saw so many handsome women with beautiful pale clear complexions; the men were often very tall and finely made and one could not help being struck by the good looks of the people which were set off by their very picturesque dress.

We saw some of the women from the mountains (Lebanon) who were remarkably fine looking; they belonged to some Prince in the mountains, but our dragoman told us with a laugh, that there were a great many princes in the mountains. The open air life of the people was very amusing; a man dressed in European clothes except that he wore a fez on his head, was calmly cutting his toe nails, sitting in the middle of the street surrounded by his friends who were eagerly discussing some interesting topic & drinking coffee.

We breakfasted at the Hotel; it was delightful sitting in the balcony of the hotel & looking across the bay to the mountains of Lebanon, which were covered in snow.

We came on board before ½ past 4 and left Beyrout in an hour's time for Scanderoon [*Iskenderun, Turkey*]. John called on the English Consul before leaving Beyrout, a funny old gentleman who had lived in the place for 22 years. His Russian wife seemed well contented with the society, and looked down immensely upon the colony of Haifa.

MARCH 14TH SATURDAY.

Scanderoon. We spent the whole day on board as the place itself seemed very uninviting. The scenery is quite beautiful at this time of year, the distant mountains covered with snow, and the near ranges purple with a sort of heather, while the sea is the most brilliant blue I ever saw. We had a magnificent sunset, when the whole sky became like sheets of gold and then turned to bright orange, deepening into crimson, the reflections on the water as bright as the sky. Scanderoon is a place of interest as being the intentional western starting point of the Euphrates Valley Railway, so long talked of, but never commenced. It is fearfully hot and unhealthy in the summer, there is no doctor in the place and anyone who falls ill there has to go to Beyrout for advice. A very handsome young mountaineer came on board going to Jerusalem on pilgrimage; I tried to sketch him and some of the boatmen who wear particularly picturesque dresses. We did not leave Scanderoon till 6 o'clock in the evening.

MARCH 15TH SUNDAY.

Reached Larnaca [*Cyprus*] about 11.30 and went on shore at once to Mr Cobham's [*Claude Delaval Cobham, 1842–1915, British Colonial Official in Cyprus and District Commissioner of Larnaca; one of the leading antiquarians on Cyprus*], where we lunched before starting for Nicosia. Mr Cobham showed us some very fine specimens of oriental needlework and a beautiful piece of Cyprus lace.

We left Larnaca about 2 o'clock; three horses being caught fortunately to drag the cumbersome old vehicle, which conveyed us to Nicosia. The ponies were all three harnessed abreast, & though small & miserable looking, brought us along capitally, doing the 26 miles in less than 4 ½ hours. Government House is built entirely of wood, and forms three sides of a square with a tennis ground in the centre; it is a long sort of Barn, with wide verandahs [sic] on each side and a red roof. The whole country is covered with wild flowers, anemones and sheets of yellow marguerites and the colony is quite lovely.

MARCH 16TH MONDAY.
Nicosia.
A high wind began to blow in the morning & continued all day, getting very cold in the evening. J.B. & I took a sharp walk before dinner.

MARCH 17TH TUESDAY.
High wind all day and bitterly cold. Our baggage arrived before 12 o'clock all right. I bought 2 buckles and a little cup of the old Cyprus work. Attempted a short walk with J.B. before dinner but were driven in by fear of rain. J.B. looked in upon the Cyprus Parliament, which seems to engross the attention of all here in the absence of papers, books & news. We were very glad of a fire in the afternoon.

MARCH 18TH WEDNESDAY.
Less windy but bitterly cold. I sat out all the afternoon sketching & burnt myself brick red as usual. J.B. called on some Nicosia people.

MARCH 19TH THURSDAY.
We all went for a ride in the morning, and I tried a new pony. J.B. got an extension of 2 months' leave, which he has forwarded to the Indian Office. Dr Owen & Dr Heidenstam signed the certificate [*Frederick Charles von Heidenstam, 1842–1909, Chief Medical Officer, Cyprus*].

MARCH 20TH FRIDAY.
Lady Bovill & her husband dined at Govt. House [*Sir Elliot Bovill, 1848–1893, Lawyer, Judicial Commissioner and Chief Justice, Cyprus*]. In the morning J.B., Mr Sinclair and I went down to the town and saw the Friday market and I bought some silk & cotton stuff and a saddle bag, after which we visited the prison and the Mosque. I find that a long spiral plant which grows all about the island is the Asphodel so much spoken of by poets, it hardly carries out my idea of its beauty and excellence.

MARCH 21ST SATURDAY.
Stopped at home all day writing & making cigarettes till about 3 o'clock when J.B. and I took a walk. Colonel & Mrs Warren, the Owens etc. dined at Govt. House.

MARCH 22ND SUNDAY.
Went to Church in the morning. Lunched with the Bovills, called on Mrs Warren, and then went to an old Church with Mr Sinclair where we sketched; a lovely bright afternoon, the hills looking so shadowy, with bright lights on the town, a most sketchable afternoon.

MARCH 23RD MONDAY.
A stormy afternoon with heavy rain and hail. A telegram arrived in the afternoon mentioning 2 fights at Suakin, a

skirmish on Friday the 20th and a bigger fight on the 21st, no mention of any loss of officers on our part. We apparently killed 1,500 Arabs on Saturday with our side killed and wounded less than 200.

MARCH 24TH TUESDAY.
Kyrenia.

Michael and Harry went off to Larnaca with their father to catch the mail for England. J.B. and I left Nicosia about 10 o'clock, and arrived at Kyrenia at 1.30. We drove to the 2nd bridge and then rode the rest of the way. Capt. Kenyon's house is a charming old house on the Quay, with bow windows and small verandahs [sic] looking right over the sea. The pass between Nicosia & Kyrenia is quite lovely when one has reached the top and one can look right down upon the blue sea with all the olive and carob trees, and the mountains themselves are very fine. Miss Houston and Mr & Mrs Templar came to tea, and afterwards J.B. & I walked over to a wreck, which is stranded on the rocks about ½ a mile from the town. Mrs Kenyon's baby was unfortunately very ailing today with a severe cold on the chest.

MARCH 25TH WEDNESDAY.
J.B. and I rode to Bella Pease [*Bellapais*] this morning, starting at 4.30. It is one of the loveliest places I have ever seen. A large Church and Monastery perched high up in the hills surrounded by orange and pomegranate trees, cypresses, almond etc. We rode up a steep path under olive & carob trees, the ground being carpeted with flowers, cistus, white and pink, cyclamen, hyacinths and many other flowers; the hawthorn trees were a mass of blossom too, and the air was so sweet with all sorts of flower perfumes. We looked down upon the blue sea, and then up to the grey rugged mountains

with clouds now and again covering them up almost entirely. We went over the old Church first on arriving and admired some very pretty silver lamps that were burning before the altar. After luncheon in the cloisters I made a quick sketch while John smoked, he then went to the school and inspected the small village and then when he returned we mounted our ponies and returned to Kyrenia by another and far less steep road. We found the Kenyons happier about the baby on our return. Miss Houston dined with the Kenyons; her brother could not come as he was in bed with influenza.

MARCH 26TH THURSDAY.
We left Kyrenia at 2 o'clock in the afternoon and rode within three miles of Nicosia where we found a dog-cart; getting into Govt. House at 5 o'clock. A number of letters were waiting for us, 2 home mails, making a budget of 16 letters altogether.

MARCH 27TH FRIDAY.
Government House, Nicosia.
    J.B. and I called on Mrs Grant in the morning. After luncheon heavy rain set in. We dined with the Warrens, who had a musical party after dinner. The native talent came out strongly, and much of the singing was really very good.

MARCH 28TH SATURDAY.
We went to the Council in the afternoon and heard Robert's farewell speech to the Council [*Lieutenant General Sir Robert Biddulph, 1835–1918, High Commissioner and Commander-in-Chief, Cyprus, and John Biddulph's elder brother*]. The Bishop made the return speech on the part of the Greek members. It was a lame sort of speech and not fluently translated, but one sentence caused much amusement; the Bishop saying the High Commissioner and himself had been chasing one object

for several days! I suppose he meant they had been agreeing on one subject, for generally they were opposing each other, the Bishop being the most factious of all the members in the Council. The Turk made a far happier speech and was very complimentary to Robert, saying all sorts of nice civil things about his good influence, his care of the interests of the island, and all the good he had done to it etc., with great regrets at his approaching departure.

[Biddulph Gate, Famagusta, Cyprus, is named after Sir Robert Biddulph.]

MARCH 29TH SUNDAY.

We went to Church in the morning, lunched with the Warrens & visited the Museum afterwards. There are many good things in the Museum and some curious jars with small figures placed on the jars holding the handle, quite unlike anything I have ever seen before.

MARCH 30TH MONDAY.

We drove to Famagusta, 36 miles from Nicosia. The road was very bad indeed after the heavy rain, and we had to ford the river as the approaches to the bridge were completely broken down. We got very wet on the road as it rained hard most of the day and were very glad to get into Capt. Young's house at Verosia [Varosha] by ½ past 5. The Laws dined with Capt. Young, and General Swinley & Major Chetwynde were staying in the house.

MARCH 31ST TUESDAY.

We walked down to Famagusta in the morning. The fort contains no end of ruins of Churches, a Palace, and a large Cathedral. The latter is called St Sophia and is a magnificent building. All the windows must have been filled with coloured glass at one time and the floor had a great many marble slabs where the Crusaders were buried beneath. These have all been taken away, with the exception of one or two, which can hardly be deciphered now. Rain came on and we had to take refuge in a big Church, which is now used as a storehouse for the locust traps! In the afternoon we walked down to the seashore where the sand is beautifully fine and hard, a grand place for bathing.

APRIL 2ND THURSDAY
We returned to Nicosia, General Swinley coming with us. We stopped for luncheon about 15 miles from Nicosia, where Madame Francesca brought us jam and glasses of water, this is the Cyprian way of greeting a guest; she had done so before on our way to Famagusta, and I appreciated the jam or marmalade very much.

APRIL 3RD FRIDAY (GOOD FRIDAY)
Went to Church in the morning.

APRIL 4TH SATURDAY
Some people dined in the evening, among them the real frisk young lady who sang, believe me, "those endearing young charms". We played tennis in the afternoon, the day being very cold and grey.

APRIL 5TH EASTER SUNDAY
J.B. & I went to Church in the morning. Called on the Warrens in the afternoon, it rained heavily about 10 o'clock at night.

APRIL 6TH MONDAY
We left Nicosia about 2 o'clock and had a very pleasant drive to Larnaca, arriving about 6.15. General Swinley travelled with us and we had to scramble across the bridge between Larnaca

& Nicosia, the late rains having caused such a high river that it carried away a great piece of the bridge; our carriage went through the river all right at the fording place. Capt. Young met us at Mr Cobham's, having ridden over from Famagusta to meet the General. No tidings of our steamer, and no telegram from the outside world.

APRIL 7TH TUESDAY

No news of our steamer at all, so we are afraid it is waiting at Jaffa or Beyrout for the pilgrims who have been spending Easter at Jerusalem.

We walked in the morning on the piers and visited the Church where Lazarus was said to have been buried, but only his tomb is there now as his body was carried off to Marseilles. I believe it was sold; the tradition says he was so extremely tiresome in Syria after his resurrection that he was shipped off by the authorities and he landed here, where he was made a great deal of and became Bishop of Kition. The Church is rather fine, ornamented with a quantity of badly painted pictures of Saints and tawdry ornaments, but there are some very handsome silver candlesticks in it. Another account of Lazarus is that he made himself so very disagreeable in Cyprus that he found it best to take himself off to Marseilles carrying a large sum of money with him. The story of Lazarus's visit to Cyprus is founded on tradition, but it is a fact that St. Barnabas's body was found at Nicosia and sold to the old Greek Govt. for the freedom of the island. Easter is a very noisy time in Cyprus as the Church bells ring incessantly, and they begin shooting off pistols on Good Friday (shooting Judas Iscariot), which they continue to do night and day till Easter Monday is well over.

The Austrian Lloyd Steamer came in about 3 o'clock for Beyrout & Alexandria and General Swinley went on board by 5 o'clock, but no tidings of our steamer, which is expected tomorrow. Colonel Ogilvy & Major Wyllie of the 60th Rifles dined with Mr Cobham.

APRIL 8TH WEDNESDAY
Larnaca.

We now hear that our steamer does not come in till the 9th and it is likely to be fearfully crowded. J.B. very anxious to get home or get news, our last telegram being March 30th.

The French Consul and his wife dined with Mr Cobham in the evening, she being Levantine spoke all languages, but he only spoke French so our conversation was carried on in this language. The French Consul told J.B. the most tremendous "corkers" saying he had been the inventor of a wonderful torpedo, besides many other things. The lady told me her husband had given her a magnificent ruby ring, which flew into powder one morning when she struck the breakfast table with it!

APRIL 9TH THURSDAY
We got our English letters and a telegram just before starting in the Austrian Lloyd Steamer. The telegram said the tension between England & Russia increasing, so of course J.B. is frightfully anxious to get out to India. We embarked on board our steamer about 1 o'clock. On board we found 2 Princes: the Arch Duke of Austria, or rather an Arch Duke being the son of Prince Charles, and nephew to the present Emperor. He has 2 Generals in his suite, one is the general who was with our army in the Abyssinian war, and he has a pretty but very tiny wife. The French Prince is the son of Jerome's and the hope of the Bonaparte party [*more likely Jerome's grandson Victor, Prince Napoleon, 1862–1926, pretender to the French throne from 1879–1926*]. The two Princes do not speak to each other

apparently. The young Bonaparte Prince has a heavy looking countenance and resembles the family a good deal in looks, he does not look clever, but they say he learnt English very well in three months at Cheltenham, which speaks well of his quickness. The Austrian Prince is clean & commonplace looking, walking with his toes well out.

APRIL 10TH FRIDAY
J.B. made great friends with the General Cultets, which is the nearest approach to his German name that I can write. I spent all day in my cabin being horribly ill, but crawled upstairs at 8 o'clock to see the Island of Rhodes. We only stopped a short time, and it was too dark to see more than the dim shadows of houses and the harbour lights and lighthouse.

APRIL 11TH SATURDAY
In the morning I made the acquaintance of Madame Cultets who is very nice and full of chat of all sorts; she is very tired of travelling and not very well, and longing to re-arrange her toilette.

In the evening we arrived at Scio, or Chios, having passed Samos and other islands in the morning. It was dark and rather cold, so Mdme. Cultets and I took care of each other on deck while J.B. went on shore with the Prince and his Generals. There was nothing very much to be seen on shore but the island is lovely to look at, with the mountains in the background and the town is in the midst of orange gardens. It is a great place for mastic, a sort of white gum looking exactly like gum Arabic, which the Turkish ladies chew; also they make a spirit like gin out of this mastic.

Mdme. Cultets told me many amusing things about the Austrian Court on account of no one being allowed to go to Court without sixteen quarterings. The lady must have it as well as her husband, as his are no use to her. This makes the Court very small and very dull. Sometimes when a great awkwardness happens, such as the Minister of Foreign Affairs not having a wife with 16 quarterings, she receives some distinguished order from the Empress, and being so ennobled is able to appear at Court with her husband, but this is only done on very, very rare occasions.

The Cook's party made themselves very objectionable on board to day, they actually go up to the Prince and take away his books and papers and maps. One dreadful old woman told Madame Cultets that she considered the prince ought to give up his chair to a lady, when he was only a young man, and there were so few chairs on deck!

The dreadful English & American tourists are clad in the most awful garments and with blue veils and large battered hats, look like nothing but themselves, they talk very loudly and shriek to each other about their travels, complaints etc., always trying to engage in conversation.

[*The 'Cook's party' would have been tourists on a package holiday arranged by the travel agency Thomas Cook & Son, founded 1841.*]

When J.B. returned we had to change our steamer, so we hurried on board another Austrian Lloyd, "The Imperial Eagle", a most disgusting boat full of Turkish soldiers and dirty Greeks. When we got on board J.B. heard more bad news; that the Russians had attacked an Afghan outpost and defeated them with great slaughter; that the French were making peace with China and that we had suffered a defeat at Suakin. All this worries us very much, and makes us still more anxious to get home.

A terrible Parson came on board the new steamer with us who drawls long stories through his nose, and is a great worry, such an awful mass of ignorance and conceit; he is lamenting at being detained so long from his Parish, I wonder if his Parish appreciates him. We left Chios about 9 o'clock.

APRIL 12 TH SUNDAY
We did not get into the harbour of the Piraeus till nearly 2 o'clock, too late for us to go into Athens, as our steamer was to leave for Trieste at 4 o'clock, such a great disappointment. It is most beautiful coming into the harbour with mountains on both sides. We saw Athens standing out very white against the blue hills, and the Acropolis and the Parthenon, I imagine, below the Acropolis. We landed and strolled about the dirty little harbour town not even able to find a paper or hear any news, so we returned to our steamer very disgusted. When we steamed out of the harbour the sun came out and shone right upon Athens lighting it up most beautifully and I sat on deck watching the mountains till it became quite dark.

APRIL 13 TH
Our wedding day. I had a bad attack of sickness and could not leave my cabin all day.

APRIL 14 TH TUESDAY
We got to Corfu early in the morning, and landed before 8 o'clock; ordered breakfast at the Hotel St. George and then took the loveliest drive to the one gun battery where we looked over the bay to the Albanian shore. It is the most exquisite place, and just now the hedges are full of roses, the orange flower is out, and the place is just like fairyland. After a too delicious drive (which J.B. could not enjoy as he was reading the paper all the time; our fears about the war being too true, and the attack on the Afghan outpost confirmed). We had breakfast at the hotel and we much enjoyed our fish and steak after the horrid fare on board the steamers; also we

drank Corfu white wine, which was not bad at all. Then we returned to the steamer, being told it was to leave punctually at 11 o'clock and after dismissing our boat and guide, were told that it would be 2 hours before the boat could leave!

APRIL 15TH WEDNESDAY
A long day on board the steamer devoted to writing letters to India and home. We have written to our cook and bearer in India to meet J.B. in Bombay next month. J.B. has also written to Mr Durand to ask for employment on the frontier in preference to Central India or Rajpootana [*Rajputana*].

APRIL 16TH.
We landed at Trieste about 12 o'clock in the morning and after posting our letters had breakfast at the Hotel de Ville. Trieste is a rather bright clean place full of markets, principally of oranges. We dawdled about on the steamer for nearly 2 hours before we were allowed to land, the Captain going on shore to say he had come, and other foolish things! The officers of the Douane [*customs*] opened all our boxes to see if we had any tobacco, at the railway station they opened them again to see if we had anything to eat, which they did again for the same reason between Trieste & Venice! We found news up to the 13th at the Hotel & found that war preparations are being made very fast on both sides. We also read of Lady Selborne's death, we had of course never heard of her illness [*the Countess of Selborne died on 10th April 1885*]. We left Trieste at 4.50 for Milan.

APRIL 17TH FRIDAY
Milan.
We arrived at the station at 6.30 and drove to the Hotel de Ville where we were glad to get bath and breakfast, and more newspapers, news up to the 15th.

J.B. telegraphed to Loui after breakfast to expect us in Eaton Place on Sunday evening. [*Loui, Louisa Biddulph, 1846–1926, John Biddulph's sister. Louisa lived at 31 Eaton Place with their widowed mother.*]

We went off to the Cathedral at ½ past 10 and J.B. was very much delighted with it. Unfortunately the day was cloudy so we had not a good view of the Alps from the roof. We had rather a good sort of guide who did not worry us; he showed us the statue that Napoleon 1st had put up of himself on the Cathedral roof, and the graceful tower designed by Raphael etc., I had forgotten that the Cathedral was commenced in the 14th Century only, Mass was going on so we heard the organ, which is such a fine one.

In the afternoon we drove to the Church where Leonardo de Vinci's Last Supper is, and had a long look at it. J.B. thought St John was a woman, & he certainly is made very, very effeminate looking; there is a very lackadaisical look about him, which displeases. We afterwards went on to the Museum, which was unfortunately closed. After a walk in the gardens and a poke into the shops, we were glad to rest at the Hotel. After dinner we got the English papers, which were to breathe of war preparations and peace in the same breath.

APRIL 18TH SATURDAY
We left Milan at 7.30 and came over the St. Gotthard Pass on a perfectly lovely day. How lovely it all is; we arrived at Basle at 7.30 and dined there, then packed ourselves comfortably into a wagon-lit and slept through the night. Our conductor was very stupid and dirty, but he brought us some coffee at 7 and we then performed a sort of hasty toilette, J.B. managing to shave himself most unsuccessfully. We arrived at Calais at 11.30 and had luncheon. A very calm passage and bright sun,

but the wind very keen. Our luggage was examined at Dover and no trouble given.

Sunday evening the 19th found us back again in 31 Eaton Place. Apparently all the papers speak of peace.

[*In March and early April 1885, the threat of war between Britain and Russia was very real. Russia's expansion towards Afghanistan was seen as a threat to India and the news received that Russia had occupied Penjdeh on the Afghan border only increased tensions. Diplomacy eventually won the day and war was avoided through negotiations between Russia and Britain, and the intervention of the Emir of Afghanistan (Emir Abdur Rahman Khan, Emir from 1880–1901) after talks with Lord Dufferin, the Viceroy of India, 'The Great Game'.*]

Chapter V

Return to India, 1885

The Biddulphs remained in England for three months before leaving for India on 15th July 1885. It would take twenty-six days to reach Bombay. Their journey included two days in Vienna, three in Venice and another couple of short stops en route.

Just as Julia had done in 1864, they travelled overland from Alexandria to Suez, despite the Suez Canal having been opened for sixteen years.

Julia and John Biddulph would not return to England until September 1889.

※

JULY 15TH 1885
Left England by the 8 o'clock Train from Victoria and had a rough crossing from Dover to Calais.

July 16th

At Cologne we had breakfast at 12 o'clock and then had a most horrible journey, the train shaking and rolling, flinging us about till I was sick & J.B. got a tremendous headache.

July 17th

Arrived at the Metropole Hotel Vienna a little before 11 very tired & exceedingly dirty. Coffee and a good tub restored us to cheerfulness and at 4 o'clock we started out for a drive. We spent some time in the Botanical Gardens, which are very fair and have some fine avenues, but not altogether well arranged. The clumps of shrubs from various countries are very untidy and the paths are very shingly & tiring to the feet. We thoroughly enjoyed the Prater [*large public park in Vienna*] and heard a very good band but on the other Prater were some curious amusements, one invention I thought quite diabolical. A large ship in a hall with seats for passengers, which seesawed up and down till I suppose everybody was sufficiently ill for their money. It never struck me that seasickness could be amusing before. We drove till 8 o'clock and came home in the cool; the middle of the day is very hot here now.

18th July Saturday

This morning we started for the Arsenal, which contains a splendid collection of armour. The halls are very fine themselves with painted ceilings depicting battle scenes and there is a great deal of gilding all in excellent taste. The armour is most interesting. I was delighted with Maximilian 1st's long, long toes, like an armadillo's tail, and some of the carved ivory powder horns were most fascinating.

We saw the picture gallery at [the] Belvedere afterwards. Rembrandt, Rubens, Van Dyke, Raphael, & all the old masters are represented there; but the Rubens are particularly fine, and the Dutch school too. The picture though is an old woman's head by Balth [*Balthasar*] Denner 1685 to 1749 the painting is quite marvellous. Every wrinkle and freckle to the life, the lips are life like, in fact the picture looks like life; one can hardly realise it is painted. There is a head of a man by the same artist, which is also excellent but does not come up to the old woman quite. Apparently there are only two portraits by this artist, whose name I had never heard of.

We drove to St. Stefan's Church, which is the Cathedral of Vienna. The outside is handsome but it is disappointing inside, with tawdry monuments. Afterwards we took a long drive to see the Danube and crossed over on a very fine bridge. The banks are very insignificant though the river itself is so broad and fine. We finished up with the Prater and heard the band again.

JULY 19TH SUNDAY

Vienna, our last day here so we spent all the morning at Schönbrunn where the gardens are very stately and stiff, with formal avenues cut out in lime trees. But the gardens are very large and grand and I like to see all the people reading and sitting under the trees enjoying the shade and quiet. The menagerie is not much, but J.B. discovered the European Ibex to his great delight.

JULY 20TH

Venice. Danieli's Hotel.

We arrived here this afternoon at ½ past 1 after a long journey as we actually left the Metropole Hotel in Vienna at a quarter to 9 on Sunday evening. We passed through the Austrian Tyrol, the woods and pine forests always delight me and I watched the scenery till my eyes ached. It was very hot the last three hours of our journey and the people of the hotel here seemed greatly unprepared for travellers, as they could hardly muster enough breakfast for us two.

When in Vienna we of course visited the Aquarium in the Prater, it was a very poor one, not to be compared with the one in Naples. All these sort of things seem to be done so much better in our own country.

JULY 21ST TUESDAY

Yesterday we walked about the Piazza St Mark before dinner and after dinner we got into a gondola and lounged till nearly 11 o'clock. We listened to various groups of singers; indeed music was everywhere & was kept up apparently all night. We floated about here & there, seeing the Rialto etc., it was a lovely moonlight night and all Venice was out enjoying it. This morning we started at ½ past 8 and first saw the Church St [San] Giorgio Maggiore where there is the most wonderful carving. All the stalls are carved with scenes out of the saints' lives and the seats have dolphins for arms; indeed every atom is most exquisitely carved. We spent some time at the Academia and looked well at Titian's Assumption and I refreshed my memory over the old Venetian School, Carpaccio, Jean [*Giovanni*] Bellini, Giorgione, Tintoretto, Paul [*Paolo*] Veronese etc. Afterwards we looked into St. Mark's and heard part of a very fine funeral Mass which was going on. J.B. looked long at the mosaics in the porch.

We met Hassan our old friend the Dragoman from Cairo and had a chat with him and we lunched at Florian's, coming home at ½ past one to rest.

JULY 22ND WEDNESDAY

We spent Tuesday evening on the Lido, where there is a bathing establishment and a band; a very Margate like arrangement altogether. We wandered on the sands and picked up shells and came home across the Lagune [*Lagoon*] in the loveliest golden red sea, the sunset lighting up the water into all sorts of rich lovely hues. We dined at Quadri's and lavished money on quails, having another turn down the Grand Canal before going to bed.

We visited today the Frari Church, the Arsenal and the Scuola Di San Rocco before breakfast. J.B. was delighted with the ironwork near the Frari and Ferdinando Borella had some excellent specimens, his workshop was close to the Frari.

We lunched at Quadri's and afterwards spent a long time going over the Doge's Palace with which J.B. was delighted. In the evening we went over Besard's shop full of lovely carvings. Dined at Quadri's and listened to music on the Grand Canal after dinner.

JULY 23RD THURSDAY

This morning we went over a lovely shop where we saw a great deal of carved furniture and glass of all kinds. J.B. gave me a sweet little hand mirror done in mosaic work. Afterwards we went over St. Giovanni e Paolo, which is said to be the Westminster Abbey of Venice, it is full of Doge's monuments. Then we had to return to Danieli's and pack and we found ourselves on board the "Lombardy" before 3 o'clock and left Venice soon after.

JULY 24TH FRIDAY

We stopped at Ancona and J.B. and I went ashore a little before 8 o'clock; but even then the sun was very hot and we were very thankful for every bit of shade. We drove through Ancona, round the Piazza Cavour and then up to the big Church, which has a fine position looking right over the harbour. The most interesting things about it are two lions, which support the pillars of the porch and which are of red granite and look decidedly Syrian, or perhaps I should say "Assyrian". Inside the Church is a curious marble screen about the crypt carved in panels with peacocks, griffins etc., apparently very old indeed. The rest of the Church was uninteresting. An old priest was gabbling over a service to one woman and one man on their knees, while a little boy rang a bell staring about him all the time and watching all our movements carefully, as did the small congregation. We left Ancona about 11 o'clock for Brindisi.

JULY 25TH SATURDAY
J.B.'s Birthday. We arrived at Brindisi about 9 o'clock but had not the curiosity to go on shore till ½ past 5 when we walked through the exceedingly dirty town, looked into the principal Church and then bargained for chairs at Cook's hotel. The hotel was apparently quite empty but a stray waiter and an odd man turned up and began producing chairs of sorts for which they asked the most tremendous prices. After a time they warmed to their work and showed us chairs from the windows of the top storey, while we stood in the courtyard and shook our heads. At last J.B. & Mr Reid walked upstairs to see for themselves, but we came away without any chairs trusting to Sunday's bringing down the prices.

[*Quite why they were attempting to buy chairs remains a mystery. Though possibly passengers were expected to provide their own chairs for sitting on the deck of the SS Lombardy?*]

JULY 26TH SUNDAY
Brindisi, on board the "Lombardy".

JULY 27TH.
Left Brindisi this morning at 4 o'clock.

JULY 28th TUESDAY

Lady Coke & Mrs Bridgeman were some of the Brindisi passengers, they were bound for Cyprus and their husbands were to meet them at Alexandria. Mrs Bridgeman was very nice & most untiring in her care for Lady Coke who was knocked up with travelling & most utterly helpless.

JULY 30th THURSDAY

Alexandria. We travelled through Egypt all day arriving at Suez about 8 o'clock. The arrangements for going on board our steamer at Suez were horrible. There were few lights and no one to tell one anything, porters running away with luggage nearly knocking everybody over. The steamer "Gwalia" was out of the harbour so we had to go in a tug to her and to get on the tug one had to cross over a barge. The deck of this barge gave way just as some of the passengers and many of the porters were on it, & they fell some 6 or 7 feet. In the dark it looked very alarming as one naturally thought they had fallen into the sea; one old man was hurt and most of us were frightened. We got to the "Gwalia" at last all right and went out to sea about 12 o'clock.

[For the next ten days Julia suffered from heat and seasickness, with only a brief respite at Aden.]

AUGUST 4th TUESDAY

Arrived at Aden, and left it after a few hours' stay.

AUGUST 10th, MONDAY.

Arrived in Bombay harbour about 5 o'clock in the morning but did not land till past 9.30.

I have said nothing about our weather from Suez to Bombay. The heat on the 1st, 2nd, & 3rd of August was very, very great indeed; on the 3rd it was difficult to breathe at 4 o'clock in the morning. We had a quiet day on the 5th until the afternoon when we came into the monsoon and after that had it rough & very uncomfortable till Sunday morning. It was fairly cool but the ship rolled horribly and twice I was thrown out of my chair on deck. J.B. played whist most days with Col. Oldham, Mr Steel & Mr Maguire; while I read through "The Voyage of the Jeannette" and other books. [The Voyage of the Jeannette, the Ship and Ice Journals of George W. Long, Lieutenant-Commander US Navy and Commander of the Polar Expedition 1879–1881. *Perhaps this book was a distraction to the heat?*]

Today we have taken up our abode at Watson's [hotel] & found letters awaiting us from Mrs Biddulph, Cunliffe & Colonel Kinloch. Jessie, Abdullah Khan and Seetal [the] bearer have turned up. We spent a couple of hours at Abdul's stables looking at a very indifferent lot of horses.

[*The Biddulphs spent one day in Bombay gathering their things together. Jessie was Julia's maid, and Abdullah Khan was John's bearer and right-hand man. They also had to buy horses and make arrangements for transporting their vast amount of baggage and equipment.*

John Biddulph would shortly resume his duties as a Boundary Settlement Officer in the Ajmer district of Rajasthan, which would involve months of travelling and camping in some of the remotest parts of southern Rajasthan. Though their camps were very comfortable, 'camp life' for weeks, even months on end could become very trying. They would also suffer from repeated attacks of 'Indian fever', John in particular. Julia often refers to his bouts of ill health as, 'a heavy cold', a 'bad liver' or 'spasms', all of which involved high fever and must have been most uncomfortable.

The Biddulphs travelled from Bombay to the hill station at Mount Abu in Rajasthan by rail, arriving at the railway station Abu Road on Wednesday, 12th August.]

13TH AUGUST, THURSDAY.

Mt. Aboo [*Mount Abu, Rajasthan*]. We left Bombay on Tuesday evening at 9.30 and travelled night and day arriving at Aboo Road on Wednesday at 5.30. There we found a pony and jampan [*a type of sedan chair*] waiting for us and came up the hill at once. It was a lovely evening, but became quite dark long before we reached half way and it was quite 10 o'clock before we got into Sir Edward Bradford's. We were desperately hungry too and most thankful for our dinner and then to bed. This morning it is very lovely but quite warm. J.B. killed a snake 7ft long before breakfast.

[*Mount Abu is the only hill station in Rajasthan.*

Colonel Sir Edward Bradford, 1836–1911 was the Governor-General's Agent for Rajputana and Commissioner for Ajmer. Bradford was an interesting character; he was later to become Commissioner of the Metropolitan Police, after first surviving a shipwreck on his way home from India aboard the SS Tasmania, which went aground and was wrecked on Monachi Rock, South Corsica on 17th April 1887; twenty-four passengers and crew were lost. Sir Edward had lost an arm after being mauled by a tiger when out tiger hunting in 1863, but continued to ride and to go pig sticking, holding the reins in his teeth.

The Biddulphs were en route to Udaipur where John would serve as Acting Resident for three months while the Resident Colonel Walter was on leave, before returning to his duties as Boundary Settlement Officer. They travelled to Udaipur via Ajmer, arriving on Saturday 22nd August.]

AUGUST 22ND SATURDAY

Arrived at Oodeypore [*Udaipur, Rajasthan*]. We had a long drive as we left Nimbahera at 9.20 and arrived at Oodeypore at 7.15. The road is very bad for the first 14 miles and we crossed the river on an Elephant but the last part of the road we got on grandly. Colonel Walter received us most kindly and Mr Evans-Jordon was in great force.

AUGUST 25TH TUESDAY

Colonel Walter left us this morning. We asked everybody to meet him at dinner last night & J.B. made a very nice little speech. I have now begun my housekeeping again.

SEPTEMBER 11TH FRIDAY

We all went out to Badi to tea. It is a very pretty lake about 4 miles from Oodeypore, but the road is very bad, almost unfit for riding and quite impossible for driving. We boated & J.B. caught a small Mahseer which he returned as it was only about 1 ½ pounds. I saw two large crocodiles swimming about which would account for the small quantity of fish. We got home quite late in consequence of the bad road.

[*Lake Badi, constructed by Maharana Raj Singh I, 1652–1680, as a reservoir.*

The mahseer is a freshwater fish found in lakes and rivers and was highly prized by fishermen at the time, and still is, I believe; they can be very large, a golden mahseer can grow to over 50lbs.

The rest of September was spent settling in, the remainder of their baggage arrived, J.B.'s new horse arrived, and many people came and went until Saturday 10th October.]

OCTOBER 10TH SATURDAY

The Grant Duffs, Dr Mackenzie, Mr Gordon, Capt. Bagot & Major Moore arrived about 4.30pm, they had left Chittore [*Chittorgarh*] at 7 and had breakfast en route so they did the 70 miles extremely well.

A Bhil dance in the evening, the Kilkee [*sic*] is a wild war cry and the Bhils scream this while dancing. When they wish to collect a force for fighting they scream the Kilkee from the top of a hill and it is taken up & answered from hill to hill.

OCTOBER 11TH

Mr Grant Duff had a visit from the Maharana in the morning [*HH Maharana Sir Fateh Singh, 1849–1930, 31st Maharana of Udaipur from 1884–1930*] and at 4 o'clock in the afternoon he returned it. Mrs Grant Duff, Dr Mackenzie, Mrs Gordon and I took a boat at the Mission house and joined the rest of the party at the Jag Manda [*Jag Mandir, the Lake Garden Palace on Lake Pichola*]. They were all very much delighted with the lake & the Palaces and all said it was unlike any other place they had seen before.

In some ways one might say Oodeypore resembled Venice and the island Palaces Isola Bella on the Maggiore, but there is really a very faint resemblance to either place. Dr Webb & Mr Thomson dined in the evening with us.

OCTOBER 12TH MONDAY

Mrs Grant Duff and Mrs Gordon & I went over the English Palace [*the City Palace*] at 9 a.m. The principal features in the Palace are the big rooms, the glass furniture and a very cleverly painted bathroom painted by a local artist with Cyprus trees and other trees and shrubs full of birds and squirrels on a green ground.

At 4 p.m. we visited the Old Palace [*within the City Palace*] and saw a room lined with Dutch tiles, the Court with mosaics of peacocks and several very beautifully cut ivory doors.

All the elephants were out covered with gorgeous trappings, the horses smothered in gold ornaments & trappings, pigeons & geese walking about among them all. The crowd of followers was most imposing. Such curious headdresses and several very fine looking men.

The Maharana courteously went all over the palace with us. We then went on the lake and Mrs Grant Duff sketched. We got home by 6.30 and at 7.30 we again embarked for the Jag Niwas [*on Lake Pichola*] where we dined. The lake was illuminated most beautifully. Such a lovely night one never can forget. Mr Grant Duff made a very nice little speech after dinner [*Mr ME Grant Duff, 1829–1906, Governor of Madras, 1881–1886 and later Sir Mountstuart Grant Duff*].

OCTOBER 18TH, SUNDAY.
We had service at 4 o'clock and afterwards drove down to a corner of the Bazaar where we watched the Rajah's procession. He was taken to a tree near our grounds where he went through some religious ceremonies, worshipping the tree and then marrying it etc. The procession was most interesting. All the Rajpoots were dressed in their petticoats and had wonderful headdresses, they rode prancing horses covered with gay trappings and all their retainers followed them. The elephants were covered with gold & silver and cloths and ornaments of all descriptions. The quivering lances were a very pretty feature in the procession and palms were also introduced. The standard was carried before the Maharana who was most gorgeous in gold and white starched petticoats. The Rajpoot dress is far prettier than the Greek. After the procession we drove in the gardens and Dr Mullen dined with us in the evening.

OCTOBER 21ST, WEDNESDAY.
Another great function took place today; the Maharana went out of the Delhi Gate escorted by all his nobles in armour and half a mile out 101 guns were fired, said to commemorate the taking of Delhi; which is a myth altogether. The armour was rather disappointing as most of it was new and the chief part of the dress was satin and silk. Mr Meade & Capt. Gordon

arrived in the evening, the latter quite ill & obliged to go to bed immediately.

22ⁿᵈ OCTOBER.

Mr Gordon heard of his appt. as attaché to the Foreign Office. Antonio the cook arrived in the evening.

23ʳᵈ OCTOBER.

We went to the Palace to see an Elephant fight. Mr Gordon and Mr Meade were with us. It was a wonderful sight. The Maharana sat with his nobles on a sort of balcony and we sat on his right hand. All the nobles and suite wore lovely pale blue, pink, green, yellow & red turbans and waistbands. All the crowd who swarmed on every terrace and vacant space wore bright turbans & sashes and the women who were opposite us on another balcony wore lovely colours. The same beautiful shades of green, blue & pink & yellow, only as veils. They stood out against the white walls of the Palace like a bouquet of flowers.

The Elephants were below us and they were loaded with chains. One was fastened to the ground by a huge chain and the other was driven to a wall, which was between them and then progged on to the attack. The huge creature goes on the wall and would soon have been over and would have killed the other if it had not been held back by the heavy chains. It was a very curious sight. The animals seemed so enormous and made such a noise when they clashed. When the inside Elephant got sulky the other was induced to leave him with great difficulty.

[After this unpleasant form of entertainment, life quietened down for a few days before the arrival of the Viceroy Lord Dufferin and his entourage.]

1ST NOVEMBER SUNDAY

Charlie Adeane arrived at 9.30 in very good force & much delighted at having seen a panther on the road.

[Charles Robert Whorwood Adeane, 1863–1943. Charles's mother, Lady Elizabeth Philippa Adeane, married John Biddulph's brother Michael (later 1st Baron Biddulph) in 1877; her husband had died in 1870. Charlie became John Biddulph's step-nephew. He was serving in India with the Suffolk Regiment at this time. Charles Adeane was later Lord Lieutenant of Cambridgeshire from 1915 until his death in 1943; he lived at Babraham, Cambridgeshire.]

2ND NOVEMBER.

Charlie and I rowed about the lake before breakfast for a couple of hours. In the evening we all three went on the lake and we saw some crocodiles and John tried his new gun at all sorts of birds. Charlie tried very hard to shoot a flying fox but did not succeed.

3RD NOVEMBER, TUESDAY.

Charlie went out after snipe with Dr Mullen. Mr Wingate arrived for breakfast. The Maharana paid J.B. a visit in the afternoon and tried the new rifle.

8TH NOVEMBER, SUNDAY.

The Viceroy, Lady Dufferin, Lady Helen Blackwood, Miss Thynne etc., all arrived about 6 o'clock. John, Mr Wingate and Dr Ffrench Mullen having gone out four miles to meet them.

They all came in very tired but said the arrangements on the road had been most excellent. Lord Dufferin was so done up with a bad headache that he went straight to bed.

I went into dinner with Sir Edward Bradford so I had the chance of a good talk with him, and on the other side I had Mr Mackenzie Wallace who is very good company

[*Mackenzie Wallace, later Sir Donald Mackenzie Wallace KCIE KCVO, 1841–1919, Private Secretary to Lord Dufferin*]. We had great talks over Laurence Oliphant's peculiarities [*the same Mr Oliphant whom the Biddulphs had stayed with at Haifa in March*], and he told me that Laurence Oliphant had a very good eye for the main chance and was always very able to take care of his own affairs, which rather surprised me. I have always thought him rather too much of a visionary for that sort of thing. After dinner Lady Dufferin came into the drawing room for a very short time and then went off to bed.

9ᵀᴴ NOVEMBER, MONDAY.

We breakfasted with Lord Dufferin and his family, Lord William Beresford and Major Cooper joining the party.

[*Lord William Beresford VC, third son of the Marquess of Waterford and brother of Lord Charles who had run the Ibis or paddy bird in the menagerie race at Cairo on 30ᵗʰ January. Lord William served as ADC to Lord Northbrook in 1874 and then as military secretary to four successive viceroys including Lord Dufferin, retiring in 1894. He won the VC during the 1879 Zulu War, having taken special leave from the Viceroy to sail to South Africa in order to serve with his regiment, the 9ᵗʰ Hussars.*]

The Maharana paid a State visit on the Viceroy at 11 o'clock. 12.30 the Viceroy returned it. I had luncheon in the tent with all the Staff etc. and at 3 o'clock Lady Dufferin, the two girls, Major Cooper & myself started for the lake.

We took boats at the Mission House and rowed up to the Jag Manda, which delighted Lady Dufferin immensely. Then we had tea at the Jag Niwas and there John & Lord Dufferin joined us; they had been riding through the City. Lord William & Capt. Harbord joined us too.

We got home by 6 o'clock in the evening. Mrs L and her sister came to see Lady Dufferin and she had a long talk about hospital work with them. All the Station dined with us so we [were] 30 to dinner.

The Maharana's band played and the thing went off very well. After dinner we had a Bhil dance, which delighted them all so much; they stayed for a long time watching it. The women especially pleased them & they all got into the centre of the circle and the women danced round them. Lord Dufferin also talked about Laurence Oliphant at dinner in much the same way as Mr Mackenzie Wallace.

10TH NOVEMBER, TUESDAY.

Lady Dufferin went out photographing on the lake before breakfast then the whole party went over the big Palace before luncheon. At a quarter to 3 o'clock we drove to the site of the new "Walter" hospital where Lady Dufferin laid the foundation.

Then off we all drove to a Pig shoot. Lord William drove the team and the young ladies. Charlie, Major Cooper, Dr Findlay and myself made up the party inside the van. We drove at a furious pace going and very nearly came to grief, which the girls seemed to enjoy.

Lord Dufferin on arriving at the rendezvous found his valet had not come up with his spectacles, horrid grief! At last after sundry false alarms the valet did arrive, but not the spectacles. The man had put a box of matches into his pocket with the spectacles and the box igniting and burning his coat, the spectacles had been lost and were never found again.

A good many pigs were driven up and 2 hyenas but of course Lord D. never even saw a pig, though he fired at several but he generally had his gun in the air and was looking quite in the wrong direction.

We had a great hustle to drive home in time to dress for dinner and then start again for the illuminations on the lake, and the dinner at the Palace. The illuminations were even lovelier than when the Grant Duffs were with us.

I had old Temple near me at dinner but could not talk much to him as Lord D. was in a story telling mood and gave me various anecdotes of French society. He mentioned the Baroness Malortie at Cairo in a very enlightening manner. We did not get home till nearly 12 from our entertainment, and were very tired with our long day.

11TH NOVEMBER, WEDNESDAY.

The whole party left after breakfasting at 8 o'clock here. Major Cooper was quite ill being knocked over by the sun, but no one else seemed the worse for the racket. Lord Dufferine's chief anxiety was to get to Chittor [*Chittorgarh*] in time to see it before it became too dark, so he rushed off without saying goodbye to John! I believe he was very much taken up with the Burma question all the time he was here but he certainly took very little interest in the Maharana. I think Bhil dances and pig shooting pleased him most.

[*The Third Anglo-Burmese War 1885; Burma declared a province of India, November 1885. The Biddulphs were now preparing to leave Udaipur and go into camp. J.B. was to resume his work as a Boundary Settlement Officer.*]

23RD NOVEMBER, MONDAY.

We started off 12 carts of luggage to Chittor. Charlie went to another pig shoot and I drove with him to the rendezvous where a whole army was collected, Elephants, the band, nobles, camels etc. Charlie very soon returned, not being able to stand 20 rifles let off in his ear almost at one pig.

We went on the lake afterwards, at least in the evening, and finished up with our last dinner party; Charlie became quite down at the idea of leaving Oodeypore. Billiards & music finished up our evening.

24TH NOVEMBER.

Charlie left at 7.30 for Chittor. In the evening I went to sit with Mrs Thomson after a drive with J.B. in the Public Gardens, and on returning home found we had two guests. Count Albiani [*Count Alessandro Albiani*] and Count De Guberantis, very unwelcome as we are packing off all our servants etc. to Chittor. We talked English during dinner but afterwards fell into French as the Counts have great difficulty in speaking English. They have come here solely for sight seeing and want to leave at once which cannot well be managed.

25TH NOVEMBER.

I had a very busy day, got up before breakfast and had a good ride with J.B. [and] wrote home letters.

In the afternoon we drove to the foot of Sajan Garh [*Sajjan Garh*] and we walked up to the Palace that is being built on the very top of the mountain; really a very wonderful work and most interesting to see, with a lovely view over the country. Some of the carving too is very clever and the thick walls are most astonishing. The women's apartments are remarkably stuffy as usual. We saw heaps of monkeys. We returned to the carriage before it became quite dark, but a wheel came off after a little time and we had to walk home.

The Counts appeared to dinner and seemed to be much pleased with their visit to the Palace, they had gone all over the Lake Palaces in the morning [*Sajjan Garh, the Monsoon Palace; building began in 1884 and is named after Maharana Sajjan Singh, 1874–1884*].

26TH NOVEMBER, THURSDAY.

I went over to see Mrs Thomson in the morning and found she had had fever in the night again. When I returned I found one of the unfortunate Counts had broken himself; tumbled off his pony and had a black eye. Dr Shepherd came to see him and said there was nothing very much amiss but he had taken to his bed.

We said goodbye to Dr Shepherd, Mr McInnes & Mr Thomson after breakfast. Mr Plowden arrived in the afternoon.

27TH NOVEMBER, FRIDAY.

Our last day in Oodeypore. J.B. received a letter from Mr Durand in the morning telling him that he was to be put on special duty in Rajpootana [*Rajputana*] until March, when Colonel Muir is supposed to leave Tonk [*Rajasthan*] and we are supposed to go there.

28TH NOVEMBER, SATURDAY.

Left Oodeypore at 7.30 & arrived in Chittor Camp by 5 o'clock. We passed Dr Mullen on the road.

SUNDAY, CHITTOR

The Coles arrived by the early train before breakfast, they and the baby were very well & in good spirits. We went up to the Fort [*Chittor or Chittorgarh Fort*] in the afternoon on Elephants and I was much surprised at the extent of the Fort. The towers of Victory are very fine and many parts are really very picturesque.

2ND DECEMBER, WEDNESDAY.

We drove in the break to a tank [*reservoir*] about 6 miles from Chittor and had breakfast there. Mrs Cole and I sat on a bank while J.B. & Major Cole shot sand grouse & snipe or rather J.B. did the shooting. When we came home we divided the game and sent some on with the Coles who left by the evening train, and we sent some to the Collins.

3ʳᴰ DECEMBER, THURSDAY.
We left Chittor by the 9 o'clock train in the evening.

4ᵀᴴ DECEMBER, FRIDAY.
Ajmer [*Ajmer, Rajasthan*].

Arrived at 6 a.m. at the Station where Mr Colvin met us, a most bitterly cold morning. We found a large camp at the Residency; Lady Bradford is looking very unwell, but Colonel Bradford looks worse. We had a great talk over many things and it is now decided that we go into camp somewhere in the district for 3 months until J.B. has a good appointment.

7ᵀᴴ DECEMBER, MONDAY.
Ajmer.

John & I went out with Colonel Bradford & Colonel Graham in the afternoon to see the City and a splendid Temple, which is a mixture of Mohammedan & Hindoo [*Hindu*] architecture. The original building being a beautiful Hindoo Temple with endless carved pillars to which the Mohammedans added a façade when they turned it into a Mosque.

Sir E. Bradford and I walked home together from the Lochs, and we talked about the future and all the present worry. Sir E was very hopeful about the future, as he said there would be so many vacancies and that J.B. was sure to get a good appointment, but we are both very low about it. I suppose it is almost certain we shall go to Deoli in March.

[*While waiting for his new appointment, John Biddulph continued his work as a Boundary Settlement Officer, settling disputes between various princely states in the region. A whole entourage of camp followers would have travelled with the Biddulphs: bearers, servants, grooms – or syces, as they were* called – and numerous horses and camels. Also, cows, sheep, goats and chickens to provide meat, milk and eggs, even elephants for transport to the more difficult places.

The tents were very comfortable and well-furnished; they had many rooms, bedrooms, dressing rooms, bathrooms, a drawing room and dining room, etc. These camping expeditions also provided great opportunity for sport, shooting and fishing. The game that they shot and the fish that they caught were always eaten and / or distributed amongst the camp followers. Quite how they were kept fresh and edible in this climate is food for thought! Big game was weighed, measured and skinned; the skins made valuable trophies.]

8TH DECEMBER, TUESDAY.
Ajmer.
The Henneys left for Jeypore and we are making a great push to get into our own camp.

9TH DECEMBER, WEDNESDAY.
We had breakfast in our own camp near the Commissionaire's house, a great business getting in all our things. We sent off a great many boxes to the Magazine and are gradually getting our camp together. We went up to say goodbye to the Bradfords at 4 o'clock, found them very busy packing for camp as they leave tomorrow.

10TH DECEMBER, THURSDAY.
We rode to the Jail [*where carpets were made by the prisoners*] in the morning and chose some carpets and dhurries for camp and I ordered 2 dhurries for Amy [*Amy Laurie, Julia's sister; a dhurrie is a traditional Indian flat woven rug or carpet*]. The Bradfords left this morning.

12TH DECEMBER, SATURDAY.

We rode in the afternoon and took the dogs for a good scamper in the country. I finished my sketch of the lake in the morning.

13TH DECEMBER, SUNDAY.

Our last day in Ajmer, we hope to leave early tomorrow morning. A thick mist all the morning till nearly 10 o'clock and very cold. We dine tonight with the Newmans and start our camp this afternoon after tea.

Our little fox terrier "Toby" ran off this morning and I am afraid it has been stolen. Mr Hallan came to see us in the afternoon and lent me his hill pony while we are in camp, a grey pony with a tremendous coat.

14TH DECEMBER.

Saradhana. [*Saradhana, Ajmer, Rajasthan*] We rode here this morning and got in by 9.30 in the morning, ten miles of good road mostly alongside of the railroad. I rode my dun pony & Abdullah Khan came on the grey; the Ayah and bearer by train.

15TH DECEMBER.

Kharwa [*Rajasthan*]

Arrived at 10 a.m. We left Saradhana at 7.30 and found a very good road all the way; it is a little over 13 miles to Kharwa. I rode Mr Hallan's white pony and it certainly has no desire to run away with its rider. We found the road very deserted, hardly passing 6 carts and certainly not a dozen people.

[*Julia was an accomplished horsewoman and it is probable that she would have ridden astride rather than side-saddle.*]

16TH DECEMBER.
Beawar [*Rajasthan*]

This morning I rode here by myself, Abdullah Khan accompanying me on the dun as I rode the grey. J.B. stayed behind to shoot ducks as we found such a quantity on the lake last evening at Kharwa. I got into Beawar before 9.30, as I was afraid of the rain coming on. Jessie [*Julia's maid*] turned up at 11 and J.B. at one o'clock having shot 12 ducks. The lake at Kharwa is a very large one surrounded on one side with pig preserves.

17TH DECEMBER.
Beawar.

We looked over J.B.'s ducks yesterday and found he had 7 different sorts. In the afternoon we walked over to the Govt. gardens and found a large tank [*reservoir*] there with several kingfishers and lots of different water birds on it. In the evening we dined with Capt. Ravenshaw. The clouds are passing away and it looks more like fine weather.

18TH DECEMBER, FRIDAY.
Beawar.

Last night it rained very heavily and the camp is in a most miserable condition this morning. The wretched Jessie got quite wet in her corner of the tent and presented a most woebegone appearance when she appeared with the tea. Yesterday Colonel Trevor arrived and we walked with him & Capt. Ravenshaw in the Bazaar. I bought some of the Beawar cloths yesterday.

19TH DECEMBER, SATURDAY.

We dined with Colonel Trevor last night and are now preparing to move from here. We send our camp on this afternoon.

20ᵀᴴ DECEMBER, SUNDAY.
Jawaja [*Rajasthan*]

Arrived here at 10 o'clock a.m. We left Beawar at 7 in a thick white mist; the distance is about 14 miles and a fairly good road. Last night we dined with Capt. Ravenshaw and met Colonel Trevor & Mr Whiteway. Our camp here is on the banks of a big tank but there are no duck to be seen. The Dak Bungalow is close to us but very much occupied. [*The Dak Bungalow was a government building, originally from East India Company days, and kept up during the Raj, providing free accommodation to government officials and, with permission and payment of a small rent, to other travellers. They had been and still were used by the postal service, which worked on a relay along the Dak routes from one bungalow to the next. There was often a resident caretaker.*]

We tried to walk round the tank in the afternoon but did not manage it. There were duck & teal on the tank but unfortunately J.B. had not taken his gun. Coming home J.B. stopped to speak to some of the people and they told him that Mohammedans and Hindoos intermarried here and lived very happily together.

21ˢᵀ DECEMBER.
Jassakhera [*Jass Khera*]

We rode here this morning a distance of 12 miles; part of the road is very hilly. We got a letter this morning from Dr Newman and he seems to have found our little fox terrier.

22ᴺᴰ DECEMBER.
Bheem [*Bhim*].

We rode the 8 miles here rather slowly at first as it is very uphill and the road winds a great deal, in fact what J.B. calls a curly road. There is a very good tank here and it is a very pretty place surrounded with hills. This is the 3rd Bungalow we have met with since leaving Beawar.

23RD DECEMBER, WEDNESDAY.
Barar. We had a very short march in here, as it is only 7 miles from Bheem. On the way we met Mr Bevan who was formerly in the 19th Hussars.

Yesterday we went to several tanks in the neighbourhood of Bheem and I walked altogether about 5 miles. We got 2 ducks, the kind with the beautiful bills which are very good eating, but there are no snipe and not many duck considering the number of tanks & jheels about [a jheel *is a pond, usually in a marshy area*]. We have seen a good many bush partridges. In the afternoon we walked over to the tank, which is a charming one and J.B. shot 6 teal, but the great difficulty was to get them out of the water. The weeds were so strong that the men could not swim well and they got nervous, besides being chilled with the cold; however after several attempts by different men all the teal were retrieved. [*Surely a gun dog would have been a more acceptable way of retrieving the game, and rather more efficient too?*]

24TH DECEMBER.
Deogarh.

We arrived here a little after 10 o'clock and the R's [*Rajah's*] son met us about a mile from the camp. The road is very bad between this and Barar, so very stony; it is not more than 12 miles.

Abdullah Khan starts back to Beawar to meet J.B.'s ponies from Bombay, my pony has a sore back.

25TH DECEMBER, XMAS DAY, FRIDAY.
J.B. and I rode to a jheel some 4 miles from here in the morning and he shot 6 teal & 3 snipe, one being a pin-tailed snipe.

There were quantities of duck on the tanks but they were very wild and never settled after the first shot. We did not get home till past 11.30.

J.B. visited the Rajah in the afternoon. I made bread sauce for the skinny chicken, which had to do duty as our Xmas turkey! We drank "absent friends" in mulled claret after dinner and talked free trade during dinner!

[*J.B. visited the Raja, Rawat Shri Krishna Singhji, born 1847, 12th Rawat of Deogarh, 1867–1900.*]

26TH DECEMBER.
Deogarh.

We went out in the morning pig shooting. We saw immense large herds of pigs but they are very difficult to shoot. J.B. shot two; one was lost in the jungle, and two hares. The beaters made such a noise & everybody talked so much and so loudly it was wonderful that we saw any pigs at all.

Our home letters came in the morning, we heard from Mrs Biddulph, Loui, Georgie & Edith, all full of the late elections & Michael's large majority of 773 [*Michael Biddulph, J.B.'s brother, elected MP for Ross, Herefordshire as a Liberal, later a Liberal Unionist, 1886*].

In the afternoon we again went out shooting & J.B. got one hare, 4 sand grouse & 1 partridge.

27TH DECEMBER, SUNDAY.
Deogarh.

J.B. went to see the hill which has been the cause of so much fighting resulting in the death of several persons. It was a great scramble up the hill and he did not get home to breakfast till 12 o'clock. In the afternoon we went out for a walk and J.B. shot 3 sand grouse.

29ᵗʰ DECEMBER.
Deogarh.

Went out pig shooting in the morning. The new horses arrived from Bombay and are very nice, "the Sheikh" & "Champion". J.B. finished his paper on "Free Trade".

30ᵀᴴ DECEMBER.
Deogarh.

J.B. went to the top of the disputed hill in the morning and I sketched.

31ˢᵗ DECEMBER.

J.B. rode over to see Colonel Trevor at Pipli [*Peepali Baori, Rajasthan*] and interviewed Mr Whiteway etc.

[*So ends 1885 – except that on 3rd January 1886, Julia records an incident that happened whilst they were at Deogarh.*]

3ᴿᴰ JANUARY, SUNDAY.
Deogarh.

A man came from the Palace to tell John that the young Rajah and his wife had been insensible from drink all day. His story was that last night the young people had gone off to their own apartments taking a bottle of native liquor with them and had locked themselves in. This morning at 10 o'clock as they did not appear, the door was forced open and they were both found insensible. John went off to the Palace and found the boy (only 16 years old) with teeth clenched and in a dying state, breathing hard. The native doctor had not been allowed to do anything though he wished to give an emetic in the morning but was prevented doing so. Some salt and water was forced down the boy's throat at J.B.'s suggestion, but too late for he died whilst John was in the Palace & the poor little wife, who was enceinté and could hardly have been more than 14, died half an hour afterwards.

[Folded into the back of this journal are several loose pages written by Julia Biddulph later in her life. I have copied these pages exactly as she wrote them, using the same names and spellings as Julia used.

John Biddulph was at Deogarh to settle a boundary dispute between the Maharana and one of his neighbours. The Maharana was at this time, Maharana Kishan Singh, Rawat of Deogarh from 1867–1900; his son and heir was Jaswant Singh, who had recently married Ajab Kunwar, a princess from Badnore. The Summer Palace is, I believe, the Deogarh Mahal, now a luxury hotel.]

I have spent Xmas in so many strange places surrounded by different peoples in far away lands but a particular Xmas in an Indian camp returns to my memory with a distinctness that never seems to wear off.

We had been living the usual delightful insouciant sort of life everybody leads in camp in the bright Indian winter; riding in the mornings to fresh camping grounds, shooting in the afternoons, dining hungrily when it became dark and sleeping soundly all night; unless a prowling Tiger roused the camp at night.

When that occurs every one wakes; the horses, elephants, dogs etc. all show their uneasiness by their cries & restlessness and one listens with a curious thrill to the rasping sound of the beast as he comes and goes; though he may be the other side of the river and the camp fires & movement keep him at a respectful distance. Still one wakes and listens and it is sometimes difficult to sleep again.

The camping ground we chose for our Xmas week was a very charming one, our tents being pitched under big mango trees and good jheels with duck and snipe not far off. While the old Rajah who lived in a queer old Palace on the top of a hill near us offered us any amount of wild boar to shoot.

The Rajah's son came out to meet us the morning we rode into camp; a good-looking slim youth with graceful manners and most beautifully dressed. I admired so much his green turban and coat with brown leather belt and boots and an emerald and diamond clasp fastening his turban on one side. He had a queer following of men dressed in every colour with shields and guns on their backs, and their horses were adorned with magenta coloured manes & tails. The cavalcade looked very picturesque in the brilliant sunshine.

Sindar Singh, the young Rajah, told us his old father was coming to see us in the evening but that he was too old to ride far now and seldom left his own Palace. He then introduced the Prime Minister to us who had a most evil looking countenance I thought, with a great deal of dark beard and moustache, and a fearful squint.

Sindar Singh chatted away merrily with my husband, and being a good sportsman told us of much that could be done in the way of shooting during the next few days. He was very anxious that I should come out too to the pig shoot he was arranging for us and he was full of young life and spirits.

Jewan the Prime Minister tried to cut in to the conversation, but was rather curtly answered I thought. Sindar Singh's young wife was not mentioned of course, but he had married a young girl, the daughter of a neighbouring Rajah, quite lately. An alliance that did not at all please the Prime Minister, there being little money in the transaction and in the old days, a good many feuds & bad blood between the two States.

When we reached our tents our young host bid us adieu, again assuring us of his great pleasure at our visit.

During breakfast my husband told me a little of the history of the old Rajah and of Sindar Singh, his only son. The young man had not had a very happy youth; his father was very suspicious and penurious, and the young one was extravagant and modern. The Prime Minister was intent on saving money and not having been consulted about Sindar Singh's marriage, he hated the bride, her family, and everything belonging to her, and was strongly suspected of making very bad blood between father and son. However, now there was a good deal of rejoicing in the Palace as the young wife was to be a mother and the direct descent was assured to the old man; the extravagant son was forgiven and made much of.

The young people lived in a summer Palace in the grounds of the old Palace, and had a separate establishment; but with the usual amount of eastern gossip & espionage, every detail of their lives was discussed in every house in the village.

It was universally agreed they were a loving couple; it was also very evident that Jewan the Prime Minister was not too much beloved. He had had all the management of the State for years during the childhood of Sindar Singh. The old Rajah being old and indolent and often drinking hard, so that gradually he depended entirely on Jewan for everything and they both combined to make the young man's life as uncomfortable as possible.

Now that Sindar Singh had passed his minority and was ready and eager even, to take the lead in the affairs of the State, and was in every way competent to do so, Jewan found himself pushed into the background, and the Rajah was jealous of his heir and annoyed at his popularity. The marriage too had added fuel to the flames for Gulab the Rose had not taken any trouble to hide her dislike to Jewan and the courtiers of course had suited their manners to that of the coming King. The old Rajah was apparently pleased at the prospect of a grandson, so he was on very friendly terms with the young couple and just at the time of our arrival it was Jewan who was left out in the cold.

By the time breakfast was over I felt quite an habitué of Deogarh and up to all its politics; my husband went off to his usual occupations, I to mine.

In the afternoon I had almost forgotten the promised visit from the Palace when I heard in the distance the sound of music. Tom-toms and shrill cries, and as the noise approached and I heard the laudatory ejaculations of the people, I remembered that the Royalties were coming to our camp.

I looked out of my tent door and saw the straggling cortege; first the runners, then some wild looking soldiery; all turbans, hair, muskets & shields, some on horses, some on camels, a confused vision of brilliant reds and yellows. And then came the old man, dressed in pure white, with a white turban in which flashed a brilliant jewel and emeralds round his neck, riding a beautiful Arab and surrounded by attendants all shouting his praises. After that came the young man Sindar Singh in a rose coloured satin coat, his pale yellow turban contrasting so well with his large dark eyes and oval dark face. He had a very grave pre-occupied air I thought and hardly looked round at all, quite different from his boyish eager manner in the morning. Jewan followed in sober brown with a turban of many colours not looking any handsomer than before, and they vanished into my husband's tent while their followers dispersed under the trees and their confidential attendants pumped our confidential attendants as to the Sahib's temper, his inclinations and general life and behaviour, even condescending to ask the same about the Sahib's Mem.

Daily newspapers not being in vogue in Indian Bazaars, it is so necessary to gather all the news and information by word of mouth and that information may be so useful, even lucrative some day; who knows?

I heard afterwards from my husband that the Royal visit had passed off very pleasantly with only one little incident; that Jewan wished to join in the conversation more than the young man thought desirable. The old Rajah seemed very feeble but was bent on hospitality, which finally took the form of a pig shoot to be arranged for the next day; to which I was especially invited.

The cavalcade departed and after that arrived a present of a dinner. Many wonderful meats and sweets adorned with silver and gold paper. Oranges, pistachio nuts, almonds & raisins and boxes of sweet Cabul [Kabul] grapes and an especial sweetmeat that was only made at the Palace, round white balls made of honey & sugar, flavoured with rose water & some indescribable essence; all these were rapidly disposed of in camp before night.

Next morning we rode out in the cool before sunrise and joined Sindar Singh in the jungles where he had arranged a beat or two for shooting wild boar. He was a charming host that morning; dressed in a peculiar leaf green with brown leather belt and boots, turban of the same green, and some beautiful old knives in his belt, the handles carved with jewels set in gold. The dress was so appropriate and indistinguishable in the jungles; an Oriental's taste in dress is generally perfect when it does not touch Western ideas. Even Jewan was cheerful that lovely morning and exerted himself to the utmost to be agreeable.

We rode through the jungles, through glades & drives cut out on purpose for the sport and then dismounted and climbed up on a little platform from which we could see down several green glades where pig were to be driven.[1]

---

[1] Every Rajput where the country allows it keeps a sort of reserve, which is full of pig and deer for his own sport. It is in fact like the hunting Park of a great English Nobleman 400 years ago. All forest and broken ground where pigs cannot be ridden but must be shot, which is very repugnant to English feelings.

There we sat some time, hardly daring to whisper even when the shouts of the beaters & tom-toms were heard and we saw an old pig cautiously stick out his head and then rush across the glade. He was followed by several others, and my husband and Sindar Singh got three pigs, much to the joy of the followers who love roast pig.

My husband did not feel much joy in the sport naturally, as he was a good pig-sticker and would have much preferred a spear to a gun. The country though was utterly opposed to pig-sticking, being broken up into ravines and generally covered with shrubs and small trees; there hardly being a flat open space which would have allowed a run.

We spent the morning shooting pig, going from one ravine to another until the sun became too hot to be pleasant, even in December.

On Xmas eve Sindar Singh told us that he and his wife were going away on a visit to his father-in-law almost immediately to receive a grant of land, and he seemed very pleased and elated about this as it was some land that had long been coveted by Deogarh and was very rich and desirable. He also told my husband some of his hopes for the future. Opening out roads for his grain to get to the large markets, deepening tanks [*reservoirs*], and adding to the prosperity of his people. He also wished to build a new Palace, and even got so far as to think of a State Railway. But at this point he found that Jewan had ridden very close to us and was intently listening to the conversation. Sindar Singh instantly stopped and his eyes blazed with anger, he said something very uncivil. Jewan's evil countenance became quite diabolic and we all cantered on rather briskly for ten minutes, changing the conversation quickly for local enquiries about trees & sport until our young host was calm again.

Doubtless their conversation was repeated to the old man with additions and he was made to believe more than ever that

Sindar Singh was longing for his death and eager to ascend the Gadi or Throne.

The incident quite threw a shadow over our bright morning as the young man seemed to recover his calm with difficulty and when he courteously bade us adieu near our camp he was still angry. He galloped off to his Palace followed by his Shikarees [*huntsmen*] and men, Jewan following at some distance, clouds of dust hiding the whole cavalcade from our eyes.

Xmas Day being Xmas Day, we feasted the whole of our camp, and ourselves had turkey & plum pudding which Antonio considered was the one unalterable feature of the Burra Dheen [*sic*] or Great Day.

We shot duck in the afternoon and spent a great deal of time receiving presents of fruit and vegetables, dālis so called. The oranges were piled up high and nests of dates, grapes, almonds & raisins, cakes and sweets, pistachio nuts and sugar accumulated. They were all distributed among the camp and Hindoos, Mohammedans, Portuguese and Christians suffered alike from indigestion.

We saw nothing of the Palace people next day, and one day of camp life is so like another, riding in the mornings, business in the middle of the day, shooting in the afternoon, that time passes only too quickly.

The second day after Xmas my husband received an intention from the Prime Minister that he wished to call on him to pay his respects on his own account, the previous visit having been paid in attendance on the Rajahs.

About 2 o'clock Jewan arrived and they talked over different matters of interest in the State. After some little time, just when J.B. thought Jewan was going, he mentioned that the young Kunwar [*Prince*] Sindar Singh was not at all well, in fact at the moment was unconscious from a drinking bout.

J.B. was much startled and asked how long he had remained in this state, and then was told the following story.

Jewan stated that the night before, Sindar Singh and his wife Jolab had retired rather early to their house in the Palace gardens and that one of the women in attendance had been ordered to bring them a bottle of liquor, and then strict orders were given that they were not to be disturbed again that night.

In the morning the women were moving about outside and all was very quiet so they did not enter the room, but sat outside. At last the young wife's favourite woman began to be uneasy and lifting up the curtain found Jolab lying on the floor by the side of the bed, Sindar Singh on the bed, both quite unconscious and they had remained so up to the hour when Jewan left the Palace.

J.B. asked if the old Rajah was not terrified and what remedies had been tried to restore the young couple, to which the Minister replied that the young man's drinking habits were so well known that no one had been frightened at all. But that as he was not recovering very quickly they began to think the young couple might have also suffered from charcoal fumes, and the Hakeem [*physician or doctor*] had been doing his very utmost for them. They had had goat's milk rubbed frequently on the palms of their hands, and all methods were being made to restore them to health. J.B. thought the whole story so very odd. First the drinking bout, never having heard of the young man's intemperate habits, though the old one was known to drink very hard. Then the introduction of charcoal fumes without apparently any reason, and the concealment of the illness for so many hours.

J.B. instantly sent up a message to the Rajah to ask if he should come up and see Sindar Singh as he had a slight knowledge of medicine and might help. Jewan rode off hastily with the note and there came an answer almost immediately begging J.B. to go up to the Palace.[2]

J.B. galloped off and rode through a crowd of people who had collected at hearing the news of the Kunwar's illness. There were all sorts of rumours afloat that the young man had poisoned himself after a violent quarrel with his father. That poison had been administered by one of the women in revenge for some insult, and the air was thick with strange stories.

Directly J.B. entered the Palace he was taken through several rooms furnished with every sort of atrocity. Satin covered sofas & chairs of every hue, large gilt mirrors and glass chandeliers etc., into a small apartment where the young man lay on a string bed (charpoy), a most utterly bare comfortless room. He was breathing stertorously like one in a fit of apoplexy, his teeth clenched, eyes with the pupils fixed upwards and his heart beating violently.

The room was crowded with people all doing nothing, and the Hakeem was standing by the bedside gazing at the boy. J.B. called for water, raised the boy's head on a pillow and told the Cabuli Hakeem to bring salt and water immediately as an emetic was the only hope. The Hakeem immediately began to protest that he had wished to try this remedy but was forbidden to do so, and was peremptorily ordered to administer it at once. But it was too late, in a few minutes all was over.

Jolab was dead, had been dead since quite early in the morning though they told my husband she was still alive but dying.

Then commenced the wailing of the women and the preparations for the funeral pyres, as the bodies were to be burnt that evening according to custom.

---

2   The Rajah's Palace was a big fortress situated on a hill above a large lake with low hills all round it covered with timber. The Rajah being on bad terms with his feudal superiors and having boundary disputes with his neighbours all round, the Palace was seldom visited by anyone.

My husband rode back to camp feeling very grieved for the lonely old man sitting weeping in his Palace, for the sudden death of the two bright young people who had so much to enjoy and live for, and with a very certain feeling that they had been done to death in a most cruel way.

I was horrified when he came into camp and told me the news and could hardly believe that I should not see Sindar Singh again, riding about full of life in lovely colours as I had so lately seen him.

That evening Sindar Singh & Jolab were burned and their ashes placed in the mausoleum awaiting for the Kings of their race.

Next morning when J.B. & I rode round that way there were only the ashes of the burnt out fires and in the brilliant sunny morning the air scented with jessamine [*jasmine*], and everything to make one feel that life was good and pleasant. We could only think of a horrible death for two young joyous creatures.

We prepared to leave camp the following morning but in the afternoon J.B. went up to the Palace to see the old Rajah who was overcome with grief apparently, but did not lay the death of his only son to anything but misadventure. Telling my husband the story of a charcoal fire in the room that had caused asphyxiation. J.B. asked him if he knew of any one who bore a grudge against Sindar Singh, if he had heard of any quarrels with the women in the Palace? But no the old man always murmured about charcoal and drink.

That evening we heard a story of the sweetmeat taster having lately gone away, for in all these Palaces there are people whose sole duty it is to taste the food, one to taste all sweets, another the meats etc. It was said that the young people were particularly fond of some white sweetmeat made with honey, sugar & spices; such as had been sent to us, and that they had eaten several sweetmeats of this kind before going to bed on their last night on earth.

The sweetmeat taster certainly had been sent away suddenly and no one had taken up his duty. I remembered that Sindar Singh had recommended these same sweetmeats to me when we were pig shooting and I had told him about the Xmas plum pudding we were making. Some of these honey balls had been sent with the dāli, they were a speciality of Deogarh.

We made all our preparations for leaving Deogarh as soon as possible. The Prime Minister paid my husband a farewell visit and was officiously anxious to ride with us the morning of our departure. He deplored the death of the young Prince and his wife but insinuated that they were both leading bad lives and that drink had certainly hastened their end, and that all his good advice had been badly received though his efforts to keep them straight had been ceaseless.

We declined Jewan's company and rode away in the morning very early. The Bazaars all shut up and the streets a dull blank of closed shutters, the sun not having risen to warm the air. The one or two natives we met in the fields were smothered up in blankets. The old castle seemed frowning down on us in isolated melancholy, and we rode hard for a mile or two when we got out of the Bazaars, trying to shake off the exceeding melancholy which had taken possession of us.

We never saw Deogarh again, but some time afterwards we heard that a neighbouring big chief had made enquiries into the tragedy and had summoned a council to discuss the matter. Deogarh was a vassal of the big State and paid tributes; the feudal system still existing in India or rather, I should say, in Native States.

When all the sad story was exposed it was found that the old Rajah had been made very jealous of his son by Jewan's frequent misrepresentations and malice; that he had been worked up to a fury by the tales of his son's anxiety to succeed him. Sindar Singh and Jolab had openly showed their dislike and scorn of Jewan, taunting him about his squint, his ugly person etc., and that at last Jewan had persuaded the old Rajah to agree to the death of the son. This was probably done in a drunken moment and Jewan had to act quickly or the consent might be withdrawn.

The young couple having arranged to pay a visit to the father-in-law hastened on matters and poison was administered in the shape of a favourite sweetmeat. Probably had we not been there at the time nothing would have been heard of this matter. Sudden deaths are so frequent in the East; cholera, fever so quick in securing victims, then comes the cremation in a few hours and coroner's inquests are unknown.

Everybody in the Palace had known of Jewan's hatred [and] of the old Rajah's jealousy. Every one had known the cause of the young man's death but no one would have said anything, for why offend the powers that be and prepare the way for one's own sudden death.

Jewan is now shut up in a gloomy dungeon, the old Rajah still drinks in his lonely Palace, there is no young Prince to shoot the pigs, who increase in numbers and destroy the poor people's fields at their pleasure. A heavy curse lies on Deogarh. Harvests have been bad the rain does not come and the people say that Sindar Singh & Jolab flit through the Palace on the night of the 25th December and pelt each other with sugar balls.

It is not surprising that Julia never forgot her Christmas of 1885. It is an extraordinary story. How accurate it is, I do not know, but it is certainly true that the young prince and his wife were poisoned.

Chapter VI

1886

John Biddulph settled his boundary dispute and on they went.

The Biddulphs would spend the next two years and four months in India before J.B. could take his next leave.

During February 1886 they arrived at Deoli where John was to act as Political Agent for nine months. He would be Political Agent at Deoli and Tonk, living at Deoli but travelling regularly to Tonk some forty miles away, a journey of about nine hours in a carriage, usually taken at night to avoid the suffocating heat of the day.

Since leaving Deogarh the Biddulphs had barely spent two nights in one place; Julia mentions several times how tired she is becoming of camp life. She writes on 15th January that 'the dust and the wind are most trying in camp now'. Julia could have opted to stay up at Mount Abu or at some other more comfortable place whilst her husband was 'at camp', but she chose to be with him and experience the less glamorous life of a Boundary Settlement Officer.

They meet few people other than the local officials that J.B. dealt with for his work. They camped one night at Asind where they were delighted to get their 'English' mail and newspapers because as Julia wrote, 'we had come to an end of our literature'.

That same night she writes:

> *Mr & Mrs Schoolbred dined with us, he is a Missionary at Beawar and his wife a middle-aged Scotchwoman, who interested us solely on account of her having had a cockroach in her ear for eight years. She told me she was very deaf as the cockroach had destroyed the drum of her ear by its long residence, and had only quite lately been ejected by vigorous treatment.*

And then:

> *Segramphur. We rode in here this morning, 10 miles. A very good road through green fields of corn, the jungles are now quite left behind.*
>
> *We have a good deal of bother with the syces [grooms], two of them lying dead drunk in the road and a third disabled by a fall.*

21ST JANUARY
Kania [*Kaniya*]

Arrived here at 10.30 a.m. a very pleasant march of about 8 miles. Our camp is pitched on a wide plain. There are no trees, houses or fields near us. Abdulla Khan [*J.B.'s bearer*] starts tonight for Nusseerabad [*Nasirabad*] to get some new syces.

4TH FEBRUARY.
Satuna [*Sathana*]

We rode here this morning a distance of 8 miles from Kania and found a very clean Bungalow. Our principal excitement was the non-appearance of our two horses "Sheikh" & "Champion" for some hours, the syces having lost their way.

5TH FEBRUARY, FRIDAY.
Bandanwara.

Rode here this morning 10 miles march along a perfectly straight road. We lost Toby for some time as he chased some antelope for a long way [*Toby, the little fox-terrier who had gone missing in December*]. We saw a good many sand grouse, wild geese and antelope and passed a very snipey [*sic*] looking tank.

On arrival here [we] found nearly all our crockery had been smashed through the camel-trunks slipping off the camel during the night's march. The bearer has gone into Ajmer in search of syces.

We are using the bungalow here and are close to a railway station & post office. The papers give the names of the new ministry formed by Gladstone, a miserable lot.

[*This was Gladstone's third ministry, which lasted for five months until July 1886. Parliament was dissolved in June after the defeat of the Home Rule Bill for Ireland.*

At last they had arrived at Deoli, thankful to be moving back into a house. The Agency House was situated in the Cantonment, which was a permanent military town in India, usually a short distance from the principal town or city in whichever princely state.]

19TH FEBRUARY.
Deoli.

We passed some Bustard on the road between this and Bogla, at the 49th milestone. J.B. saw 8 Bustard and rode quite near them.

We are encamped within a mile of the Cantonment and this afternoon we walked over and saw the little palace. Capt. Bell showed us over the agency house, which is a very nice one with an upper storey and is in very good repair. There is a profound respectability pervading the atmosphere of Deoli, with its miniature Cathedral and neat barracks.

21ST FEBRUARY, SUNDAY.
We went to Church this afternoon at 4.30 and were introduced to all the Deoli society afterwards.

26TH FEBRUARY.
Deoli.
We moved into the Cantonment on Monday the 22nd and have now made the acquaintance of all Deoli including the Agency house and grounds.

[*After settling into the Agency house Julia leaves to spend a month with her brother Cunliffe in the Punjab. Colonel Cunliffe Martin CB commanded the Central India Horse.*]

28TH FEBRUARY.
I left Deoli this afternoon at 4 o'clock and drove with J.B. to the river [*the Banas*] which I crossed in a doolie [*a doolie, or dhooly, is a type of covered sedan chair carried by bearers*] and then came to Kekri in the Camel Carriage with Jessie [*Julia's maid*], just getting into the Dak Bungalow at 8 o' clock.

1ST MARCH.
Nusseerabad [*Nasirabad, Punjab*]
I arrived here at 12 o'clock in the day and found all the trains had been changed so that it would be impossible to get on to Augar [*Augarh, Punjab*] by an evening train. The Dak Bungalow is very stuffy and the weather has become quite hot.

3ʳᴅ MARCH.
Augar

My long journey has come to an end at last. Since leaving Deoli I have been in a carriage with horses, a doolie, a camel carriage, a dak carriage with horses, 24 hours of railway carriage, then a bullock carriage for 6 hours, then a double dogcart. The latter was the most exciting as the horse kicked and reared so frightfully that I had to get out of the carriage once. The second time I got in, he kicked the splashboard to a limp condition and it hung down forever after, broke the trace and nearly upset us.

I had a very hot journey from Nusseerabad to Fatehabad [*Nasirabad and Fatehabad, in the Punjab*] and had a dinner breakfast at 5 a.m. in the station waiting room.

[*There is a section missing here from this journal, some pages have been removed. It would seem that Julia had gone to see her brother while he and his regiment were at camp. Meanwhile, J.B. was still waiting for a permanent appointment.*]

[No date.]

The tent pegging and feats of horsemanship were first rate and Cunliffe's horse "King Arthur" took the jumps most beautifully, it was quite a cool afternoon after a very hot day. The rain, which has been going on since the 4ᵗʰ is now over.

24ᵀᴴ MARCH.

Heard from J.B. that he had refused Jodhpur on account of the heat, and it would be only till December when we should be again moved. Have made all my arrangements to join J.B. on the 30ᵗʰ at Nasirabad.

30TH MARCH, MONDAY.
Met J.B. at the Nasirabad station at 10.30 a.m. We spent the day in the Dak Bungalow.

1ST APRIL.
Deoli.

Last night we reached this at 7 o'clock, we left Nasirabad at 5 o'clock and reached Kekri at ½ past 9 a.m. We breakfasted at Kekri and left in the Rajah of Boondi's [*Bundi*] carriage at 4 o'clock getting into Deoli at 7 in the evening. Dined with the Bells, the poor Boilians having heard of their son's death in Burma.

[*After another twenty-four hours of travelling, Julia was back at Deoli where she would remain until August. The climate would become hotter and hotter before the rains came. Her life was taken up with tea parties, dinner parties and receiving people when they arrived to stay en route to wherever. J.B. continued his work while Julia ran the house and carried out her duties as Memsahib.*]

11TH APRIL, SUNDAY.
Deoli.

J.B. went off on tour of Boondi [*Bundi*] & Kotah [*Kota*] this afternoon, starting at 5 o'clock.

17TH APRIL, SATURDAY.
J.B. returned today from his expedition to Boondi etc., and came in about 9 o'clock in the morning. He is quite charmed with Kotah and its surroundings. I sent a horse to meet him in the morning (Sheikh) and he came in quite fresh.

28TH APRIL, WEDNESDAY.
John left yesterday morning for Tonk starting in a carriage with 4 horses at 4 a.m. The heat has become intense and last

night my punkah rope broke in the night, alarming me a good deal. [*A punkah is a large fan made from a light frame covered with cloth and hung from the ceiling; it is pulled backwards and forwards to cool the air. The man pulling the rope is known as a Punkah-wallah.*]

We dined at the Mess on Monday 26th and heard the bagpipes to perfection.

1ST MAY, SATURDAY.
J.B. returned from Tonk, and was in here by 9.30.

9TH MAY, SUNDAY.
Mrs Wyllie came in from Kotah [*Kota*]; it was a very cool morning and she had had a very fair journey. In the evening we went to Church and Colonel Greenfield & Capt. Bell dined with us.

10TH MAY, MONDAY.
Capt. Wyllie arrived to early breakfast; Mr Bonnar & Dr Harrington also came over. The Wyllies left us about 5 o'clock for Nasirabad [*Rajasthan*]. I heard from Dr Shepherd this evening that poor Mr Campbell Thomson was living at the Residency at Oodeypore [*Udaipur*], his wife died at Marseilles on her way to England; her little baby is living I believe. Mr Wingate is now acting Resident of Mewar [*Rajasthan*].

[*Captain William Hutt Curzon Wyllie KCIE, 1848–1909, later Lieutenant-Colonel Sir William Curzon Wyllie, was first a soldier and afterwards held different civil and political appointments throughout India. The Curzon Wyllies were good friends of the Biddulphs and they later travelled to Japan together.*

Curzon Wyllie was assassinated on 1st July 1909; he was shot dead as he left the Imperial Institute, South Kensington by Madan Lal Dhingra, an Indian student. There is a memorial to him in the crypt of St Paul's Cathedral, London that was unveiled by Earl Roberts on 19th October 1910; both Julia and J.B. attended the ceremony.]

25TH MAY.

Yesterday being the Queen's birthday we had "the Station" to dinner, which consisted of only the Sutton Jones & Colonel Greenfield. Before dinner John had a small Durbar and received all the Vakeels [*native agents, etc.*] and Native officers. He made them a little speech, which was answered by one of the Vakeels and "God Save the Queen" on the pipes ended the ceremony.

31ST MAY, MONDAY.

We have had storms now for three days, the first was on Friday 28th and the heaviest was last night when we had heavy rain which continued till nearly 5 o'clock this morning. The heat had become almost unbearable and we are now only beginning to feel alive once more.

Our thoughts are constantly at home with the Irish Bill. Home Rule seems just now in the ascendant.

This morning I received a photo of Aggie in her presentation dress. [*Agnes, Julia's niece, eldest daughter of her sister Amy. Agnes was about to be eighteen; she was born on 19th July 1868.*]

We have not had good use of our tatties for quite a fortnight, and the heat has really prevented one being able to think even.

[*A tattie is a type of screen made from scented cuscus grass and placed in doorways or windows; it is kept damp to cool the breeze and freshen the air. The rains continued but had little effect on the stifling heat.*]

1ˢᵀ JUNE, TUESDAY.

Yesterday we had another tremendous storm in the afternoon with torrents of rain, the whole place looked like a sea; I hear we have had nearly three inches of rain.

[*For the remainder of June and July, the heat and humidity were almost unbearable; the rain, when it came, though torrential did little to relieve the oppressive humidity. At last, at the beginning of August, the Biddulphs headed to the hill station at Mount Abu, where they would stay for two weeks, leaving Deoli on 3ʳᵈ August.*]

3ᴿᴰ AUGUST, TUESDAY.

J.B. very seedy all night with fever. We left Deoli at a quarter to 6 a.m. and drove to the river in the Kotah carriage, crossed the river on an Elephant and then drove to Kekri where we had breakfast.

J.B. was very unwell with a bad headache all the time; I am afraid he has had a touch of the sun. We got to Nasirabad at 2.30 where J.B. was able to lie down and eat some luncheon and we were here (Ajmer) at 5.30 p.m. Colonel Trevor was very kind in asking us to stay on here as J.B. had to send for Dr Crofts who gave him some medicine and told him to take quinine.

6ᵀᴴ AUGUST, FRIDAY.

Mt. Aboo [*Mount Abu*].

We left Colonel Trevor yesterday and started from Ajmer by the 12.30 p.m. train which arrived at Aboo Rd. at 2.30 next morning [*Abu Road is the railway station for Mount Abu*].

J.B. had a headache, but was rather better on the whole.

We got into Aboo Rd. Station this morning and I left at 4 o'clock in a Palkee [*a type of horse-drawn* gharry *or* cab *for one person*] for Mt. Aboo, leaving J.B. to have a good sleep and then he rode up and came in to the Residency half an hour after I did.

The weather is horrid, pouring rain & clouds, and Lady Bradford ill in bed, Mrs Spencer in attendance.

9TH AUGUST, MONDAY.

A lovely evening, J.B. & I started off to walk to the Temples and on our way met a Miss Phillips & Miss Bell Irving, the latter a young artist. We found two obstacles on the way in the shape of running streams, which were sufficiently broad to make us very wet if J.B. had not carried us over them. Miss Phillips, a stout lady, preferred to walk through them.

The Temples are wonderful, with an extraordinary mass of carving.

12TH AUGUST, THURSDAY.

Lady Bradford got out of doors for a short time this afternoon. We all walked round "Bailey's walk"; a very pretty walk and had tea at a damp place called Toad's Rock [*Toad's Rock, Mount Abu*] provided by Miss Phillips. Miss Deedes arrived. Received new photos of Amy & Robert from Bath [*Julia's sister Amy and her husband, Robert Laurie; Robert Laurie had been elected as member for Bath at the recent general election*].

14TH AUGUST, SATURDAY.

Miss Deedes and I went to the Dilwara Temples [*Dilwara Temples, Mount Abu*] before breakfast. These Temples were built by some rich merchants and were supposed to be finished about 1140, though begun more than 50 years before that. We looked over every part of the Temples, especially behind the screen where there are ten dear little white marble elephants.

Coming back, Miss Deedes got kicked by her pony in trying to get on it, and we had to wash her wounds in the priest's drinking water!

[*The Biddulph's holiday was over and they were now returning to Tonk and Deoli.*]

17TH AUGUST, TUESDAY.

We left Aboo after breakfast and had a very fair journey down the hill. We saw some large monkeys and met a number of invalid soldiers coming up. The rain has commenced again and we are in for a spell of it.

18TH AUGUST, WEDNESDAY.

Arrived at Jeypore [*Jaipur*] at 9 a.m. having left Aboo Rd. at 5.30 p.m. yesterday. The Henneys are very well & the Residency is a charming house. I went to the School of Art & the museum with Mrs Baines in the morning, to the Palace Gardens & Albert Hall with Mrs Henney in the evening.

19TH AUGUST, THURSDAY.

John and I did the Jail before breakfast and ordered durries [dhurrie, *a type of Indian carpet which was often made by prisoners*]. The Jacobs dined at the Residency in the evening. J.B. & I drove to the Palace in the afternoon when he went to see the Maharajah.

20TH AUGUST, FRIDAY.

We left Jeypore at 11.30 a.m. and drove the first 25 miles in a Jeypore carriage, then stopped for luncheon at a small bungalow and got into a Tonk carriage [*a Jaipur carriage, or a Tonk carriage, was the equivalent to a stagecoach*]. The rain commenced about 3 o'clock and when we got to the river it was very full and we had to cross over it in a big country boat. We got into Tonk about 6.30 p.m. just before the very heavy rain set in.

22ND AUGUST, SUNDAY.
Tonk.

Our luggage arrived in the afternoon; it had been detained on the banks of the river as no boat could go across, the river was running at such a pace.

1ST SEPTEMBER, WEDNESDAY.
Tonk.

J.B. has finished most of the important work here and we are arranging to return to Deoli soon. There has been a great deal of rain here during the last few days & it is very cool & pleasant.

5TH SEPTEMBER, SUNDAY.
Tonk.

J.B.'s work being now finished for the present here I am going to return to Deoli tonight in a palkee, and he is to ride over tomorrow morning to breakfast.

Since I have been here I have done most of the drives and have visited the girls' school. My livestock is now increased by the addition of two Minas [*myna, or mynah birds, from the starling family; kept as pets, they are good mimics and can learn to talk*].

6TH SEPTEMBER, MONDAY.
I arrived in Deoli about 6.30 a.m. and J.B. came in about 9.30, he rode but I travelled all night in a palkee and left Tonk at 9 p.m. on Sunday evening.

8TH SEPTEMBER, WEDNESDAY.
Deoli.

J.B. had a narrow escape from a bad accident, he went into the stables and found "Champion" humbugging about in his stall so he went in to him and the horse came right down on his back, knocked him over and hurt his side, or at least it is very bruised and sore from the fall.

26TH SEPTEMBER, SUNDAY.
This week we have had quite a dissipated time for Deoli. Monday the Wyllies, Bells & Dr Harington dined with us, Tuesday we dined at the Mess, or rather with Dr Harington at the Mess. Wednesday we dined with the Bells and had tennis at home. The Boileans left us for Abu that afternoon. Thursday we went down to the river & had tea on the banks & Mrs Wyllie & I sketched, the others went in a boat. Friday was the Mess afternoon & tennis. Saturday all the gentlemen went out to Rajmahal with the exception of Mr Bonnar, who had breakfast with Mrs Wyllie and me. Mrs Wyllie also spent the day with me & she sang for nearly 2 hours. The gentlemen all came back from Rajmahal about 6.30 in great force having had a very jolly day there. Mrs Wyllie & I have sketched the little lake Temple three times now. Tonight Mr Scott, Mr Bonnar & Dr Harington dine with us; I have not gone to Church this morning. Toby is at last getting better having been very ill, poor little dog.

[Rajmahal, on the Banas River, now very near the Bisalpur Reservoir; the Bisalpur Dam was completed in 1999. Rajmahal was a favourite place for fishing at the time.

Julia now returns to Tonk for three weeks.]

1ST OCTOBER, FRIDAY.
I leave for Tonk this evening; all the servants, horses [and] cows have gone on and J.B. rides over tomorrow morning.

We dine with Mrs Wyllie who dined with us last night, her husband having gone to Jhalrapatan [*Rajasthan*].

2ND OCTOBER, SATURDAY.
Tonk.

J.B. rode over very comfortably this morning and was in by 9.30.

4TH OCTOBER, MONDAY.

J.B. visited the Nawab who brought him back in his carriage and afterwards we both went to the Band and drank tea in the gardens, being received by Obeidullah Khan [*the Nawab of Tonk, HH Sir Hafiz Muhammed Ibrahim Ali Khan, 4th Nawab of Tonk, 1867–1930, born 1849*].

20TH OCTOBER, WEDNESDAY.
Tonk.

My last day here; I leave this evening for Deoli.

26TH OCTOBER, TUESDAY.

This afternoon Mrs Wyllie and I drove out to Rajmahal in the little carriage; J.B. and Capt. Wyllie went in the dogcart and Tonga [*a tonga is a two-wheeled cart or wagon drawn by two horses, still in use today in India*]. We got into our camp about 6 p.m. and found everything so comfy and nice, our tents pitched under some very big trees; so cool and pleasant sitting out under the trees drinking our coffee after dinner.

[*A few days fishing and shooting had been arranged at Rajmahal on the River Banas.*]

27TH OCTOBER, WEDNESDAY.

We rode on the Elephant down to the river and then embarked for the "hole in the wall" in Capt. Wyllie's boat, which was a very charming one and held us four, two boatmen and another man. We stopped at the hole in the wall till eleven o'clock and fished, I caught two fishes, which I felt was about as much as I should do in the morning, and took to sketching. J.B. caught about 6 nice ones, none very large. In the evening we again went on the river and back to the hole for a short time.

[*The 'hole in the wall' was clearly a favourite place for the fishing parties. Perhaps it was part of a ruined temple or building on the banks of the river now lost when the reservoir was built?*]

THURSDAY 28TH
Mrs Wyllie and I left J.B. and Capt. Wyllie on the banks as they were going for a drive after Sambar [*a large deer, native to the Indian subcontinent*] and having deposited them we rowed up to Begelpore [*another place perhaps lost to the dam*] where the boatmen got 2 fish and we rested in the shade; such a quaint old Temple in front of us, and a beautiful piece of water for fishing. The gentlemen returned after we had had breakfast and came back empty handed. In the evening we all rowed up to Begelpore again and did not get back till very late, very tired and very glad of dinner.

29TH OCTOBER, FRIDAY.
Mrs Wyllie and I sketched on the little platform in the hole in the wall and the gentlemen again went after Sambar but got nothing. In the evening we went out on the river again, a most lovely evening. Capt. Wyllie hooked the biggest fish and played with it for a little when it broke the line and got away, however he got a very fair sized fish, which was good for dinner & J.B. caught half a dozen of sorts.

30TH OCTOBER, SATURDAY.

We drove back into Deoli, arriving here at home exactly at 9 o'clock a.m.

4TH NOVEMBER, THURSDAY.
Kotah [*Kota, on the River Chambal*].

Mrs Wyllie and I arrived here early in the morning; we got into the steam launch at 6.30 and met Capt. Wyllie paddling his canoe. 2 p.m. we started in the steam launch for a panther, the Maharao joining us at the steps nearest the Palace, he is a very toothless old man [*Maharao Shatrushal Singh II, 17th Maharao of Kotah, 1866–1889, born 1837*].

We saw a magnificent panther; it came and stood quite quietly on some rocks near us, the Maharao shot its tail! Then Capt. Wyllie gave it a ball right in the shoulder and it rolled right over and down the rocks but it sprang up again and gave a great bound, another shot bowled it over and it rolled down into a steep place where it was not found for ½ an hour.

Friday, we went to Aklera in the evening where we saw the crocodiles fed, a wonderful sight; three great beasts came close up to the steps of the tank and were fed with the insides of sheep; I must have seen nearly 20.

The Henry Wylies arrived on Sunday and we went down the river after service not coming back till quite late; the river was dotted over with little lights, oil put into orange skins and floated down looking so pretty.

[*To avoid confusion, the spellings of Wylie and Wyllie are correct. Mr Henry Wylie worked as a colonial administrator.*]

Tuesday we went to a perfectly lovely glen called Gaipernath; it was full of monkeys and ferns, with a little hut belonging to a Fakir [*a holy man*], and a great deep pool, into which a waterfall fell. We had tea there after descending 180 steep steps [*the Gaipernath Waterfall, Kota*].

Wednesday we drove to Suasāger [sic] and Mrs Henry Wylie had an unruly Elephant; we were obliged to ride on Elephants part of the way and her Elephant turned cross and gave no end of trouble. At last we got down from our Elephant (Mrs Curzon Wyllie & I) and then it was taken near to the unruly one, whose hind legs were tied with stuff got out of the nearest village & Mrs Henry was taken down, the Elephant kneeling down at last.

[*From Kota the Biddulphs return to Deoli, arriving there on 12th November before moving on to Bundi.*]

22ND NOVEMBER, MONDAY.
Bundi.

Enjoyed coming through the town immensely, the old Chief had a most quaint retinue. J.B. went to the Palace in the afternoon.

[*HH Maharao Raja Ram Singh ji Sahib Bahadur, Maharao of Bundi, 1821–1889, born 1811.*]

23RD NOVEMBER, TUESDAY.
Bundi.

We are living in a summer palace on the lake, it is very pretty. The old Chief called on J.B.

24TH NOVEMBER.
Bundi.

Today John went to the Palace on a private visit and was much pleased with his interview with the old man. I drew two of the Camel Corps.

25TH NOVEMBER.

John had fever all night with ague [*a malarial fever*]. I had fever after visiting the Royal Mausoleums in the morning. The Chief came to see J.B. in the afternoon.

26ᵀᴴ NOVEMBER, FRIDAY.
Dablana [*Rajasthan*]

I came here partly by palkee, the rest of the way in a Bundi carriage. J.B. went out Sambar shooting but as the Chief with all his retinue went too, it is not surprising they saw no Sambar.

It rained very heavily in the evening.

[*The Biddulphs were about to move back into camp and J.B. to resume his work as a Boundary Settlement Officer.*]

27ᵀᴴ NOVEMBER, SATURDAY.
Dugari [*Rajasthan*].

A long 14 mile ride with a very bad road. We went round the lake in the evening, where the inhabitants fished two crocodiles out of the lake for our benefit, one was 12 foot long.

29ᵀᴴ NOVEMBER, MONDAY.
Nynwa [*Nainwa, Rajasthan*].

We rode over here very comfortably, I on Punch as the Witch had been kicked; the march was about 8 miles. The town here is very quaint with a great many gates, the Governor is never allowed to go outside the gates of the City. We bought two bits of brass & copper work from a Fakir.

1ˢᵀ DECEMBER, WEDNESDAY.
Kattoli [*Khatoli, Rajasthan*].

A very easy march and excellent road all the way. The Bundi Vakeel has left us as we are now in Tonk territory.

J.B. went shooting with one of the Tonk gentlemen, Mohammed Khan, who was so fat he could not walk & tumbled about into every hole. He was got up in khaki and was a most absurd looking figure; waddling about like an old goose.

3ʳᵈ DECEMBER, FRIDAY.
Alyghar [*Aligarh, Rajasthan*].

We came in here early in the morning; the march seemed only six miles for we were in before 9 o'clock.

Yesterday we came across a very old well said to be 800 years old. It had been a large covered building with a great many staircases and cool rooms to rest in by the well. From the ruins one could see it had been extremely well built, the pillars supporting the roof of the outside corridors bore traces of deep carving. A little distance from the well was a Chuttree [*Chuttri, a dome-shaped pavilion*], which looked perfectly new but had been built 150 years ago. In the evening today we went to see a large garden near the camp, full of orange and date trees, a few cocoa nut palms and a good deal of wilderness.

4ᵀᴴ DECEMBER, SATURDAY.
Alyghar [*Aligarh*]

I enjoyed the unusual treat of a long morning in bed.

5ᵀᴴ DECEMBER, SUNDAY.
Kairod.

We rode over here early and at 11.30 started off on a shooting expedition. The stout Sahib Zada [*sic*] came out in his beautiful khaki shooting dress and a number of followers of all sorts. To commence with we all trooped through the town and about a mile & a half beyond, J.B. got off his horse and stalked some Black Buck [Antilope cervicapra, *also known as the Indian antelope*] at a long distance; I could see a large heard running about. J.B. shot a buck and then we went on into the jungle for about another mile when we all got off our ponies and scrambled up a steep hill. At the top we found a shooting place and we waited there for the drive.

A number of pigs passed but J.B. would not shoot at them. I fired once and was told I had wounded the pig but anyhow I did not kill it. The drive was stopped too soon and after we had descended to the bottom of the hill, two Sambar passed on the top. We all got on our ponies again and rode for another mile and there dismounted and scrambled up to the top of another high hill where J.B. perched himself on the very top of a slab of rock. He saw a Sambar coming down on the opposite hillside and fired, wounding it, then ran round to another point where he fired again and shot it dead. A number of pig then passed, and one pig came up to a few yards of where I was lying down. We got nothing more out of the beat and came down the hill & rode home, getting into camp about 5.30, a very jolly day, so exciting watching for game and seeing owls flying through the woods, & quail under one's feet occasionally.

6TH DECEMBER, MONDAY.
Tonk.

Capt. Pears met us about five miles from Tonk and the Nawab and all his suite came out too to meet J.B. We are encamped under some trees close to the river.

14TH DECEMBER, TUESDAY.
Tonk.

We very nearly had our camp burnt down this evening; the Pears were dining with us and we left a lamp burning in the little drawing-room tent when we went to dinner. I heard a great smash and a great deal of noise and Toby barking loudly, but did not make any remark as apparently no one noticed it. Presently in came the bearer to say Toby had pursued a jungle dog into the drawing-room tent who had knocked over the lamp and set fire to a chair and the carpet, but they had put out the fire with only the loss of the chair.

I sent off a large number of chickens to Mrs Boilean this morning.

22ND DECEMBER, WEDNESDAY.
Duni [*Dooni, Rajasthan*].

J.B. shot over the Tank after breakfast and I sketched. It is a very pretty place with a big fort and massive walls to the latter. The weather looks very rainy and is much warmer.

CHRISTMAS DAY. DEOLI.
We had Church in the morning at 8.30 and in the afternoon drove down to the river in the dogcart. Dr & Mrs Harington, Capt. & Miss Bell, Mr & Mrs Bonnar dined with us in the evening. My table was a mass of roses of every shade and really looked very pretty. After dinner we played a round game. Mrs Bonnar, the bride, was hardly at her ease and J.B. found conversation during dinner somewhat fatiguing while Capt. Bell got into many complications not understanding her broad Scotch.

28TH DECEMBER, TUESDAY.
We rode over to Jahazpur, a big Fort on the top of a hill. It was very picturesque riding up to the place as it is surrounded with big trees and gardens. J.B. went to see the army in the afternoon and the Adjutant received him in a pale blue silk helmet & scarlet coat, holding his sword as if it was a wet umbrella. Just as J.B. rode up to him the Adjutant's horse stood upright, the syce hung on to its head, and the unfortunate man presented his back to J.B. by way of reception! I rode up to the gates of the fort by myself, but did not go in.

29ᵀᴴ DECEMBER.
Bheelri.

We had a most charming road here from Jahazpur, quite flat and very soft. We passed a number of buck & J.B. tried to get a black buck, but they were too much on the move.

30ᵀᴴ DECEMBER, THURSDAY.
Shahpura.

We rode half way & then the carriage met us and J.B. got into the carriage with the Rajah. There is a very good Bungalow here full of mirrors and chandeliers. The country is perfectly flat all round, just a big bare plain.

Chapter VII

1887

The Biddulphs continue their camping for the first three months of 1887. At the beginning of March, they would be back at Deoli, where they would remain until July. It will be another eighteen months before J.B. could take his next leave and by then they were both becoming very tired with this way of life, Julia in particular. John Biddulph would spend as much time as possible shooting and fishing, which for him was a distraction. It was with great relief when in July they head for Mount Abu, where Julia would spend two months away from the heat and the flies and the dust, and live in a comfortable house. J.B. would spend a fortnight at Mount Abu before continuing his work.

The New Year would begin at Shahpura, Bhilwara, Rajasthan.

1ST JANUARY 1887.
Shahpura.

J.B. went for a ride in the morning with the Rajah; the other day he visited the Jail and was given the list of prisoners in English – "2 bloody prisoners" stood for 2 murderers!

In the evening we went for a stroll & J.B. shot 3 snipe close by. The Rajah & his little son came to wish us the good wishes for the New Year at dinner time, and the Rajah drank a glass of Champagne to the Empress's health; after dinner we had feeble fireworks. [*HH Rajadhiraj Sir Nahar Singh, Sahib Bahadur KCIE, 13th Raja of Shahpura from 1870–1932, born 1855.*]

3RD JANUARY, MONDAY.

We went out pig sticking with the Rajah, driving with him to the meet about a couple of miles off. J.B. had such a stiff neck that he couldn't ride and had to sit on an Elephant with me. We saw three fine boars killed but to please the people J.B. had to shoot one before the real sport began.

We really saw a number of pig. The Sowars [*a mounted orderly or attendant*] got rather excited & wild and in the end a poor horse belonging to the Rajah got badly speared; no one knew how. Four boars were killed before we left off and our camp had pig enough to eat to satisfy them for some time to come.

5TH JANUARY, WEDNESDAY.
Shahpura.

We again went out pig sticking with the Rajah but this time J.B. rode and the Doctor carried him very well, I was on an Elephant alone. Abdullah Khan rode "Sheikh" and got one great tumble, but was not at all hurt. "Sheikh" did not like the pig much, but behaved better than I expected him to.

A big boar that had been shut up for some time was let loose and we expected him to show great flight, but he was most indifferent, trotting along quite carelessly or remaining perfectly still. The Minister, Ram Jewan said that, "if he oppose, he will be formidable" but he appeared to have no intention of opposing.

After that they had two good runs after pig, getting them each time. A quantity of young pigs kept running about at odd times, getting quite under the Elephants at times. A large sounder [*a herd of swine or pigs*] was dreadfully missed by the Sowars getting so excited that they rode over them & scattered them, missing the big boar completely. We left off about 11.30.

In the afternoon we went to the Summer Palace to fish out of the windows. The fishing rods were painted so that the paint came off, the lines were bad and knotted and there were no fish! The Rajah & J.B. each got a small one.

We had rain on Tuesday night (4th Jan) and it has made the ground very pleasant, getting rid of the dust for a time; this is the second time we have had rain since we've been in camp this season.

8TH JANUARY, SATURDAY.
Dikola [*Dhikola or Dheekola*].

We came out here this morning, I driving in the Shahpura carriage with the family, which consists of Toby [*Julia's dog*]. There was not much to see at the place, a number of tanks scattered about, a Fort on the hill, supposed to be the abode of a marvellous serpent or snake, and some pretty little Chuttries [*Chuttri, a dome-shaped pavilion in Indian architecture*] which I sketched. Ram Jewan's horse put his foot into a bees nest coming along with John; he was nearly kicked off but fortunately the bees did not attack any of the other horses or men.

9TH JANUARY, SUNDAY.
Mowa.

We had another very short march and again I drove with Toby while John rode to see a boundary on the way. There is nothing of much interest in this place except the tomb of a Capt. Waugh, who commanded Tod's escort and died here in 1829. [*Captain Patrick Waugh, 1788–1829, who travelled with Lieutenant-Colonel James Tod through Rajasthan during the 1820s. Tod published the* Annals and Antiquities of Rajast'han *in 1832.*]

10TH JANUARY.
Bilwarra [*Bhilwara*]

Capt. Meade joined us here at 8 p.m., our camp is exactly facing the railway station – hideous country.

12TH JANUARY, WEDNESDAY.
Gangara.

John, Capt. Meade and I rode in here this morning, the Rao of Bedla and his son met us some miles from the camp in a carriage. [*Rao Bahadur Takhat Singh, 13th Rao Sahib of Bedla, 1880–1892.*]

13TH JANUARY, THURSDAY.
We had rain in the morning but it cleared up by 2 o'clock. We went out after pig and Sambar with the Bedla Rao and his son. We had a long beat and only one fine boar turned out, quite out of range; then another beat when a lot of pigs were seen in the distance, but nothing came near us. A panther broke out below, near where the Elephants were waiting for us and went across country, but not in our sight. We returned home on Elephants and introduced the Bedla Rao to Vermouth, which he much approved of.

14TH JANUARY.
Chittore [*Chittorgarh*]
   Bitterly cold here, J.B. and I went down to the river in the afternoon.

15TH JANUARY, SATURDAY.
Satkhanda.
   Capt. Pears came over to breakfast, it was bitterly cold leaving Chittore in the morning and I wrapped myself up in furs and shawls and yet was not warm till the sun was quite high.

17TH JANUARY, MONDAY.
Nimbahera.
   We rode in here, Capt. Pears meeting us half way. Our camp is away from the village near the river. Capt. Thornton dined with us in the evening.

22ND JANUARY.
Nimbahera.
   We left this night for Jaora [*Madhya Pradesh*] by the 12.30 Train.
   [*The Biddulphs were going to Jaora to meet Julia's brother Cunliffe, whom she had last seen when she had visited him in the Punjab in March 1886.*]

23RD JANUARY, SUNDAY.
Jaora.
   We arrived here at 7 a.m. & drove to Cunliffe's camp, which we found being pitched. I made tea in a small tent that was ready and we waited till Cunliffe & Fanny [*Cunliffe's wife*] arrived at about 10 o'clock. They were looking very well and were delighted to see us.

J.B. called on the Nawab in the afternoon and he returned the call afterwards, such a funny looking person dressed in a velvet coat, gold cap & hunting breeches; he talked very good English. We drove through the town in the afternoon and sat over the stove after dinner gossiping. [*Major HH Ihtasham-ud-daula Nawab Mohammed Ismail Khan Bahadur Firoz Jung, 3rd Nawab of Jaora, 1865–1895, born 1855.*]

24TH JANUARY.
Nimbahera.

We had to leave Jaora very early this morning and the train being late did not get here till 2.30, & with the shaking of the train & waiting for breakfast, I got a very bad sick headache & had to go to bed at once. Mr Loden arrived soon after we did, and he & John went out shooting before dinner.

26TH JANUARY, WEDNESDAY.
Mulliakera [*Malya Kheri*].

I rode half the march with J.B. & Mr Loden, and drove the last four miles or so. John had a bad cold, which increased towards night very much so that he could not go out fishing in the afternoon with Mr Loden. Mr Loden went out to the river but was not successful; the fishing is said to be good about here.

27TH JANUARY, THURSDAY.
Morwan.

Mr Loden and I rode over here alone for J.B. was so very ill in the night with almost congestion of the lungs. I put two mustard plasters on his chest, the second relieved him a little but he was in great pain. He drove over in the pony carriage when the sun had risen rather high and it was tolerably warm. Mr Loden went out shooting all day [and] saw a good many deer, sand grouse etc., but was very unsuccessful. John kept at home in the Shamiana and we put turpentine on his chest morning and evening, which relieved him greatly. The Shamiana becomes very hot at night with the stove and it is difficult to moderate the heat comfortably [*a shamiana is a flat-roofed tent or marquee*].

28TH JANUARY, FRIDAY.
Morwan.

Mr Loden and I went out to Mangalwar for duck shooting; the jheel was covered with duck & teal & there were many snipe too. Mr Loden got 1 duck & 2 snipe; we did not get home till 11 o'clock.

Toby [*Julia's dog*] nearly had a fit with the dust and heat. In the afternoon a frightful wind sprung up ending in a perfect gale, the Shamiana nearly came down; the dust and discomfort were horrid. John was better in the afternoon and we went over the village and strolled about till nearly dark. English letters arrived after dinner.

29TH JANUARY, SATURDAY.
Dungla.

I drove over here, the march being only 7 miles I was in by 9 o'clock. Mr Loden went out after Black Buck and had 2 shots, but as he tried at a distance of 400yds it was not extraordinary that he came back empty handed. John rode over slowly and is much better but not quite well yet, he had a very sleepless night.

30TH JANUARY, SUNDAY.
Chikara [*Chikarda*].

John and I rode over here very slowly, a short distance of 8 miles, J.B. still feeling very weak. Mr Loden went out again after deer but did not get anything. At the last place (Dungla) we visited the village where the Johar [*Jauhar*] took place last September. That is two women burnt themselves to bring down a curse on the Government for not allowing them (the village) to cultivate their fields without rent being taken from them. Four old women offered themselves but two got frightened and ran away, while the other two were burnt [*Jauhar is a custom, similar to sati, an act of self-immolation*]. We saw the place where the sacrifice took place; the ashes were still lying there. We also saw the two women who had escaped, they would not show us their faces but sat near me while I sketched the place and then I tried to sketch them themselves, but they were mere heaps of clothes.

[*For the next two weeks they would move every day, riding up to twenty miles a day before eventually arriving at Pirawa on Saturday 12th February.*]

12TH FEBRUARY, SATURDAY.
Pirawa.

We had a very long stony march of 17 miles; a very bad road all the way here, dogs and bullocks very lame from the stones and rocks; servants & cattle all pretty well tired out, but we halt here for a week or more. The place looks pretty, and the trees and poppy fields, with large fields of young wheat, make many little bright pieces of colour to sketch.

16TH FEBRUARY, WEDNESDAY.
Pirawa.

Jubilee Day 1887

We rode out at 7 o'clock and inspected the ground for rifle practice. Then we went down to the ground at 2 o'clock and stayed till 5.30.

J.B. started all the men shooting, the children ran races, & finally he and I shot with the native officers & Vakeels etc. J.B. made some capital shooting, and I got an average of centres.

We came home to tea and soon after started on an Elephant through the City, which was illuminated in a poor little way in honour of the Jubilee. After going through the streets we got off our Elephant and mounted on a platform in the middle of a sort Place. We listened to loyal speeches, J.B. making one in return; witnessed some very feeble fireworks and had some truly terrible scent poured on our handkerchiefs & had wreaths put round our necks of strongly scented flowers. We left when the last firework had fizzed out and got home on the Elephant very tired indeed, and very thankful to drink the Queen's health in Champagne.

20TH FEBRUARY.
Magispura [*Magishpur*].

We marched here this morning; not a long march, about 10 miles but the days are getting very hot. We have heard of Sir E Bradford's appointment in London and are feeling very low about ourselves, having a bad fit of loathing for Deoli & Tonk.

[*Sir Edward Bradford returned to London in 1887 and was appointed Secretary of State at the India Office. The Biddulphs were becoming depressed with the endless travelling, repressive heat, bouts of ill health and camp life in general.*]

22ND FEBRUARY.
Jhalrapatan.

We rode part of the way and then drove; the young Chief met J.B. with all honours and was excessively civil. [*HH*

Maharaj Rana Zalim Singh Bahadur, 3rd Maharaj Rana of Jhalawar, 1876–1896, born 1865.]

The Abbotts received us most kindly; they have a very nice house with the most lovely verandah [sic], and the garden is very pretty with quantities of nice flowers, violets in abundance.

23RD FEBRUARY.
Jhalrapatan.

Mrs Abbott took me for a long drive in the morning; J.B. went out shooting with the young Chief and he shot a very fine hyena and a Nilgai [the largest Asian antelope]. We dined with the Miles in the evening. [Major Abbott was Political Agent at Jhalrapatan.]

24TH FEBRUARY.
The Durra Pass.

We drove here after luncheon and arrived at our tents about 6 o'clock. It is such a beautiful pass, and we had a very pleasant drive. We have been warned to look after our dogs as the place is full of panthers, but we have seen nothing worse than peacocks.

The Jhalrapatan Chief came to see John in the morning, and has shown him every attention; this is probably to pique Major Abbott, to whom he is behaving very badly indeed.

25TH FEBRUARY, FRIDAY.
Mundana [Mandana]

We rode through the Durra this morning and enjoyed it so much; it is very picturesque and was deliciously cool & shady. Here it is very hot and we have had a disagreeably dusty day with much wind.

26TH FEBRUARY.
Jagpoora [*Jagpura*]

This is a very pretty place, the tents are pitched in a grove of trees and I have been sitting underneath a tree all day long sketching. The trees are full of monkeys & the dogs are nearly driven wild with them. We have been feeding the monkeys with oranges & grapes. In the afternoon we walked out in the jungle, to the consternation of some of the people, as a tiger had been seen about in the direction we went.

27TH FEBRUARY, SUNDAY.
Kotah [*Kota*]

We rode half way & then drove; and meeting the Bayleys in the public gardens, took a walk with them before breakfast. In the afternoon we went to see all the mares. The heat is now very great.

Wednesday. We left Kotah this morning for Bundi; John was very seedy last night and could not dine with the Bayleys but had to go to bed before dinner. We had a terrible jolting this morning and John has had to lie down all day long, feeling his head so very bad. I caught quite a big fish in the lake in the afternoon.

4TH MARCH, FRIDAY.
Hindoli.

We got over our journey from Bundi more comfortably as we travelled in a big carriage, but we remain here all tomorrow as the Maharaja comes to see J.B.

5TH MARCH.
Hindoli.

The Maharao came in 5 miles to see J.B. & was very nice and courteous [HH Maharao Raja Ram Singhji Sahib Bahadur,

21st Maharao Raja of Bundi, 1821–1889, born 1811]. J.B. is looking better but is by no means all right and I shall be glad to get into Deoli. [*On Sunday 6th March, the Biddulphs arrive back in Deoli where J.B. will resume his duties as Political Agent at Deoli and Tonk until the end of November.*]

6TH MARCH, SUNDAY.
Deoli.

Here we are at last; we had a terrible road to drive over from Hindoli this morning, but we got over it somehow. Capt. Bell came over to see us in the morning, Dr Harrington in the afternoon, also the Boileans & Mr Bonnar.

11TH MARCH, FRIDAY.
We drove over to Tonk this afternoon and got in at 7 o'clock. The Nawab had been waiting on the road since 4 o'clock and seemed very glad to see John again.

20TH MARCH, SUNDAY.
Tonk.

We have been quite upset over the terrible tragedy that has taken place at Anjar, poor Major Neill being shot dead at parade (field firing) by an insane Sowar [*Indian Cavalryman*].

Colonel Miles being appointed to Oodeypore [*Udaipur*] there is no chance of us leaving Deoli for some time.

21ST MARCH, MONDAY.
Deoli.

We left in the evening for this & had a very long drive.

Servants all very tired & beat. The horses felt the heat very much and one may now say the hot weather has begun.

22ND MARCH.
Deoli.

My birthday. J.B. and I did a lot of poking about the house and have been madly busy all day. I sat with Mrs Boilean who is far from well before dinner.

23RD MARCH, WEDNESDAY.
J.B. left for Shahpura at 6.30 riding Sheikh.

25TH MARCH, FRIDAY.
The Sutton Joneses dined with me. I bought a new Mina [*myna bird*], 2 Bulbuls [*native songbirds*] & 2 Chukors [*chukar partridge, the national bird of Pakistan*].

28TH MARCH, MONDAY.
John came in early from Shahpura; he has had capital sport, 11 boars & 1 panther in two days; only 4 other Englishmen beside himself of the party, Mr Trevor, Capt. Meade, Capt. Salmon & Mr Stratton.

7TH APRIL.
Deoli.

Yesterday we had a violent dust storm about ½ past 6 o'clock in the evening, which lasted for some time. Mrs Bonnar dined with us, her husband having gone to Rajmahal [*on the River Banas*] with Col. Bayley, they all three dine here tonight. We have begun punkahs at night now and have them all day long.

13TH APRIL.
Deoli.

Our wedding day. J.B. is going off to Rajmahal to meet Mr Bonnar for 2 days fishing and will be back on Friday. We had a great dust storm in the night but it is not much cooler.

15ᵀᴴ APRIL, FRIDAY.
Deoli.

J.B. returned from Rajmahal this evening, I drove with him when he went out on the 13th & came in for a tremendous dust storm. I was out in it two hours and had to go to bed instead of dining with Mrs Bell. Mr Dyson also arrived this evening from Agra & has brought tons of luggage with him.

21ˢᵀ APRIL, THURSDAY.
Col. Boilean dined with us for the second time since his wife left for Mussoorie [*a hill station in Uttarakhand, Northern India*]. Mrs Bell & Harington also dined here. Mrs Bonnar was very ill on Tuesday night, but was able to drive with me this evening. We heard the news of the wreck of the Tasmania on the shores of Corsica; this is the steamer in which the Bradfords & Mrs Neill went home.

[*The Tasmania went aground and was wrecked on Monachi Rock, South Corsica on 17th April 1887; twenty-four passengers and crew, including the captain, were lost. This was the shipwreck that Sir Edward Bradford and his wife survived on their return to London.*]

22ᴺᴰ APRIL, FRIDAY.
Colonel Bissett arrived in the early morning and after dinner, J.B. went off with him as far as Bundi, Col. Bissett is going on to Kotah [*Kota*]. We have had tatties for the last 5 days, but they do not work properly as there is so little hot wind.

We have discovered that J.B. has 2 months more furlough leave than he thought, and we hope to go home for good in January '89.

[*The Biddulphs did return to England in 1889 but not for good; they returned to India in 1892 for J.B.'s final posting as Resident of Gwalior and then Baroda.*]

25ᵀᴴ APRIL, MONDAY.

Mr Dyson came back from his shooting trip & J.B. turned up from Bundi before I was up in the morning. Mr Dyson got 8 Cheetah, but nobody got any Tigers.

We are now having tatties & thermantidotes all day long. [*Thermantidotes are another cooling device, a rotary wheel fitted into a doorway or window and encased in wet tatties, the cutting edge of air-conditioning!*]

5ᵀᴴ MAY, THURSDAY.
Tonk.

We arrived here at 11 o'clock this morning; we dined with the Bonnars last night out of doors, the heat being so great in their dining room. Then we went home and tried to sleep for a couple of hours and at 1.30 a.m. we started for Tonk. We got on capitally till within ten miles of this and then one of the carriage wheels came to bits and we had to send in here for another carriage; we, sitting waiting under some big trees for several hours. A man brought us some melons to eat; the heat was tremendous before we got into the house.

7ᵀᴴ MAY, SATURDAY.
Tonk.

J.B. had a great meeting of the Bankers and has nearly finished now his business with them; today it was the Nuttra [*sic*] Banker who was being interviewed.

11ᵀᴴ MAY, WEDNESDAY
Tonk.

We have decided to return to Deoli on Friday night. Yesterday Mrs Henney sent us "Living or Dead" which we both read straight through in a few hours. [Living or Dead *by Rabindranath Tagore. Rabindranath Tagore, 1861–1941, Indian writer, poet* and philosopher; he was the first Asian to win the Nobel Prize for Literature in 1913. Knighted in 1915, he renounced his knighthood after the Amritsar or Jallianwala Bagh massacre on 13th April 1919, when British troops massacred some 400 Indian demonstrators.]

14TH MAY, SATURDAY.
Tonk.

We are to return to Deoli tonight, or rather tomorrow morning, as we cannot leave till 2 a.m. when the moon rises. J.B. has done a great deal of work here and has settled his bankers; also arranged the Council more satisfactorily and started good men to Pirawa to settle matters there.

24TH MAY, TUESDAY.
Deoli.

The Queen's birthday. A tremendous dust storm in the evening. J.B. was seedy with a sprain, but we had to go at 6.30 to lay the foundation of the new tank [*reservoir*] in the Main Park, or Vakil's [*Vakeel*] garden. At 8 everybody assembled here and we had a Durbar in the garden on the tennis ground, all the Native officers and Vakils attended. We had dinner rather late, the Bonnars, Bells & Mr Scott made the party.

8TH JUNE, WEDNESDAY.
Dined with the Haringtons; quite fearful heat now, day & night; the Monsoon has burst in Bombay.

15TH JUNE, WEDNESDAY.
Last night the heat was so terrible we sat up all night & kept wet handkerchiefs round our heads and then sat under the punkah; sleep was quite out of the question. I mixed some Bay rum [*an aromatic stimulant distilled from rum and the leaves or berries of the West Indian Bay tree*] in a bowl of water and

constantly dipped our handkerchiefs into this, and so kept our aching heads cool.

This morning Colonel Bayley arrived from Kotah looking terribly white & done up. In the afternoon we had a storm, which relieved us all immensely, about an inch of rain fell and we opened out all the house to the cool air.

28"ᴴ JUNE, TUESDAY.
Deoli.

The rains have not properly set in yet; yesterday we had a great storm of wind & thunder but hardly any rain. Rain has fallen both at Bundi & Tonk. Today is terribly stuffy. J.B. & Mrs Harington went for a ride in the morning and could not do anything hardly but walk. We have decided to go to Tonk on the 5ᵗʰ, then on to Abu.

30ᵀᴴ JUNE, THURSDAY.
The rains have begun here; a good fall of rain came down at 3 p.m. but after that the heat was too fearful.

3ᴿᴰ JULY, SUNDAY.
We had a terrible hot night & I could not sleep, we spent the night tossing about & I sat on the varandah [sic] for a long time; today we have rain falling. Yesterday I paid up all the servants.

6ᵀᴴ JULY, WEDNESDAY.
Tonk.

We left Deoli in Palkees last night about ½ past 8 or 9 and arrived here comfortably at 6.30 a.m. I never had a more comfortable journey for I slept most of the way, and as we had a great deal of rain, we had no dust or heat. The place here is looking at its best, so green & such lovely cool breezes.

11ᵀᴴ JULY, MONDAY.
Tonk.

The Bearer left us this morning on a month's leave and is to join J.B. at Ajmer on 10ᵗʰ August. We heard that the Banker of Ratlam [*Madhya Pradesh*] had lost his son, who had died of a curious illness through eating enormous quantities of Musk. Musk is very expensive, and they say this young man ate £6,000 worth in two years; he ate it in enormous quantities.

The weather is now delightful, it rains every day and there is always a cool breeze.

12ᵀᴴ JULY, TUESDAY.

We had 7 ¼ inches of rain last night; it began last night about 9.30 and it continued nearly without stopping till 10 o'clock this morning. It was tremendous rain & the country looks quite flooded.

14ᵀᴴ JULY, THURSDAY.

We have had 16 ½ inches of rain during the last 48 hours; this morning it cleared up. We went to see the Pukka Bund, over which the water was pouring, falling in great cataracts the other side and making a tremendous noise. I saw several very large fish carried against the edge of the wall and very nearly being swept by the current over the Bund.

20ᵀᴴ JULY.
Tonk.

Our portmanteaus went off to Jaypore [*Jaipur*] this morning.

J.B. had a frightfully tiring day yesterday, beginning by having the Nawab with him from 7.30 a.m. till 11.30 and going on all day seeing people; this morning the Nawab was here again for sometime.

The servants have been more or less ailing with cold & fever etc. Now the Ayah says she is very ill, unable to go to Abu, she says she has been made so ill by two cats, which came into my room!

24TH JULY, SUNDAY.
Jaypore.

We drove here on Friday the 22nd and had a capital journey escaping with only one heavy shower on the road, though it looked threatening at starting. J.B. is particularly pleased at this last visit to Tonk as things went so much more smoothly, and he got so many things done that he wanted; the Nawab & he are on the best of terms now.

Yesterday morning we went to the gardens before breakfast and had a good look at all the birds; there are some most delightful ones and a great many rare ones. There is a very fine Sambar there too, which is said to be 20 years old.

25TH JULY, MONDAY.
Jaypore.

This is J.B.'s birthday & we spent the morning together looking at the Museum and driving about the gardens; the School of Art was unfortunately shut up. We leave this evening for Abu.

26TH JULY, TUESDAY.
Abu. [*Mount Abu*]

We arrived here about 4 o'clock very comfortably, no rain to speak of on the journey up the hill. Colonel Walter received us very kindly and Major Wyllie was also in the house. [*The same William Curzon Wyllie as previously mentioned; Captain Curzon Wyllie became a Major in 1886.*

The rainy season was just starting and the Biddulphs had come to the hill station at Mount Abu to escape the heat. John

Julia Biddulph

John Biddulph, 19th Hussars

*Lady Martin,
Julia's mother*

*Sir James Ranald Martin,
Julia's father*

Amy Laurie, Julia's sister

Colonel Cunliffe Martin, Central India Horse

Maréchal Canrobert

*Leila Canrobert & her
daughter Angelique
aged 6 months*

Cav. Alessandro Tomea-Albiani and Count De Gubernatis

The calling card of Counts Albiani
and Count De Guberantis

1

I have spent Xmas in so many strange places, surrounded by different peoples in far away lands — but a particular Xmas in an Indian camp, returns to my memory with a distinctness that never seems to wear off — We had been living the usual delightful insouciant sort of life everybody leads in camp i' the ~~bright~~ Indian winter — riding i' the mornings to fresh camping grounds, shooting i' the afternoons, dining hungrily ~~at~~ — Then it became dark and sleeping soundly all night — unless a prowling tiger roused the camp at night — When that occurs every one wakes, the horses, elephants

Julia's handwriting

Biddulph stayed for about a fortnight before returning to work; Julia remained at Mount Abu till early September.]

11ᵀᴴ AUGUST, THURSDAY.
Abu.

J.B. is going down the hill today, he stops at Ajmer for two days and then goes on to Nimbahera [*Rajasthan*]. We had a fine afternoon yesterday for the 2nd time since we came up; it has simply rained all day, every day and all night too, but this morning there are signs of a break, just as John must go down. I go over to the Wyllies after luncheon and stay with them all this month. Yesterday I walked with Mrs Spencer to enquire after Mrs Temple whose child was born dead a few days ago; she is apparently recovering rapidly.

We have had nearly 40 inches of rain since we came up I believe.

25ᵀᴴ AUGUST, THURSDAY.
Mt. Abu, Lake House.

Mrs Wyllie is now quite jolly, just a week ago she was badly bitten by Rose the greyhound, who also had been bitten two days before by a Pie dog [*pariah dog or wild dog*]. Rose was bitten on Tuesday the 16th, Major Wyllie left the next day for Simla [*Simla, Himachal Pradesh, the summer capital of British India*].

Mrs Wyllie was bitten on the 18th and we at once sent for Dr Spencer, but before he came the bite had been well burnt out with caustic. However he cut more & burnt very freely, leaving a very nasty place on the poor arm [*this very unpleasant process was supposed to prevent rabies*]. Rose has been perfectly well and she really only bit because she was in pain, the sore having been accidently touched by Mrs Wyllie.

It has rained here steadily since Monday night almost without ceasing, and it is still pouring without the least chance of clearing, yesterday we stayed indoors all day long. I have finished one sketch of Abu and given it to Mrs Wyllie. I have not had any letters from J.B. for 2 days.

Mrs Pears had a child born in Neemuch [*Madhya Pradesh*], a son, but it only lived two days.

[*This is very sad; first Mrs Temple and now Mrs Pears. Julia mentions one or two other occasions when either a mother or her child, or both, did not survive.*]

26TH AUGUST.
Abu.

I heard last evening of J.B.'s long & adventurous journey to Tonk; the river and Nullahs were so full they had to swim the horses and literally carry the carriage over the Nullah. The rain continues & we had 5 inches here last night.

Mrs Bayley has had another daughter (the 5th) and is going on all right.

[*A nullah is a watercourse, similar to a wadi, which is usually dry, but torrents of water rush down it during the monsoons.*]

30TH AUGUST.
Abu.

I have heard from J.B. that I am to meet him on Saturday the 3rd at Ajmer.

Pouring with rain, we have now had over 80 inches of rain here.

1ST SEPTEMBER, THURSDAY.
Abu.

I had a telegram from J.B. yesterday telling me not to leave this tomorrow as he is going to stay on at Tonk till the 5th and

I shall not probably go down now till the 7th. We had such an exquisite sunset last night but today the rain has begun again and it is very close and muggy.

4TH SEPTEMBER, SUNDAY.
Mt. Abu.

I am really now to go to Ajmer on the 7th, and hope to be at Deoli on the 10th. The weather is better but still very damp & uncertain, 85 inches of rain have fallen here. The traffic between Jaypore & Ajmer was stopped for a little time owing to a bridge giving way on the line.

I have consulted Dr Spencer about my health and he has given me arsenic to take for three months. [*This seems rather alarming; it is a wonder that Julia lived to such a ripe old age!*]

8TH SEPTEMBER, THURSDAY.
Ajmer.

I left Abu yesterday at 12 o'clock, Major Wyllie rode down with me, it was very hot indeed, quite exhausting to the dandy bearers. [*A dandy is a type of sedan chair carried by four bearers who would have carried Julia down the hill from Mount Abu to the railway station at Abu Road. It would seem, thanks to Major Wyllie, that Julia had her own carriage on the train from Abu Road to Ajmer, quite a luxury, but a great relief from the heat.*] I thought at one time they would give in quite completely. I had tea at Abu Road and Major Wyllie got a carriage put on for me; J.B. met me at 4 o'clock. We are staying with Colonel Trevor. Ajmer is pretty now and very pleasant.

11TH SEPTEMBER, SUNDAY.
Deoli.

We arrived here last night and had a very hot but otherwise successful drive from Ajmer yesterday, getting in here at 7 o'clock, or rather before. The river was quite low but our Elephant nearly got into a quicksand and frightened me very much.

[Ajmer to Deoli is some eighty miles, a long journey in a horse-drawn carriage; the horses would have been changed at least three times. The elephant was used to ferry them across the river at Deoli.]

12TH SEPTEMBER, MONDAY.
Deoli.

John is very far from well and we have had Dr Huntley here twice to see him. He had a bad night with colic and was in great pain till 2 o'clock this morning when he got some sleep at last. [John Biddulph's bouts of ill health are becoming more regular, mostly related to 'Indian fever'.]

13TH SEPTEMBER, TUESDAY.
Deoli.

J.B. is not all right by any means & Dr Huntley is so much engaged with Mrs Bonnar who has been ill since 3 o'clock this morning that he can't give him much attention.

16TH SEPTEMBER, FRIDAY.
Mrs Bonnar was very ill all day and in the afternoon her child was born dead, a son. We were told that she could not live and all hopes of her recovery were over, but quite late in the evening she rallied.

17TH SEPTEMBER, SATURDAY.
Mrs Bonnar had a peaceful quiet day, sometimes conscious and able to talk to those around her. Mr Bonnar was very hopeful and went out with us for a 20 minute walk.

18TH SEPTEMBER, SUNDAY.
Deoli.

Poor Mrs Bonnar died at 4.30 p.m. she was never conscious, suffered no pain & died at last in convulsions. Colonel Bayley took Mr Bonnar away to his own house, and Dr Shepherd has been telegraphed for from Oodeypore [Udaipur].

[*How desperately sad; Mrs Bonnar was the young bride whose broad Scotch had been so difficult to understand at Julia's Christmas party nine months earlier.*]

19TH SEPTEMBER, MONDAY.

We all attended Mrs Bonnar's funeral this morning at 9 a.m. Mrs Boilean and I made wreaths of jessamine [*jasmine*] & white roses & oleanders, and crosses & laid them on the coffin. The native Christian women wailed in a most distressing way at the funeral, which upset us all a good deal.

24TH SEPTEMBER, SATURDAY.
Deoli.

Dr Shepherd called in the afternoon; he has arranged to take Mr Bonnar back with him to Oodeypore. [*Dr Shepherd being a doctor of divinity.*]

25TH SEPTEMBER, SUNDAY.
Deoli.

Dr Shepherd read service in the Church at 7 a.m. & I took a wreath before service to put on Mrs Bonnar's grave. I met Miss Onbridge there and we both went for a little drive till it was time for Church. [*Probably in a dogcart, pulled by a pony and driven by Julia.*]

8TH OCTOBER, SATURDAY.
Deoli.

We have heard that Charlie Adeane comes out here in November to shoot. My pony "Robin" has gone off to Major Vincent, and the Sheikh has been sold, so our stables are now much reduced; Punch, the Doctor & the mare are left to us.

14TH OCTOBER, FRIDAY.
Deoli.

We have heard that Richard & Mary Martin will be in India on Monday, and that Marie Adeane has been made Maid of Honour; two pieces of news received this mail.

We are much shocked to hear of poor Mrs George Money's death after the birth of a baby.

[*This is the fourth such tragedy in as many months. Richard and Mary Martin were in Egypt with the Biddulphs in 1885.*]

18TH OCTOBER, TUESDAY.
Tonk.

We drove over here this morning and arrived about 12 o'clock, we were both very tired in the evening. The road from Deoli to Tonk is pretty bad, and it got hot before we got in.

20TH OCTOBER, THURSDAY.
Tonk.

Col. Trevor comes to us on the 5th, or a day or two later, so that our party is gradually being settled for Rajmahal.

[*The Biddulphs are planning a few days fishing with friends at Rajmahal, where they would camp by the Banas River.*]

29TH OCTOBER, SATURDAY.
Tonk.

We are trying to arrange the dāk [bungalow] for Richard & Mary to arrive on Tuesday; they have made some extraordinary mistake about dates and write & telegraph about Tuesday the 2nd; Tuesday being the 1st November, so that it is very puzzling to know what they really mean to do. I am wildly writing from this place to everybody to help them on the road, as we hear Mary has been much knocked up by the heat in Bombay.

I have advanced the baker 10 rupees for flour for camp.

31ST OCTOBER, MONDAY.
Tonk.

This is our last day here; we are to drive over to Deoli tomorrow morning. Yesterday the Nawab was ill and John had to go over and see him in the afternoon. He found he was suffering from a bad pain in his waistcoat and his Court were all wringing their hands and giving him scent and water to drink out of a big teapot. J.B. insisted on a dose of castor oil. [*There is nothing like a good dose of castor oil to sort out a bad pain in your waistcoat, either that or arsenic!*]

1ST NOVEMBER, TUESDAY.
Deoli.

I drove over here alone this morning, leaving John as the Nawab was so ill he did not like to leave Tonk till the Nawab was decidedly better; Capt. Pears was also very seedy. I made all sorts of preparations for Richard & Mary, and kept carriage, elephant, and Abdullah Khan waiting till 8.30 p.m. at the river; but they did not come.

6TH NOVEMBER.

Richard & Mary arrived here on Wednesday the 2nd, J.B. came over in the morning. I sent off everything on Tuesday to meet Richard, so I was very anxious when Wednesday afternoon arrived, and could hardly believe they had really turned up.

We went to Tika [*Teekar*] on Thursday afternoon, and on Friday Richard shot snipe with J.B. – or rather went out with J.B. after snipe.

Saturday morning (yesterday) Colonel Trevor arrived and we had tent pegging etc. for Richard's amusement.

7TH NOVEMBER, MONDAY.

Rajmahal [*on the Banas River*].

We said goodbye to Richard and Mary this morning; they left in the Bullock Shigram soon after 7 a.m., with the top on the Shigram as there was rain falling [*a shigram is a two-wheeled covered wagon pulled by two bullocks*].

Colonel Trevor & I drove over here, and Mr Egerton & John rode. Colonel Bayley arrived for breakfast.

It rained a little all day, sometimes quite smartly; I spent the day in the hole in the wall, the others went after trout. We all had tea in the hole in the wall, coming home in time for dinner – whist after dinner.

8TH NOVEMBER, TUESDAY.

Rajmahal.

Colonel Bayley left us in the morning; John & Mr Egerton got 4 brace of snipe before breakfast. Colonel Trevor & I took a stroll. We had a glorious day, I sketched all day till teatime, which we had in the hole in the wall. The men got a lot of trout and Mr Egerton caught a big fish of 11 lbs. and several others.

9TH NOVEMBER, WEDNESDAY.
Rajmahal.

We had breakfast at 10 o'clock and went down for the day to Byselpore [*Bisalpur*], and had a most charming day, the men caught some very nice trout; Colonel Trevor caught a fearful fish, which he called the Jabberwock, and a turtle.

[*What type of extraordinary fish was it that Colonel Trevor had caught? The 'Jabberwock' is the strange dragon-like creature from Lewis Carroll's* Through the Looking Glass and What Alice Found There, *1872.*]

10TH NOVEMBER, THURSDAY.
Rajmahal.

We had breakfast at 10 and in the morning we all fished down stream below the bathing place. Afterwards we went up to the hole in the wall and John and Mr Egerton got some good fish spinning. We played Knaves after dinner.

11TH NOVEMBER, FRIDAY.
Rajmahal.

We had breakfast at 9 and fished till 2 o'clock, then we returned to camp and Colonel Trevor & I started to drive home at 3.30. We got into Deoli at 5 p.m.

John was very lucky getting one very large fish of 9 ½ lbs, also Mr Egerton brought in two big fish, one weighing 7 lbs.

[*After five days fishing, they return to Deoli, where for the next fortnight they would prepare to move back into camp and their travels would begin again.*]

24TH NOVEMBER.
Sawar [*Saver*]

Arrived here at 10 a.m. I rode the first five miles on "She" and finished up in the carriage; Toby was so wet after unwillingly swimming across the river, that he had to run all the way.

We got our home letters last night; Annie gave us an alarming rumour about Fanny Martin, which has greatly concerned us.

[Fanny was Julia's sister-in-law, married to her brother Cunliffe. I think the rumour may have been that Fanny was expecting a baby, which as we have heard was always a risky business in India.]

LASARIA.
John got some good shooting here and bagged nine duck, most of them big grey duck & one mallard, he lost several more in the water. In the afternoon we took a stroll through the fields but got nothing.

Poor Mrs Money contracted the fever she died of in the hospital at Ootacamund. [*Ootacamund, or Ooty, Ooty Hill Station in the southern Indian state of Tamil Nadu, known as the Queen of hill stations. The Ooty Club was where the rules and game of snooker were first recorded in 1882.*]

26ᵀᴴ NOVEMBER.
Kadisaina [*Kadisahana*]

J.B. went over to Shahpura in the afternoon to pay a visit of condolence to the Chief there on the death of the Ranee.

27ᵀᴴ NOVEMBER, SUNDAY.
Kadisaina. John shot both morning & evening. We wrote our Xmas letters home & I wrote to the Mystole children.

[*These were Julia's nieces and nephews, her sister Amy's children; they lived at Mystole Park, Kent, England. A letter written on 27ᵗʰ November 1887 in deepest Rajasthan would arrive in the UK in time for Christmas – remarkable. The* recommended last posting date for standard surface mail to India for Christmas 2018 is 28th September, a whole two months earlier; even by airmail it is 7th December – how things have changed!]

28TH NOVEMBER, MONDAY.
Bari-Kunesau [sic]

John shot ducks in the afternoon, the Rajah of Shahpura has joined us and means to stay with us in camp for the next few days. We have still a few very hot hours during the day, as we never get any trees to camp under.

My larder is so full of game I know not what to do with it all; we have made game pies, potted game, stews, hare soup etc., & are still crowded with ducks.

29TH NOVEMBER, TUESDAY.
Phooliya.

We had a very short march of about 6 miles here. This is the principal town in Shahpura but it is very uninteresting and there are no manufacturers of either cloths or brass; or indeed anything.

We walked through the town in the afternoon and looked at an old bowree [sic] or well, and strolled about in a good deal of dust.

30TH NOVEMBER, WEDNESDAY.
Phooliya.

This morning we went out to Dhunope [sic] a tank about four miles from here, and a very bad sandy road for the carriage. We started at 7.30 and got back to breakfast at 10.30, the Rajah joined us there and John shot one duck & one snipe. It was too large a piece of water to shoot over; the duck & geese went off at the first shot. We had a most dismal account from the Wyllies last night; all their servants down with fever, their best tent burnt down and their Chuprassee [Chuprassi, *a servant or messenger*] bitten by the cook's dog! No game except 2 grey partridges and Mrs Wyllie ill herself with fever. I made a sketch at Dhunope of a little temple, my first sketch in camp this season.

14TH DECEMBER, WEDNESDAY.
Kanti.

We went after a Panther with the Rajah this morning, but we never saw the Panther. We saw a very big Hyena, some lovely black buck, a porcupine and a huge Boar which J.B. shot. The men beating made so much noise the Panther must have been driven back.

15TH DECEMBER, THURSDAY.
Kachola [*Kachhola*]

We had a tiresome march this morning though a short one, as we had to cross the river on starting and then come up a ravine & my mare became very fractious indeed and I was very miserable.

This place is very charming on a lake, and we hope to have some good shooting. Mr Bonnar and I went out about half past two after duck & J.B. went in his canoe. I shot my first duck on the wing and was much pleased. Mr Bonnar shot several duck & teal, but we lost them in the reeds & water and only brought back three; J.B. brought home 6 duck & 7 snipe.

16TH DECEMBER, FRIDAY.
Kachola.

We went out at 11 with the Rajah for a panther beat. Before breakfast I made a slight sketch of the lake; but it became so bitterly cold with an east wind I could not finish it.

The first shooting box we came to was a tower with a fearful staircase of stones outside the building. Here a stone, there a stone, impossible for me to climb up. So I stayed inside with Mr Bonnar & we saw nothing, but John saw a fine panther just for a moment between the trees; also a Boar but he did not get a shot at either.

We then got on ponies and rode to another tower, and this one with the help of a ladder, I got up to the top of. Here we again saw nothing. I saw a mongoose & Mr Bonnar saw a pig! After the beat we sat down in the shade and had some soda water. Then we mounted tower No: 3. After a short time a panther crossed slowly over some open ground; we had a beautiful view of him and J.B. shot him, wounding him mortally. He fell over & roared, then presently all the beaters came howling down. We shouted at them to stop but they wouldn't hear, one old man got hurt by the panther, fortunately very slightly; and then they all began shooting into the panther's dead body! At last J.B., the Rajah & Mr Bonnar rushed off to stop the firing & see the beast, and one of the Shikarees [*native huntsmen*] came breathlessly up to me to know where all the gentlemen were! I was afraid for a moment there had been an accident, for everybody was shooting so wildly, but it really was to announce the death of another panther. Then a hyena was brought up; a big white one, and we went down the hill & examined the two panthers, which had been dreadfully shot & the skins spoilt. We rode home & got into camp at 4.30.

17ᵀᴴ DECEMBER, SATURDAY.
Mandi [*Mandi Gusaiyan*]

Rather a long march of 14 miles, but a very good road and I only rode five miles, the carriage bringing me here comfortably at about 10.30. John & Mr Bonnar fished all day, or rather all the day they had; for with late breakfast etc., they did not start till one o'clock, and then they had to walk down to the river for about a mile. They got some lovely trout, Mr Bonnar brought in 6 dozen & 3, and J.B. three dozen & a half which we distributed all over the camp. The wind was east all day, if it had been in the west the bags would have been much bigger. The rivers meet here and it is the best water for fishing that J.B. has seen on the Banas.

18TH DECEMBER, SUNDAY.
Mandi.

J.B. went down to the river before breakfast and got three lovely Mahseer. The biggest was about 3 lbs and the next very near it, he also got fourteen trout, most of them very large & fine ones; we had a great fish breakfast. In the afternoon I went down to the river to watch J.B. fish and he was very successful. His bag for the day was 6 dozen & 5 trout & 6 Mahseer of which the biggest was 3 lbs., the smallest 1 ½ lbs. Just as the sun set J.B. hooked a huge Mahseer but it got away through the reel coming into contact with J.B.'s knuckles.

19TH DECEMBER, MONDAY.
Mandalgarh.

J.B. and Mr Bonnar fished in the morning at Mandi and John got 3 Mahseer & 11 trout. The biggest Mahseer was 6 lbs., the next 4 lbs. and the small one over 1½ lbs. We had breakfast under some trees in a delightful place and after breakfast I drove over here, leaving John to follow when his fishing was over. Mr Bonnar went on his way to Chittor [*Chittorgarh*]. This is a most picturesque place, there is a great fort on the hill and we are encamped under beautiful trees. Quantities of big monkeys in the trees watch the camp & sometimes try to snatch the food from the servants when they are cooking it. We have been ordering a brass lamp to be made here; there is a kind of lacquer work made here too, but it is very rough.

21ST DECEMBER, WEDNESDAY.
Bijaollie [*Bijolia*]

We had a short march here over a very bad road, quite impossible for wheels. It was a very pretty march though, and when we got up to the top of one of the passes there was a delicious breeze that reminded me of home somehow. Here there is a big fort and the camping ground is very picturesque with palms & big trees. The Rajah was anxious to salute J.B. with 21 guns; but fortunately the gun burst before the 5th salute, it made such a terrible noise; the fort being just over our camp.

The Rao's son met us about three miles from Bijaollie, and the old man himself came to see J.B. at 2 o'clock; afflicted with bronchitis & gout [*Sawai Rao Govind Das, 14th Rao of Bijolian, born c. 1828*].

We went out at 3 to see the Temples of Siva [*Shiva*], which are quite close, and then we rode on to another place about ½ a mile off where there are ruins of 5 more Temples. They are small & insignificant, but the inscriptions on two slabs of rock are very wonderful. They are written in Sanscrit [*Sanskrit*] about 1150 A.D. and are in very good preservation, they are simply cut out on the bare rock.

23RD DECEMBER, FRIDAY.
Gererda [*sic*]

We had a march of 12 miles here through a jungle forest of small trees & grass, with quantities of huge slabs of stone. In one place these slabs were so polished & slippery from the water going over them & were highly unpleasant to ride over; otherwise it was a charming march, which I enjoyed very much. Our camp here is pitched in the open, just beyond the forest and hills.

24TH DECEMBER, SATURDAY.
Gererda.

We went out at 10 a.m. this morning to see if we could get a bear or a tiger, and rode an Elephant for about a mile & then scrambled through the jungle to a place where they had tied a charpoy on to the top of a tree, just over a stream. I was expected to get up the tree, but I had to have the charpoy moved lower down & then I did scramble up. J.B. & I sat up there with our rifles but nothing came and the beaters turned up nothing at all. We got down & walked about a mile down the bed of a river, & then on its bank, till we came to a lovely large pool where there were red rocks & beautiful foliage, and one of the big green & blue kingfishers, such a lovely spot.

J.B. shot a crocodile there & we brought it home to make soup for the camels! I sketched it after tea.

[*I wonder if camels like crocodile soup?*]

CHRISTMAS DAY 1887
Gererda.

John and I started off at 10 a.m. on an Elephant and went about 2 miles into the jungles and then got down & walked another 2 miles till we came to a tree, up which I had to climb. From some mistake the head Shikar [*huntsman*] did not come with us & in consequence the arrangements were very bad, this beat proving useless. We had a frightful scramble over rocks, through bushes & up a hillside covered with high grass & thorns to another tree, up which I got – another blank beat!

We then had a third even worse trudge up another hill side, and through terrible thorns, to tree no: 3! This time

I sat at the foot of it & J.B. got up with his rifle. We sat on & on, the sun disappearing behind the hillside till we were fairly worn out & no sound of beaters; at last J.B. said, "We'll go and leave them all," to which I promptly agreed, being dead tired. We had hardly left our post 5 minutes when a shot, 2 shots were fired by the Tonk Vakil [*or Vakeel*] & J.B. saw a black bear disappearing & I heard the grump of the bear twice repeated. Of course there was a chance of the bear being turned by the beaters on us, as they now made their appearance. So I got up another tree & J.B. stood guard with his rifle; but the bear went over the opposite hill & we returned home after sunset, much dejected. I then distributed plum puddings to the camp, and a good dinner a little comforted our wounded feelings.

26TH DECEMBER, MONDAY.
Gererda.

J.B. went off early to try and get a bear and had to ride a good 9 miles before he got on to his ground. He was away all day working hard, but never saw a thing, and returned home at sunset without having let off his gun.

27TH DECEMBER, TUESDAY.
Gererda. We had a quiet potter in the afternoon and went over some extraordinary ground. I never saw anything like the slabs of rock about here, very tiring to the feet, and most horrid to ride over.

28TH DECEMBER, WEDNESDAY.
Kullianpore [*sic*]

J.B. and I rode half the march here together, then he went off on another bear hunt and I rode on here alone and got in about 9.30, the march being 10 miles.

At 3 o'clock J.B. came in having had a most capital day, bringing in 2 very big black bears. The bears are very good specimens; one measures 66 ½ inches and the other 68 inches from end of nose to tip of tail. I sketched the place where we are encamped a short time before sunset; the lights were so pretty, but I had no time to make a finished sketch.

29TH DECEMBER, THURSDAY.
Borkhera.

Not a very nice march here, rather long and tiresome and not a very nice camping ground, and a horrid wet night, everybody dripping & the tents soaking. The bears' skins a great anxiety on account of the rain.

30TH DECEMBER, FRIDAY.
Bundi.

I came in here in the Shigram as the morning was so damp & uncertain, and the roads very muddy, J.B. rode in by himself. It is very cold and windy & disagreeable.

31ST DECEMBER, SATURDAY.
Bundi.

A frightfully cold, misty morning, we were so cold we could do nothing till we had breakfast, and everything looked most miserable. We had very unhappy letters from Deoli; things are very uncomfortable in the Regt. and seem to be getting worse. J.B. and I drove out in the afternoon when it cleared up, and the sun cheered us.

I have written to Mrs Hall to send off all my things by the middle of February without fail.

So ends 1887; it is now only four months until John Biddulph can take his much-needed leave. The past two years have taken their toll on both Julia and her husband, and they are longing for a change. They have both suffered repeated bouts of ill health. John in particular; he has fever, rheumatics, sciatica and goodness knows how many other complaints. I suspect all largely due to 'Indian fever' and suffering from any of these illnesses in the heat and humidity of Rajasthan 130 years ago must have been very trying. Julia complains very little about her own health, other than occasional attacks of fever; she will have just completed her three-month course of arsenic prescribed by the doctor in September, which I am sure will have much improved her constitution!

Just as the last two years, 1888 begins 'in camp', and by the end of February, they are back at Deoli and Tonk.

Chapter VIII

1888

1ST JANUARY, SUNDAY.
Bundi.
 The New Year has begun with a lovely morning; the wind & rain having gone, everybody is again very cheerful.

5TH JANUARY, THURSDAY.
Bundi.
 Colonel Walter and all the camp came in early, the Frasers, the Spencers & the Marshalls. A most lovely sight, all the Bundi Chiefs following to meet Colonel Walter. The Camel Corps in orange & red, with guns; then a Corps on horseback in orange with gold & red paggries [Pagari, *a turban*], & numbers of horsemen, men on camels etc., in gorgeous colours. Mrs Spencer & Mrs Fraser went out with me in the afternoon to the Bund, and we saw the old Chief and all his retinue again in the streets of Bundi [*Maharao Raja Shri Sahib Bahadur, 1811–1889, Maharao Raja from 1821–1889*].

7TH JANUARY, SATURDAY.
Dublana.

We all marched here in the morning making a very early start. I drove over in the pony carriage. Mrs Spencer is very far from well [and] the Marshalls often have headaches. Mrs Fraser has left with her husband for Abu [*Mount Abu*], being in delicate health, but robustness & health are represented by Capt. Meade who arrived here yesterday morning.

The death of Capt. Salmon from a fall at polo has been a terribly sad thing; he was pig-sticking with J.B. last March at Shahpura & was very popular with everybody.

11TH JANUARY, WEDNESDAY.
Indoghur [*Indergarh*]

We came by the wrong road and had a terrible bumping over a stony road. We all however had headaches; at least both the Spencers, the Marshalls & I felt seedy.

I sketched all day nearly, trying to get the castle & fort of Indoghur, which is on a hillside & looks very picturesque. We have quite a charming camping ground with fine trees. Mrs Spencer looked worse than ever after dinner; she is certainly very seedy.

12TH JANUARY, THURSDAY.
Lakheri.

We had quite a bad march here; on leaving Indoghur the Sowars took us on a wrong road and landed the pony carriage in a quite impossible place. I got out & walked & J.B. sent the carriage back & round another way, but it got broken en route and we had a lot of bother to prevent the Shigram following. The road all along is quite impossible for driving [and] the big camp went off in another direction.

We said goodbye to the Spencers & Marshalls this morning. It has turned quite hot suddenly.

We went to see a pawn [sic] garden in the afternoon; the gardens are the neatest things in gardening I have ever seen out here. The plant is grown like rows of peas, carefully guarded from the sun by a roof of dried grass and surrounded by a high fence or hedge of the same grass, so that the garden is in perpetual shade. The rows of pawn are trained on to sticks and every row is as regular as possible, not a weed growing anywhere. A Bigah [sic] employs 25 labourers and produces about 300 Rupees profit yearly. There were a good many nice mango trees near the garden; altogether Lakheri struck us as a very pretty place.

We noticed one Sati Stone, which represented 7 women and the big man on horseback; this meant 7 wives were burnt at his death. [*Sati is a funeral custom where the wife commits suicide on her husband's death, often by burning.*

I believe that the Biddulphs had visited a 'Paan' garden or betel leaf garden. Betel is a climbing plant that is cultivated for its leaf and grown in rows as Julia describes. The heart-shaped leaves are used for medicinal and culinary purposes; it is a mild stimulant often chewed with betel nut as a mouth freshener.]

13ᵀᴴ JANUARY, FRIDAY.
Khera.

I rode here with John, a very good road only 7 miles march. We went out for a walk in the evening and Toby [*Julia's terrier*] attacked a wolf, which fortunately fled from Dingo [*Julia's other, larger dog*] who came up to Toby's rescue.

14ᵀᴴ JANUARY, SATURDAY.
Dehkhera [sic].

I rode Doctor half the march here, about 5 miles, and liked him much. Clouds are gathering & every day looks like rain.

15TH JANUARY, SUNDAY.
Kapren.

I rode She part of the way & the rest on Doctor. I only met the carriage close to camp, as there were two roads here, which made great confusion.

The Thakur here is a great man & very disobedient and disloyal to the Durbar, so J.B. has had to sit on him; he came out to meet J.B. with a tremendous following [*Maharaj Raghuraj Singh, Thakur Sahib of Bansi, 1884–1906*].

18TH JANUARY, WEDNESDAY.
Patan [*Keshoraipatan*]

I drove here, but it was such a cold morning that J.B. got off his horse & proposed a walk, so we took a sharp walk on the way to warm us. The distance is said to be 12 miles; the road was good all the way.

We went to some wonderful Temples on the banks of the river [*the River Chambral*] in the afternoon; they had been whitewashed so often that all the carving had disappeared & the Temples were quite disfigured. Inside the Temple were dancing girls dressed in brilliant colours, red, yellow, pink, all trimmed with silver and musicians who played drum & fife. These girls danced and sang to amuse the Gods. There were crowds of people looking on, some of them very gaily dressed. These Temples are very richly endowed and attract a great many Hindoo [sic] worshippers.

22ND JANUARY, SUNDAY.
Kutkar [sic] *Khatgarh*.

J.B. got a very good Cheetal stag [*or chital, spotted or axis deer*], he was out all day and had a tremendous walk. I sketched the pass [and] in the evening we had a big storm and tremendous hailstones as large as very big marbles.

23ᴿᴰ JANUARY, MONDAY.

Kutkar. I went out with J.B. today and he got three Cheetal Stags, and the old Rajah a hyena. The stags were better ones than yesterday and in prime condition; unfortunately they died before their throats could be cut, so no Mohammedan will touch the meat.

I finished my sketch of the Pass; when I came in it had turned so very cold after the storm that I could not get warm till I had sat almost into the stove.

24ᵀᴴ JANUARY, TUESDAY.

Ramghur [sic] Ramgarh.

We marched here during the day, having breakfast half way (the march being only about 6 ½ miles) and J.B. shooting till nearly 4 o'clock. After breakfast I rode on and got into camp by one o'clock. J.B. had no sport, the old Rajah shot at a fine panther, which got away and J.B. took a long shot at a Nilgai Bull. J.B. came in quite fagged and knocked up by the heat and tremendous grind up a hill just at the last. The Pass is exceedingly pretty and full of game, it is a first rate place for Cheetal & Sambar but the drives are so badly managed that the Sambar stags always break back, and J.B. has not had a shot at one yet. I saw a baby Sambar this morning; it came quite close to us.

Ramghur looks very pretty, we shall stop here two days as the carriage & shigram etc., have gone round another way & will meet us.

25ᵀᴴ JANUARY, WEDNESDAY.

Ramghur.

J.B. went out shooting after breakfast, and came back at 12.30 with a panther and a sambar. He had a great encounter with the panther; he had just shot the sambar, and had fortunately re-loaded when a panther appeared quite close to him. J.B. fired and wounded it really mortally, but it sprung upon him and he fell, slipping on his stick, just as the animal pounced. The panther was on his foot when J.B. gave it a thrust with the barrel of his rifle down its throat, and it fell down dead. The panther was 6ft 5, with a very good skin, so nice & bright. The sambar stag is not a very large one. All last night different noises kept one awake; we heard a tiger or a panther very close to camp making that peculiar sawing noise, which is horribly creepy. Then the rain came & all things had to be moved from the shamiana; altogether a most disturbing night.

27TH JANUARY, FRIDAY.
Banjeri [sic]

I came here on the Elephant being afraid the horses would all be so fresh after their long holiday and the intense cold. It was lovely leaving Ramghur, the end of the Pass is so very, very pretty; we had a beautiful sunset this evening.

1ST FEBRUARY, WEDNESDAY.
Kakor

On our way here, and within a mile of Kakor we passed a very curious statue of an Elephant carved out of solid rock [*the stone elephant at Hathibhata Kakor*]. The Elephant was not in relief, but a statue of the animal 15ft high or so, and in a very life like natural attitude. There were several large rocks near the statue and one imagines that this particular piece of rock must have borne the resemblance of the animal, and so put the idea of the complete statue into the artist's head. It is very cleverly done and comes upon one as a surprise in a rather bare looking plain.

The weather is particularly disagreeable, windy with occasional showers. J.B. has not been able to shake off his rheumatism. The English mail came in this afternoon.

2ND FEBRUARY, THURSDAY.
Bhambor [sic]

J.B. rode here but found he could not go out of a walk. Rain and wind as usual, we are within 5 miles of Tonk and have determined to break up our camp there and remain in the place till Colonel Walter arrives on 20th.

3RD FEBRUARY, FRIDAY.
Tonk.

We drove in here this morning and the weather was delicious; but soon after breakfast a fearful storm came on and we were flooded.

John's rheumatism is very bad indeed this evening, and the damp everywhere & the soaking ground are about as bad for him as bad can be. The Nawab met him and was very friendly this morning, but the discomfort of this deluge is most trying to everybody.

7TH FEBRUARY, TUESDAY.
Tonk.

Mr Ney Elias arrived here for breakfast [*Ney Elias, 1844–1897, explorer, geographer, diplomat and member of the Royal Geographical Society, who travelled widely in China, Kashmir and Chinese Turkestan*]. J.B. is still on the sofa but in less pain.

16TH FEBRUARY, THURSDAY.
Tonk.

J.B. is now almost well. Home letters came today with news of Cunliffe's new daughter. [*Cunliffe Martin, Julia's brother. It would seem that the alarming rumour that Julia had heard about in November had come true. Sensibly, Fanny had returned to England to have her baby.*]

19TH FEBRUARY, SUNDAY.
Tonk.

Colonel Walter, the Spencers and Capt. Meade arrived here this morning.

John and I drove down to the river to meet them and Mrs Spencer came back with me; she is not at all well and even thinner than ever.

23RD FEBRUARY, THURSDAY.
Tonk.

Colonel Walter and all the party left us this morning. Mrs Spencer drove all the march, she is very seedy indeed.

25TH FEBRUARY, SATURDAY.
Tonk.

We had rain several times in the night, and now again it is pouring this morning; the clouds are very heavy and it looks very stormy. We have had rain for a month now and it is very bad for the country; there has fortunately been no hail.

I am sending all our baggage to Deoli, and we ourselves go on Monday.

27TH FEBRUARY, MONDAY.
Deoli.

We came in here this morning, or rather afternoon, having smashed one carriage en route & finishing up with a drunken coachman in the other carriage.

11TH MARCH, SUNDAY.
Mrs Bullen and I went to church in the morning. In the evening J.B. & Colonel Bullen arrived quite knocked up by the heat & fatigue of the last few days, though they had enjoyed

themselves very much indeed [*pig sticking*]. They got 14 boars in the 2 days; Capt. Meade and Mr Hallan got bad falls, but no bones broken fortunately, and the whole thing was a great success.

[*The next few weeks are spent at Deoli; John Biddulph has applied for three months' leave. Their plans for a trip to Australia hang in the balance, depending on what dates the leave is granted.*
On Sunday 25th March, Julia writes:]
We have given up all thoughts of Australia and are now going to Japan most likely. Our application for leave has gone to the I.O. [*India Office*] any time after 20th April.

[*Then, after weeks of uncertainty, she writes:*]
1st May, Tuesday
Our baggage for Australia leaves this evening.
[*Having given up all thoughts of going to Australia, they had now packed and were preparing to leave. John Biddulph's three months' leave had been granted in time for them to catch their intended steamer, and they were off to Calcutta.*

The Biddulphs had been in India since their arrival on 10th August 1885. John Biddulph had been working continuously for nearly three years as Acting Resident, Boundary Settlement Officer or Government Agent in Southern Rajasthan.

For a great deal of this time, the Biddulphs had been living in camp, often moving daily. There is no doubt that these camps were extremely comfortable and well-equipped, but I would imagine the excitement of camp life would soon weary even the most ardent of traveller. The heat and humidity, and the potential for any type of ghastly disease must have been a constant burden. As we know, Julia and John Biddulph both suffered from repeated attacks of 'Indian fever'.

This sudden change to their lifestyle, as they leave the Indian summer for three months of Australian winter, must have felt quite extraordinary.

It would take them eight days to reach Calcutta from Deoli.]

Chapter IX

Australia

8TH MAY 1888, TUESDAY.
Calcutta.

Arrived here early in the morning. We are staying with Mr Lambert who lives over the police station and has charming rooms with big verandahs [sic]. [*Possibly Mr John Lambert of the Indian Police Department, later Sir John Lambert KCIE.*]

In the afternoon we went to the zoo and to the Belvedere where we saw Sir Steuart Bayley [*Sir Steuart Colvin Bayley, 1836–1925, Lieutenant-Governor of Bengal, 1887–1890*]; the ladies were away.

The Belvedere is charming with lovely grounds and such a delightful comfortable house, much more attractive than Govt. House [*the Belvedere was the Lieutenant-Governor's residence, now home to the National Library of India*]. The zoo was very attractive and I enjoyed the evening drive and the band very much.

9TH MAY, WEDNESDAY.
Calcutta.

This morning J.B. and I went to the Botanical gardens, starting at 6.15 a.m. and going down the river [*the Hooghly*] in Mr Lambert's steam launch. The gardens are beautiful; the orchid house is full of lovely things, orchids and ferns, and everywhere the wonderful vegetation strikes one. The variety of trees and flowering shrubs, and the biggest Banyan tree in the world; it is a hundred years old and spreads over a vast space, a very favourite place for picnics in the winter [*the Great Banyan Tree at the Indian Botanic Gardens, Kolkata, is now over 250 years old and remains a huge tourist attraction*].

After breakfast we went to some shops and had our hair washed.

I forgot to say that yesterday morning we went over Government House before luncheon and I was very interested in all the portraits of the former Governor Generals, many of them are very fine. I was more interested in seeing the room that J.B. occupied for 4 years when with Lord Northbrook. [*Lord Northbrook was viceroy from 1872–1876; John Biddulph served on his staff during those four years. Government House, now the Raj Bhavan, Kolkata, opened in 1803 (architect Charles Wyatt, 1758–1819), the house where Julia had been so royally entertained by the Lawrences in 1864.*]

After luncheon today I had a great pack & then we drove to some nursery gardens with Mr Lambert. These nursery gardens are the property of a Bengali Baboo [*or* Babu, *a title corresponding to Mr, or a native clerk in India*], and are quite as well looked after as they would be at home. The Baboo himself was a very pleasant little man, thoroughly up to his business; he or his brother had travelled all over the world in search of curious plants and trees, and had spent a week in Covent Garden learning to make button holes.

Calcutta was very hot & steamy all today; but the heat though exhausting, is nothing like so disagreeable as it is in Rajputana [*Rajasthan*].

10TH MAY, THURSDAY.
S.S. Brindisi [*3,542 tons, built 1880*].

We came on board at 6.30 as we were told we should start at 7 a.m. About 4 p.m. we stopped and spent the night in the river as the navigation is dangerous and we could not get out to sea at night.

There are some very nice people on board. Mr and Mrs Heilgers, she is a very pretty young woman, half French, half English. Mr Heilgers is the Austrian Consul and a merchant. They have been all over the world and of course talk all languages. There is a German lady & her husband. She is quite a girl with very pretty fair hair and she has an extraordinary duenna [*governess or guardian*] who possesses the most beautiful appetite; the husband is a Saxon officer on 2 years' leave. The lady is the daughter of a very rich man, [the] proprietor of a newspaper, and the duenna is supposed to hold the purse strings.

11TH MAY, FRIDAY.
S.S. Brindisi.

We could make no start till 9 a.m. this morning on account of the tide, for which we had to wait. The day is hot but the evenings are cool, even last night in the river was not at all disagreeable.

This morning the German lady sought in vain for her husband, and told J.B. that she had been everywhere over the ship to find him but that he was lost, dead she feared; when just then J.B. discovered his boots sticking out of a long chair, he was fast asleep. When he was restored to his spouse, she burst into floods of tears and I came upstairs just at that moment and could not imagine what had happened.

We all felt rather uncomfortable this evening, at least we ladies, and did not appear after dinner.

[*Julia had not been to sea for three years; as usual, seasickness was to blight the early part of her journey.*]

12TH MAY.
S.S. Brindisi.

An uncomfortable day, feeling decidedly miserable.

14TH MAY, MONDAY.
S.S. Brindisi.

We have all perked up and are quite lively.

15TH MAY, TUESDAY.
S.S. Ballaarat [*4,752 tons, built 1882*].

Came on board at 4 o'clock p.m. from the Brindisi. We got into Colombo harbour at 12 o'clock and J.B. went on shore very soon to secure our cabin. It was a mercy he did so, for otherwise I should have been put into the cabin with the 2 German ladies and he would have had 2 Australian companions; but he managed capitally and we have got a capital cabin to ourselves with 4 berths. We did not go on shore to see anything as J.B. said the heat on shore was intense and we are to leave Colombo at 8 p.m.

This ship is fearfully crowded as it contains 2 mails and all the passengers out of a steamer that was run into by another off Aden. The passengers in the "Garonne" were mostly 2nd & 3rd class, but of course they have to be put into 1st class cabins when the others are full, and I hear there are 40 children on board [*the SS Garonne had collided with the cargo ship* Lucinda *in the Red Sea on 1st May 1888*].

I was quite sorry to say goodbye to the Heilgers, Mrs Heilgers gave me quite a lesson in judging sapphires today; we hope to meet them some day again.

18TH MAY, FRIDAY.
S.S. Ballaarat.
Disagreeable weather, the ship pitching and everybody rather out of sorts, myself especially.

19TH MAY, SATURDAY.
S.S. Ballaarat.
Still feeling very seedy.

23RD MAY, WEDNESDAY.
S.S. Ballaarat.
We are now having charming weather, last night was our first cold night and I slept under a blanket. We had a most horrid day on Sunday, it poured all day long. I was the only lucky person who had my chair in a dry place and was able to stay on deck all day long, but it was thoroughly miserable. John has been playing in a whist tournament and won everything till the very last when he lost as he had such bad cards, never holding a trump even.

I have quite recovered my sea legs now and am able to amuse myself with letters home. Last night there was a concert after dinner and some very fair singing. Mr Fischer, a professional, sang two songs and a Miss King, a handsome Irish girl who is going out to Australia to be married, plays extremely well. The passengers on board are very funny; one young lady with a cropped head who sits opposite J.B. at dinner remarked to his neighbour that the "H'ice generally found out one's 'ollow tooth," and one finds the H's flying about everywhere.

J.B. has found the acquaintance of everybody on board. There is a Mr Moore who has led a strange life in India, France & Peru; and the last few years in Australia. Here he discovered the mines and has been making a large fortune, £150,000 a year for the last two years and has just bought back the old family property in Ireland. Mr Maude is a young fellow going out to a Brewery in Australia, and Capt. Mague, a cousin of Charlie Mague's, has all his family settled in Melbourne.

28TH MAY, MONDAY.
S.S. Ballaarat.

We had a concert in the 2nd class saloon on the 24^{th,} which was a much better one than the concert in the 1st class. Some of the singing was very good & the man who played all the piano accompaniments was quite a musician; I believe he is a 3rd class passenger. We had a very painful piece of recitation, both as to subject and delivery. At dinner the Captain proposed the Queen's health and some of the people were very anxious that J.B. should return thanks.

John discovered a son of Col. Cookson's on board, a 2nd class passenger. He is going to New Zealand as a doctor and seems a nice manly boy, full of pluck, and likely to get on.

We have had some very rough days and are now in regular winter weather, wearing all our warm clothes and wrapping ourselves in furs. Today I saw an Albatross for the first time, there were four following the ship, they skim the waves most gracefully and it is wonderful to see how they can keep up with the ship.

I had a very amusing conversation with a certain Mrs Plunket on board, a vast lady, who is accompanied by a red nosed husband and a terribly vulgar daughter. Mrs P is full of pride at having been presented at Court by the Duchess of Buccleuch; and told me she was returning to Australia with engravings of all the family portraits, "which it was just as well to have about one". She was loud in her praise of England and Ireland and very complacent that she had not gone about to see things, "along with the other colonials".

Her excuse in speaking to me she said was to apologise for her daughter who sits opposite me, and who has got into discredit on board through some escapade with one of the ship's officers. The mother said the young lady was so innocent and unsophisticated that she couldn't understand anything and was, "too stupid for anything". Mrs P told me Sydney was by far the nicest of all the towns in Australia being, "so English" and that the people there had no connection with, "those that used to be sent there" (meaning Botany Bay); though to be sure there were some of their grandchildren in very high places, very high places indeed.

We arrived at King George's Sound [*Albany, Western Australia*] on Saturday night, the 26th, but as we didn't get into the Sound till 10 o'clock at night, of course there was no landing again for me. It is a very fine harbour within another; the town is a very small poor place. A coach takes on passengers to Perth, but there is not much going on I fancy in the place.

We left at 4 a.m. and most of the people stayed on deck till all hours. The European telegrams seem very warlike, the Emperor of Germany much better [*Emperor Frederick III, 1831–1888*]. I posted letters here to Mrs Biddulph & Annie.

31ST MAY, THURSDAY.
York Hotel, Adelaide.

We left the Ballaarat after luncheon yesterday and got out at Largs Pier, taking all our luggage with us in a little steamer tug. The Thomsons, Plunkets, Martins, Ieichmanns etc. were with us, and all but the Plunkets had perfect piles of luggage; so that at least, we had 48 pieces amongst us. When we got to the Pier there was only one porter for the whole of us. He had actually been telegraphed for by the Thomsons from King George's Sound, but in our necessity he had to look after us all, and like the patient ant, roll each box and portmanteau up to the Custom House and then bring it on to Adelaide, which is ½ an hour by rail from Largs.

The Thomsons were in great wrath of course; but there was actually no help for it.

We had our boxes examined by the Custom House officer and he immediately pounced upon my new boots and said they would be 4s duty a pair, and as I had several just on the top of my box, I felt rather low! But J.B. said immediately he was an officer travelling for his pleasure for a short time and the man shut up the boxes and let them all pass without any more bother. Then we rushed off to the train, leaving the one man to bring up all the luggage, and we ourselves got into Adelaide about 3.30 but our luggage never turned up till 9 o'clock.

We found the York Hotel very full, crammed, but we managed to get 2 single rooms, which do very well.

The Elwells have very kindly introduced us to some of their friends and we are to go to a big sheep farm in the country on Saturday, belonging to a Mr Hawker.

Adelaide strikes J.B. very like a seaside town at home, like St. Leonards or Worthing. Straggling streets, very broad though, but the houses and shops have a very country look, and the carts & butcher's carts etc., look like the provinces.

Mr Hawker called on us yesterday and later on, Mrs Hawker and her daughters, but we missed the latter as we walked down to the railway station with the Elwells. Our dinner was much appreciated last night; I felt tremendously hungry and the turkey and apple pie, with delicious pears at dessert seemed a tremendous treat after board ship. We dined with the Thomsons who are travelling round the world for the 3rd or 4th time apparently. They are very much at home here, but as they seem to know America, Japan, India & New Zealand well, I suppose they would be at home everywhere.

We had a very disagreeable row on board the Ballaarat the last evening we were on board. Some of the gentlemen gave a dinner party and most of them drank too much, so that when the ladies started dancing it was quite a riot. The Lancers were attempted but had to be given up (I went to bed and did not see anything, but heard quite enough) and later on there was a great deal of fighting and rowdyism, very disgraceful indeed; the noise went on till 2 o'clock in the morning and the Captain did not interfere at all. Young Mr Cookson had a bad time of it, being attacked by some of these drunken men, knocked down and his neck hurt.

Mrs Thomson has told us some amusing accounts of the ladies from the Colonies who boast of being presented at Court. One lady mentioned one day that her husband was "decomposed" (indisposed), & on board ship she said, she should be thankful to find herself once more on "terra-cotta". They are always photographed in their court dresses and the picture forms the principal ornament of the drawing room.

1ST JUNE, FRIDAY.
York Hotel, Adelaide.

Yesterday we went to the Briars with Mr Hawker and lunched there, spending some time with Mrs Hawker & her daughter. The house was crammed with pictures, some lovely water colours, and a great many good bits and sketches by good artists. Everything showed that the owners were wealthy people. The rooms full of expensive ornaments, the furniture from Shoolbred [*James Shoolbred & Co., Tottenham Court Road, London*], & large gardens and grounds round the house. But there were only three maid servants in the house; an old nurse who did the cooking, and two raw girls who did all the waiting at table etc. Mrs Hawker & her daughter did all the dusting of the drawing rooms and had to look after all the arrangements of the dinner table, and teach the girls everything. These maids, even the most inexperienced, get their food, 15 shillings a week, & two holidays in the week & are never expected to sit up after 9 o'clock in the evening. They will not go one mile out of Adelaide, and the Hawkers, who spend 6 months at the seaside or in other colonies have to get new servants every 6 months. Miss Hawker told me she had 5 sisters, they have all been educated abroad and are apparently very accomplished; there are several sons too. Mr Hawker is a member of the House of Assembly and is entitled to the distinction of being an Honourable out here.

The grounds round the house seemed very nice and there were many strange trees to see, palms and firs and a very big orangery. Mrs Hawker drove us down to the Botanical gardens and Miss Hawker went over them with us. They are very pretty and well laid out, but are insignificant after the Calcutta gardens. Some of the tree ferns from New Zealand are very fine and the palms from Malay; but this is not the time to see the gardens in their beauty. Miss Hawker went afterwards to rink; there is a famous rink here, which can hold a thousand rinkers comfortably. [*This was roller-skating, known as rinking, which had become very popular at the time.*]

J.B. and I walked about the streets till nearly time to dress for dinner. The principal street is King William St., a great wide street full of shops and businesses, Govt. House being at the end of it.

The rain has only just come in time for the country, it is rejoicing all hearts but those of travellers like ourselves. The rain never lasts here more than three or four days at a time.

The shops here are very poor after the London ones, and everything is very expensive, except meat and fruit and the necessaries of life. We sent a letter to the Briars yesterday morning and it cost 4 shillings, there are no messengers, so that a note has to be sent in a cab.

[*Mr and Mrs Hawker, who had been introduced to the Biddulphs by the Elwells, had kindly invited them to stay for a few days at Bungaree, their home in the Clare Valley, some ninety miles north of Adelaide.*]

3RD JUNE, SUNDAY.
Bungaree.

We meant to arrive here last evening at 9 o'clock, but as the train we were told to take, the 2.30 p.m., does not go on Saturdays or Sundays, we had to wait till 4.45 p.m. and consequently did not arrive at Farrell's Flat [*Farrell Flat*] station till 9 p.m. We had a 20 mile drive before us; but the horses being good as well as the road, and the trap light, we got in here to the Hawkers about 11.30.

We found them very unhappy at having made the mistake about the trains, which they had only discovered themselves about two hours before. They gave us a capital supper and then we went to bed; having a roaring wood fire in our bedroom for the night was very cold. I had been afraid of starving on the railway as we missed our dinner, and my appetite is quite immense here; but I need not have been alarmed for there are refreshment rooms at several places between Adelaide & Farrell's Flat, and at one place we got a capital cup of tea and an excellent hot mutton pie.

All the stations were full of people; it is a great amusement to them to come down and meet their friends and see who is in the train, and the platform seemed the great promenade.

This morning was beautifully clear and bright, very cold wind and a hot sun. I went for a stroll in the garden with Mrs Hawker and met J.B. and Mr Hawker & Mr Michael Hawker in the vinery where there were still some bunches of grapes, white & blue, the white with a real muscatel flavour.

We went over the barn where the sheep are sheared and had all the mysteries of sheep shearing explained. It is so extraordinary to hear them talking of 100,000 lambs as an everyday occurrence. And Mr George Hawker mentioned one proprietor who had only 380,000 lambs last season, which he was lamenting as it was a bad season and he expected 450,000. In this property there are 300 miles of wire fencing and everything is on such a large scale.

The house is a very comfortable double storied one with every comfort, but the usual paucity of servants; and the cook who is decidedly moderate, gets 1£ [sic] a week and everything found her. The living is always excellent out here as far as good meat, poultry, fruit, vegetables, bread and butter; but one can see that no great talent is displayed in the kitchen.

After luncheon Mr George Hawker drove us out in a buckboard buggy! It is a very light carriage or cart, unlike anything I have ever seen before, on four large wheels very far apart. One sits rather low, two in front and two at the back, dos à dos, and it is the lightest springiest thing I have ever been in. We went at a capital pace across grass country, the horses jumping over any little ditches and flying over any little humps & bumps as easily as possible. We were well wrapped up, and though the air was so cold I enjoyed it immensely.

We saw a number of sheep & lambs and some shepherds' cottages at long distances. The trees were all gums I think, and the country about here is well wooded, but further on it is very like the Sussex Downs without any trees at all. Just near the house here are a good many firs and carobs, but everywhere else there are only gums.

The garden is full of chrysanthemums, Japanese of all colours, the large marguerite & hollyhocks, and still looks very gay. We have a great bunch of violets in our room too. The chrysanthemums are most lovely, red, yellow, white and purple.

On Thursday the day before we came here, we went over the Zoo in Adelaide and were a good deal interested in it. It has only been established 5 years and has some very fine tigers & animals, all looking so clean, fat and well cared for; indeed the hyenas look as if they were brushed & combed every day. There are not so many kangaroos as I expected, they are becoming quite scarce now in Australia as the settlers advance further into the interior.

The birds are very good and among them are some doves from the Philippine Islands, called bleeding heart doves. They have a bunch of red feathers in their breast just the shape of a heart, and look exactly as if they were bleeding, I never saw anything more curious; these birds cost 20 guineas a pair, even here. We got hold of the secretary of the Zoo and J.B. got a black buck, which had been misnamed & put down as coming from Africa, its proper title and country.

The secretary offered us a pair of dingoes; they are very handsome dogs, but would be rather in our way! The secretary complained a good deal of the way people promised animals to the Zoo, taking some in exchange, and then never sending any after all.

We went over the museum afterwards which of course is very small, but the public library is a capital one, free to anybody to go and read there, and there is a small collection of pictures, a few good ones.

4TH JUNE, MONDAY.
Bungaree.

J.B. went out duck shooting this morning and got 9 duck and saw two wild turkeys. The duck are found in small holes & pools of water, and the gentlemen drove from one place to another, wherever the duck were to be found.

This estate is 100,000 acres and there are 80,000 sheep on it. Mr Hawker has two other estates, one of 1,000 acres & another of 1,500.

There are 13 of the family living, 7 sons and 6 daughters, but there have been 16; all are educated at home for some time, and the girls entirely so.

5TH JUNE, TUESDAY.
Bungaree.

It rained all last night and is very cold this morning. Mrs Hawker has been showing us some beans, which are to be bought in Sydney and which make charming matchboxes. Beans and native peach stones for necklaces I must look out for.

We were told yesterday of a man in Queensland who owns 3,000,000 sheep, he is a great misanthrope and woman hater but enormously rich. The size and numbers of everything out here is so great that one is almost afraid of repeating what one hears for fear of making mistakes.

Poultry thrives here splendidly and this morning at breakfast Mr Hawker mentioned that from the little station here (Clare) 12 tons of eggs are sent every month to Melbourne. In the seasons everything thrives in this country in a wonderful way.

We went for a drive yesterday afternoon, again in the buckboard, and saw a good deal of country. Of course nothing living but sheep, crows and a few plover; but we were shown the native honeysuckle, it has a curious burr inside of which is a smooth pod just like a piece of brown chenille.

6TH JUNE, WEDNESDAY.
York Hotel, Adelaide.

We returned yesterday, leaving Bungaree at a quarter to two and catching the 4.30 train at Farrell's Flat, which got into Adelaide at 8.30.

It rained all yesterday in the country but here it has been beautifully fine, the rain though is much wanted everywhere.

This morning Sir Samuel & Lady Davenport called on us [*Sir Samuel Davenport KCMG, 1818–1906, landowner and parliamentarian, born Oxfordshire, England. Married 1842, Margaret Fraser, only daughter of William Lennox Cleland, a barrister of Calcutta* (Australian Dictionary of Biography)], they were both very nice indeed & regretted very much we could not go out to them, but their house [*Beaumont House*] is some miles out of Adelaide and we must go on to Melbourne tomorrow. Lady Davenport said she was so sick with exhibitions that she felt truly thankful her husband had declined to have anything to do with the Melbourne one; but she said the Melbourne people expected great things of it [*the Melbourne Centennial Exhibition, opened 1st August 1888*]. Also she told me I must not entirely take the house at Bungaree as a specimen of South Australian country life, as it was a good deal more comfortable and luxurious in every way than the homes further off. The wages I hear at Melbourne are much higher than here, and quite a plain cook there gets 65£s [*sic*] a year and a kitchen maid, of course being found in everything.

8TH JUNE, FRIDAY.
Menzies Hotel, Melbourne [*demolished 1969*].

We left Adelaide yesterday at 3.30 p.m. in the express, getting here at 9.15 this morning. The express is a most excellent train, so smooth & comfortable and though the sleeping cars are not so good as Pullman's, everything is very well managed. We had a capital tea, so called, but really dinner, getting fish, meat, stewed fruit etc. at 6 o'clock at Murray Bridge. Only the 20 minutes allowed was rather a limited time as it included running down a long platform & back again to one's carriage.

At Geelong this morning we got a very nasty breakfast at 8 a.m., another time it would be better to go to the "light refreshments" and get a cup of tea & some bread and butter, but I don't suppose I shall see Geelong again.

At the Custom House we had a horrid time, all our boxes nearly being turned over and ransacked to see if we had any plate or jewellery. In fact they were very uncivil and tiresome. We had to pay 8 shillings for our cabs (2) as we had too many things for one trap and the distance from the railway station is about a quarter of a mile. So we have made up our minds to leave some of our luggage at the P & O office and pick it up when we return.

We met several of our fellow passengers of the "Ballaarat" at this hotel. After luncheon J.B. went to Govt. House & wrote his name in the book. Sir Henry Loch [*Sir Henry Loch, Governor of Victoria, 1884–1889*] is at Ballarat [*some sixty miles north-west of Melbourne on the Yarrowee River*], but Lady Loch is here; she receives on Thursdays.

We then went to the Museum and looked at the picture gallery; and on returning home I thought we should be run over by the Trams. These Trams are very noisy, pass up & down the principal streets every instant and are rather a nuisance. The streets are very broad & the shops are better than at Adelaide, but the town is dirty and dusty. I returned home with my face covered with smuts and I think we are both a little disenchanted with Melbourne!

The last day we had in Adelaide we had luncheon with the Hawkers & I made the acquaintance of the laughing jackasses [*laughing kookaburra*], one of them was a great pet and laughed long and loudly for our benefit. And Miss Hawker had a lovely pink & white cockatoo, which came from Bungaree scrubland. After luncheon we went to the tennis ground. There were heaps of girls and no men; there are no idle men hardly in the colonies. Then we looked in upon the rink, which is the greatest amusement of the ladies of Adelaide just now, I went again yesterday morning with Miss Hawker.

Lady Davenport sent me an Emu's egg and a box of the wild peach stones. There was a Ball at Govt. House last night, but the Hawkers would not go as Mrs Hawker objected to meeting Lady H......m [*sic*] the wife of the Chief Justice, who was a notoriously bad character for many years and was never admitted to any society in consequence. Indeed a committee of ladies wrote to Govt. House some years ago begging she might not be asked there.

I must mention here that Mr Tyson, who owns the 3,000,000 sheep, has also 600,000 head of cattle. He is the wealthiest squatter in Australia and began life as a gentleman's coachman. He has made this huge fortune entirely by stock, none by speculation, and he came forward handsomely during the Egyptian campaign and paid £1,000 a month towards the expenses of the Australian contingent.

[*Mr Tyson, the man that Julia refers to as the misanthrope and woman hater who owns 3,000,000 sheep, is Mr James Tyson, 1819–1898; whether he was a misanthrope and a misogynist, who knows? He died unmarried and intestate on 4*th *December 1898. The son of a convict, his mother, a Yorkshire woman, had* been sentenced to seven years' transportation in 1809 for theft. By the time of his death he held over five million acres freehold. He had also donated money to many charitable causes including, as Julia mentions, the New South Wales Sudan Contingent. Tyson was a byword for wealth and a legend in his own lifetime (Australian Dictionary of Biography, Volume 6, 1976 by Zeta Denholm).]

10TH JUNE, SUNDAY.
Menzies Hotel, Melbourne.

Yesterday morning was wet, the Elwells & Ieichmanns came to see us in the morning and after luncheon it cleared up. We went over a big Bank in Collins St. (the English, Scottish & Australian, I think), it was very handsomely decorated & looked far more like a Church than a Bank. The doors and all the divisions and wood work in the offices were made of a very lovely Australian wood. Then we went by tram to the Natural History Museum, which is a good mile & a half from here. It is a very interesting one I think, the skeletons of snakes & fishes and animals are so good, and the stuffed specimens too; but there is altogether too little room and in some cases birds and beasts are muddled up in one case, and the specimens are often badly stuffed too; still it is quite worth going to see.

We came back by tram, & by tram found our way to the Elwells for tea. They are living in a suburb, "Fitzroy" and are not settled yet in their house. We gave up the idea of going to the Opera, as Saturday is the worst day to go to the theatre, it is the night all the shopmen etc. go, & it is very crowded & disagreeable.

12TH JUNE, TUESDAY.
Menzies.

Yesterday I went out shopping in the morning. In the afternoon we went to the Zoo with the Carvers and Mr

Breeds. The gardens are larger than those of Adelaide but I don't think them so well cared for.

We saw several curious animals, amongst them a small buffalo, which seemed very fierce. Miss Carver had never been to a Zoo in her life before. She told me that the Sunday meals here are called "Tea muddles", and that she had suffered from a fearful indigestion after her first tea muddle.

After dinner last night we went to the Prince's theatre, which is considered the best in Melbourne; it is very prettily decorated in blue & buff, but was very empty. The piece, an old one, The Lady of Lyons, did not attract, and Charles Warner who acted as Claude Melnotte, said he had never acted to such an unsympathetic audience [*The Lady of Lyons by Edward Bulwer-Lytton, 1838; Charles Warner, actor, 1846–1909*]. We went in a tram & returned in a cab.

This morning we have been to fur shops with Mrs Elwell, and I have ordered a set of opossum skins for a jacket and a muff, and a rug for Mrs Wyllie, and have bought her some beads. We ordered the fur set at Green's, the fur sets seem to be very reasonable, but a good dark Tasmanian opossum rug costs 17 guineas, the grey only 3 or 5£s [*sic*].

The next big hotel to this is the Grand. We passed it on our way to the Exhibition on Sunday, and at Adelaide I found that the Botanical was considered a good one, though the York is quite the best; but the Botanical is thought very nice for ladies.

13TH JUNE.
Menzies, Melbourne.

We heard this morning that the Emperor of Germany was dead.

Yesterday we did so much during the day. We went to the Elwells after luncheon and went with them to the South Yarra

Rink, where a large party was given by 40 young ladies. The whole thing was very well done; refreshments all round the hall and a band, the hall itself being very prettily decorated with flags etc.

The young ladies were all over the place, but three or four stood by the entrance & received everybody. Very few people were rinking but some of the girls did it very well and several pretty children.

The Australian girls have no complexions, and though there were many pretty faces yesterday, and good figures, there was nothing very distingué.

After that we took the train to Windsor and accomplished our visit to the Magues, which was somewhat depressing as Miss Mague looked so very ill and Mr Mague was in a fog about our mutual relations, and India in general. We got home at 6.15 and had a scramble to dress by ½ past for dinner. A very bad dinner indeed, the cuisine here seems to get worse every day somehow. Then we went to the French play, "Le Voyage de Monsieur Perrichon" at the Freemasons' Hall [Le Voyage de Monsieur Perrichon, *a comedy in four acts by Eugène Labiche & Édouard Martin, 1860*]. It was most excellent, capitally acted and very amusing altogether. Sir Henry & Lady Loch were there and a pretty good audience.

This morning has been wet & gloomy. We called on the Ieichmanns and found the ladies at home and had a little chat, they are not more in love with Melbourne than I am as far as the gay appearance of the town, but then the weather is decidedly dull.

15TH JUNE, FRIDAY.
Government House, Melbourne.

We received a kind invitation from Lady Loch to stay here for a few days yesterday and we came over at 5 o'clock. It was Lady Loch's reception day, but nearly everybody had left before we arrived. This house is very charming & comfortable with delightful views of the gardens and the city beyond.

The day before yesterday we went all over the Botanical Gardens and were delighted with them. We walked home by a pretty walk on the banks of the Yarra. The days are cold and grey, but very pleasant for a good walk & I have gone all over the town almost.

Capt. Keith-Falconer is the A.D.C. here and Mr Fort the secretary. There is a very fine Ballroom in the public part of Govt. House and all the rooms are very large and the private rooms extremely nice. The suburbs here are all called after English places, Brighton, Windsor, Kew, etc. The trains run very conveniently every 10 minutes or a quarter of an hour.

Last night there was a dinner party of 16 and two very pretty Australian ladies among the guests. Lady Loch is so very kind and gracious in her manner to everybody, I do not wonder at her popularity.

John and I have ordered a very nice foot muff to be made for Mrs Biddulph, to be sent home to her. We took a long walk in Melbourne yesterday, ending up by having tea with Mrs Elwell, who has asked us to stay with them the next time we stop in Melbourne before going back to India.

Green, the shop in Gertrude St. where we have ordered our furs is very fascinating. We have also invested in a carved Emu's egg, which is carved like a cameo, and is the work of one man in the Bush, a native who draws out the designs and does the carving entirely himself.

Today we have heard of the Emperor of Germany's death; the first report was not true but now it is a fact. Lady Loch has to go into mourning of course and we cannot go to the theatre this evening. All entertainments must cease until after the funeral.

I have begun to read Robert Elsmere [*Mrs Humphry Ward, 1888*], which is most interesting; the review by Gladstone of this book has just come out. This morning I have had a drive with Lady Loch and then a walk through the Botanical gardens. I am more in love with these than ever, they are so beautifully situated and have such lovely peeps of the town.

[*Emperor Frederick III, 1831–1888, was emperor for three months, 9th March–15th June 1888. The first report of his death, which arrived on 13th June via telegraph from London, had been 'false news'; the first telegraph message from the UK to Australia was sent in 1872, making the world a much smaller place. Frederick was married to Victoria, the Princess Royal, and eldest daughter of Queen Victoria. Their son, Wilhelm II or Kaiser Wilhelm II, 1859–1941, succeeded him and was Germany's last Kaiser. He abdicated in November 1918 at the end of the First World War and died in the Netherlands aged eighty-two in 1941.*]

18TH JUNE, MONDAY.
Govt. House, Melbourne.

We went to the Scotch Church yesterday and heard a preacher of the name of Clarke, who is considered very wonderful here, I thought him a little commonplace; but he has a very fine voice and a good delivery and one listens to him, which is what I do not generally do to a sermon.

Yesterday Sir Henry Loch had a busy day. A meeting with the Ministers, and perpetual telegrams being received and sent on account of the Emperor of Germany's death. Today is the funeral and the 58 guns were fired at 12 o'clock; the number of the Emperor's years.

I have been all over the gardens today with the curator, (the Botanical gardens) and we have been promised all sorts of seeds and plants for our Indian garden. We had a most charming stroll through the gardens and we saw one of these extraordinary Mantis; like a leaf, it is almost impossible to discover the insect he is so exactly like a leaf. This one came from the Seychelles; indeed there are two in a glass case feeding on a shrub. I am going to try and grow the rice paper plant from Japan & China at Deoli [*Rajasthan*].

[*Note in margin:*]
Mr Guilfoyle, Curator, Botanical Gardens, Melbourne [*William Robert Guilfoyle, 1840–1912, director of the Royal Botanic Gardens, Melbourne from 1873*].

22ND JUNE, FRIDAY.
Empire Hotel, Sydney.

I must go back to our last days at Melbourne. On Monday afternoon I went out shopping with Lady Loch and I ordered a tweed dress for myself to be ready for me on the 9th July. We spent a long time at Green's the furriers; and there Sir Henry & Mr Frost joined us, the latter immediately ordered a foot muff like the one I have had made for Mrs Biddulph and Sir Henry ordered a set of opossum like mine for a jacket.

We went to prize giving to the Fire Brigades in the evening after dinner. Sir Henry had to give the prizes and make speeches & Lady Loch was very anxious to go too, so we went with her. The function took place in the Town Hall, where there is a very fine organ.

The Mayor was in full force and he and others made several H-less speeches, but all sensible enough. The different bands played and there was a recitation, "The Fireman's Wedding" which brought the house down. The Mayoress & her daughter received Lady Loch and the body of the hall was full of firemen. In physique they were not much to look at, and several of them looked very delicate; many were very young. It seems there is no good fire escape in all Melbourne, or Sandhurst, or Ballarat; so a suggestion was made that three should be telegraphed for from America. In case of fire at a big hotel or theatre, it would be disastrous having no proper fire escape. The Mayor was induced to promise 1,000£ [sic] from the Corporation towards one by Sir H. Loch.

On Tuesday we went to the opening of Parliament. Sir H. Loch in gorgeous array & a good big attendance of ladies in the House, so much so that it looked like a ladies' Parliament. Sir Henry made a diplomatic speech, skirting the Chinese question by saying his advisors or Ministers had done all they thought was right on this occasion.

After the opening of the House we returned to Govt. House to pack. Lady Loch had a reception of French ladies, the ladies of the Thèatre Francaise etc., and we left by the express, 5 o'clock p.m. for Sydney.

We travelled in a reserved compartment till 12 p.m. and then we had to get into sleeping cars in another train. Here I was wretched; in an upper berth, with no air, and a lady in another berth below who said she had heart disease & sometimes when travelling fainted, and could not come to for hours. She took charge of the key for our compartment and we were locked in for the night. But in the morning she found she had mislaid the key and we could get no air till the conductor came to our rescue! Consequently I was violently sick, for the stuffiness beat all description. At 8 o'clock we got some tea & J.B. and I travelled to Sydney in a carriage to ourselves. We arrived at Sydney at 12.30, the train being half an hour late.

Sydney station arrangements are admirable; cabs & porters & carts for one's luggage ready.

We found our rooms ready for us at this hotel, "The Empire", but the hotel is not nice, quite a tavern, and the smell of gas, beer and food overpowers one.

We went after luncheon to the Admiralty and found the Admiral & Mrs Fairfax at home [*Admiral Sir Henry Fairfax*

KCB, *1837–1900, commander-in-chief Australia Station, 1887–1889*]. They were very kind to us and we had a nice afternoon looking at all the curiosities, which had lately arrived from Samoa, and particularly the ladies' skirts or fringes! Sometimes the ladies put on 8 of these fringes, one over the other, as they are very full they must stick out for yards! The fringes are made from grass & strips of paper.

The Fairfaxes had some lovely shells and a great many ferns and plants from the islands; they have quite a charming house & grounds. The New South Wales Govt. spent 20,000£ [sic] in buying the house & another 20,000£ [sic] in furnishing and making the grounds & gardens, very generous I think. The Nelson was in the harbour & several other big ships [*HMS Nelson, a Nelson-class armoured cruiser, 7,593 tons, flagship of the Australia Station*].

Some of the views from the Admiralty House are most lovely. We returned across the harbour in the Admiral's own boat.

After dinner we went to the theatre. We could not get in at the Criterion so we went on to Her Majesty's and saw a fearfully sensational drama called "The Orphans", everybody fainted & tumbled about in every scene but it was really well got up; scenery & dresses very good indeed, and some of the acting quite good. There was a coach drawn by four live horses introduced, which is considered a great thing, and duly advertised.

Yesterday J.B. met Miss Carver, her brothers, & Mr Dunsmere in the morning. We called at Govt. House and left Ethel Baring's note for Lady Carrington [*Lady Baring, wife of Sir Evelyn Baring*].

The grounds seem very charming belonging to Govt. House and there are such splendid trees in the grounds. Then we went to the Zoo after luncheon with the Carvers and Mr Dunsmere. We went by tram, the cold was quite intense, such a bitter, bitter wind, I was quite chilled to the bone and I think everybody else was the same. We found the Zoo very inferior to either the Adelaide or Melbourne gardens. The animals all seemed to be suffering from the cold and they were neglected and wretched. The gardens are in the most exposed place, and the whole place looks like a country fair sort of arrangement.

We could not pick up a tram to return by until we had waited in the bitter cold wind for at least 20 minutes, by which time we had all caught cold. We rushed into a shop in King St. for tea and got some very good tea & cakes which we were most thankful for and which partly restored animation. Afterwards we found a very fascinating arcade for photos and rubbish of all sorts.

We went to a play afterwards & saw "As You Like It" by Bacon, at least J.B. says so [As You Like It *by William Shakespeare (or Francis Bacon?)*]. The theatre was crammed and we could only get seats quite at the back. The Carvers & Mr Dunsmere were with us.

Rosalind was a very pretty girl, "Miss Essie Jenyns" and the piece was well got up [*Elizabeth Esther Helen Jennings, 1864–1920, actress known as Essie Jenyns*], but a good deal of the acting was very inferior. Still we enjoyed it very much and are going again to see "Romeo & Juliet" on Tuesday.

We have taken rooms at the Crown & Anchor which is now called "Robert's Hotel" and which is infinitely nicer than this. We like the looks of Sidney very much better than Melbourne as it is so much more old fashioned and far lighter and livelier. The streets are not so wide, but they are not at all narrow. There are fewer trams and the up & down hill streets make the town picturesque rather, while many of the buildings are really handsome, especially the Post Office.

The Fairfaxes have gone to Brisbane I am sorry to say and we shall not see them again.

I have bought some of the shells that Mrs Wyllie wants and shall poke about for a few curios, but we are told they are now very difficult to get. In one shop one reads, "Passion fruit & cream", "Strawberries & cream", the Passion fruit comes from the Islands and is very big, like a melon; all the very good fruit comes from Queensland.

24TH JUNE, SUNDAY.
Robert's Hotel, Sydney.

We came here on Friday and were delighted to leave the dirty uncomfortable Empire hotel. On Friday John got a very pleasant little invitation for us to dine at Govt. House and we found them quite alone [*Lord and Lady Carrington; Lord Carrington, 1843–1928 was governor of New South Wales, 1885–1890*]. Govt. House is a charming one, the rooms are delightful and the quantities of flowers (pink camellias) struck me at once, everywhere pink camellias, double and single.

Unfortunately yesterday John's cold was so very bad he could not go out of the house and we had to doctor him up with quinine, hot whisky & water, mustard leaves and strong remedies. He had quite a go of Indian fever on Friday night; today he is much better.

Lord Carrington gave us his pew in the Cathedral today and I went there with a Mr & Mrs Newton who are stopping in this hotel. We had a very good service, nice singing and quite a good sermon. The Ieichmanns came to say goodbye to me soon after I had left the hotel. They are stopping at the Empire, unfortunately recommended by us! But they are off to the Blue Mountains tomorrow.

We are going to stay at Govt. House for a few days, and go there on Wednesday and intend to start for the Blue Mountains tomorrow week.

This afternoon John and I walked for a good long time, starting immediately after luncheon. We had a good look at the harbour and found out Mrs Macquarie's Chair and sat on it and walked through the Botanical gardens; home by Bourke's Statue. The wind had quite gone down and it was deliciously comfortable for walking.

George St. is the swagger street here, but Pitt St. has no end of good shops in it, and to my eyes looks every bit as good. The Cathedral is a fine Church and full of modern coloured glass windows.

On Saturday afternoons the streets are perfectly deserted, everybody goes holiday-making. Football and races and other amusements take place on Saturday afternoon so that all shops are shut; and on Sunday mornings it is difficult to get hot water early for one's bath as everybody is late. This morning we couldn't get any hot water at 8 o'clock, but had to wait till nearly 9 and then at breakfast we had to wait again for our poached eggs! The waiter said it was "disgasting" which amused us a good deal.

There is no dinner here on Sundays but tea muddle at 6.30 p.m. Mr Newton said last night at 9.30 p.m. the streets were so crowded with people one could hardly get along. Though there are no express trains on either Saturdays or Sundays, there are heaps of excursion ones, & steamers ply to all the little seaside places and coves in the Bay. The National Art Museum is open too, and I heard a Band playing in the gardens, also I saw a Concert advertised for Sunday evening. It is only that all business and work are stopped on these days; I imagine an Express train is considered business.

I have ordered a Covert coat here, it is too cold to be able to go about without a warm jacket and the shops here are extremely good, though it is the fashion in Australia to think there are no good shops except in Melbourne.

The Botanical gardens here have not struck me as nearly so nice as the Melbourne ones, but tomorrow we go over them with Mr Moore the Curator and perhaps we may see them to more advantage.

25ᵀᴴ JUNE.
Robert's Hotel, Sydney.

This morning we went all over the Botanical gardens with Mr Moore, the curator [*Charles Moore, 1820–1905, director of the Botanic Gardens, Sydney*], a prosy old gentleman rather, but his reminiscences of Sydney 40 years ago were very interesting. The numbers of different trees are very striking, and the position of the gardens is very beautiful indeed. But as the garden is so much cut up, it does not seem to me so beautiful in itself as the one at Melbourne, and the number of rubbishing statues placed in it by Sir Henry Parkes [*Sir Henry Parkes, 1815–1896, five times Premier of New South Wales between 1872 and 1896*] give it a tea-garden sort of look.

We did a little shopping afterwards. J.B. ordered a great coat and then, after a hasty luncheon, we started off in a steam launch round the harbour.

It is impossible to describe how beautiful it is; one is always turning into some new Bay, out of which again are little coves, and the forest comes right down to the water's edge. It is 32 miles up to the head of the harbour & back, and it is a most delightful excursion. We didn't get back till a quarter to six and walked briskly to the hotel to get warm. The day has been most lovely, perfectly still and a bright sun and cool clear air. The sunset on the harbour was lovely, and we stopped for a quarter of an hour at a funny little landing place where there was an Inn, and we got a cup of tea; such scalding tea as it was, with only three minutes to drink it.

I heard a letter read from Albury [New South Wales] yesterday where there is a plague of mice. The young man [who] wrote it was most dreary, nothing to be seen but sheep and mice, with a dreary drizzle of rain all day. At night his head came down with a bump, as the inside of the bolster had been eaten by mice while he was sleeping. They killed usually 1,000 a day and still there was no decrease. The mice had eaten everything food, clothes, and everything they could find!

Several people called on us today while we were out, & John has been made a member of another club in Sydney.

We ought to have gone to tea with Mrs Plunket today, but we both thought we could not stand Mr P's red nose and the story of Mrs P's presentation at Court again, so we got out of it.

The Carvers and Mr Dunsmere came to 5 o'clock tea with us yesterday, and we have quite decided to start for the Blue Mountains on Monday next.

Memo for the Fish River Caves: An old hat, an old dress & a Pair of canvas shoes perfectly necessary, everything one wears will be completely spoilt.

28TH JUNE, THURSDAY.

Government House, Sydney.

We spent Tuesday in a loungy [sic] way. Miss Deverell came over from Melbourne and J.B. met her at the station, brought her to luncheon at the hotel, and her brother; immediately after luncheon I took her to call on Lady Carrington. We returned to tea at the hotel & then J.B. had to go off with the young people to start them off in the steamer for Brisbane. I meanwhile had a long visit from Lady Darley and one of her daughters, a very nice woman and very kind. The girl too was very chatty and told me a great deal about the Fish Caves and the clothing that was necessary for it. Sir F. Darley is the Chief

Justice & ranks next to the Governor [*Sir Frederick Darley, 1830–1910, Chief Justice, New South Wales, 1886–1910*].

Wednesday we shopped in the morning; but I have forgotten about our theatre on Tuesday night. We went to see "Romeo & Juliet", Miss Essie Jenyns being Juliet. Mr Dunsmere dined with us and went with us and we enjoyed our evening very much. Miss Jenyns is very pretty indeed, she looked very charming and acted on the whole very intelligently but we did not always like her interpretation of the play; she is inclined to rant and rave too much. There was not a vacant seat in the theatre.

On Wednesday we did some shopping in the morning, then we packed. We went to the Museum and spent a good couple of hours there. They have a very fine collection of skeletons of animals and whales and crocodiles etc., and a grand collection of birds. The shells too are most lovely and though I know nothing about them, they always are very fascinating to me.

After that we came on here and received an invitation to a Ball given by 6 bachelors, Messrs Alison, Billyard, Evans Fairfax, Riddell, Street & Weston. We dined a little earlier and started off for the Ball almost at 9 o'clock. Lady Carrington looked most sweet in white with the loveliest diamonds. I danced a quadrille with Lord Carrington and a set of Lancers with one of my hosts; but John took the floor with Mrs Newton and danced a gallop! There were many very pretty girls, the Belle being a Miss Cox, daughter of a doctor here, a very lovely girl. The floor was exceedingly good and everybody danced well and with a great deal of spirit. We came away after supper; the only drawback to the festivity was that the rooms were rather cold for non-dancers.

Today I have written a number of letters and we have taken our tickets to the Blue Mountains.

We made the acquaintance of Mr Conder, the son of the traffic manager in Ajmer [*Ajmer, Rajasthan*] & have promised to go and see his studio tomorrow morning. [*Charles Edward Conder, artist, 1868–1909, a key figure in the Heidelberg School. His father, James Conder, was a railway engineer in India.*]

Lady Carrington had a reception this afternoon. Heaps of people came, the Newtons and Lady Darley were nearly the only people I knew, but I was introduced to one of the Queensland leading men & tried to talk intelligently about Stations, droughts & sheep.

Lord Carrington has his brother Rupert as A.D.C.; Lord Bertie is another [*Montague Bertie, 1861–1938, later 12th Earl of Lindsey*], and Mr Wallington the private secretary. Nothing could be more charming than the Carringtons' kindness, they make one so at home and are very delightful altogether. The three little girls are dear little people, very fair.

There is an expedition being made up for the National Park on Saturday; but as it is a riding expedition and I have no habit, I shall probably go on the harbour with Mr Carington [*Rupert Carington*]. I was introduced to a Mr Read at the Ball last night, he is the most eloquent speaker, quite an orator in New South Wales, and he is very anxious I should go in his steam launch on Saturday.

30TH JUNE, SATURDAY.
Govt. House, Sydney.

On Thursday I wrote an immense number of home letters and in the afternoon we took our tickets for the Blue Mountains; returning to Lady Carrington's reception in the afternoon. A great number of people turned up and some played tennis and others strolled about the garden. In the evening Sir Patrick Jennings ex Prime Minister dined here [*Sir Patrick Jennings, 1831–1897, Premier New South Wales,*

1886–1887], he is a Roman and a great enthusiast about his religion. He told us how he had been in Rome just about the Pope's Jubilee, and went into minute descriptions of a Mass he attended in the Pope's private Chapel. Afterwards when he had gone, Lord Carrington told us of how he had once been "Bones" in a Christy Minstrel troupe when he had been very hard up, and now he sat at the theatre next to Lady Carrington, in true Bones style with his knees and arms out.

Friday I went with J.B. to Mr Conder's studio and looked over his drawings. We gave him a commission for a sketch of the Sydney Harbour and I tried to like some of his sketches in vain. Our sketch is to be in black & white and will not be bad.

Afterwards J.B. went for a ride with Lord C. and I went for a drive with Lady Carrington and the children. I have never done anything so grand before. 2 Postillions, 4 horses and 2 footmen behind the carriage with an escort. We called on Lady Darley who was not well enough to see us unfortunately.

Today J.B. went to the National Park with the Carringtons & Newtons etc., and had a delightful ride; and I went down the Parramatta River with Mr Carington on the steam launch. It was Mr Read's party and we had tea on board. Miss Essie Jenyns and her mother Mrs Holloway, the three Miss Coxes, Lord Bertie, Sir G Ennis, Sir Edward Strickland, Mr Salomans, Mrs Willis & Mrs Ogilvie etc. were the party. I had a long talk with Miss Essie Jenyns on her art and she told me she was so anxious to do Lady Macbeth, but her friends would not allow it. She said she liked tragedy best but she was supposed to do better in comedy, which is certainly the case. A Mr Nathan sang several songs on board the steam launch in a very rich voice and very correctly, without any accompaniment. We got back to Govt. House about a quarter to 6 o'clock; by which time it had become cold.

1ST JULY, SUNDAY.
Government House, Sydney.

I went to the Cathedral this morning with Lord & Lady Carrington and the children. We had a very long prosy sermon, but some rather good singing. We walked home from the Cathedral and it commenced raining just as we got home. After luncheon J.B. and I went to return Mrs Philip King's call at Double Bay. It was a very wet afternoon and we drove in a hansom. The streets were very slippery and we had a long drive as the driver lost his way and drove us for an hour before we got to our destination; we passed Darling Point & Double Bay was just beyond. The house the Philip King's live in is a very small one, and Mrs King, her daughter, 3 small children and a visitor quite filled up the room.

The rain continued all the afternoon and I spent the time before dinner with Lady Carrington in her own little sitting room which is full of papers, books, prints, screens, photos etc., a very delightful room. Lady C told me the whole story of Mrs Langtry who she knew as a girl of 14 in Jersey [*Lillie Langtry, Emilie Charlotte Le Breton, 1853–1929, actress and mistress of the Prince of Wales, later Edward VII*].

2ND JULY, MONDAY.
The Royal Hotel, Oberon [*New South Wales*].

We left Govt. House at 8.40 a.m. and caught the 9 a.m. train. The Carvers turned up and we had a pouring wet morning, which lasted, as far as the rain went, all day. Lady C had given us an excellent luncheon in a basket with good brown sherry, which proved a great comfort. The Carvers got out at Mt. Victoria and had a grand luncheon of beefsteak pie and puddings etc., but we remained cosily in the railway carriage.

We got out at Tarana at 4 p.m. and found a fearful old shandrydan [*a light two-wheeled cart or similar type of rickety, horse-drawn conveyance*] with a pair of rough horses; this was to convey us to Oberon, 18 miles. We pushed all our bags and umbrellas and baggage generally into the trap, then we poked ourselves in and as it was bitterly cold, we covered ourselves up with rugs and two eiderdown quilts which Lady C had lent us. Four of us managed to get inside but the Carver boys took turns to sit outside & freeze. The rain fortunately stopped but the roads were in a pitiful condition and it was very heavy work for the horses to pull us up the tremendous hills. There was very little flat at all, we were always going up some tremendous hills or going down them, but chiefly going up.

At 8 o'clock, stiff and tired out, we arrived at our hotel, which is the roughest one I was ever in. We found the hotel made of wood, with tiny rooms opening into a gallery. Every one with a double bed & a single one, and about three square yards to stand in and wash or dress; no tubs were forthcoming. We had a very good substantial dinner of turkey & apple pie, and a roaring fire, which was most comforting. I went to bed soon after dinner and our neighbours in the bedroom next door to us seemed to be throwing grand pianos and dining room tables about, judging from the fearful noise they made. J.B. came to bed rather soon and said all the arrangements were the very roughest he had ever seen.

3ʳᴅ JULY, TUESDAY.
The Cave Hotel, Jenolan [*Jenolan Caves House*].

We left Oberon this morning at 5 minutes to 11 and had a seventeen-mile drive in a most curious old trap with a hood and 4 horses. The 2 Carvers sat outside and J.B., Miss Carver and I sat inside. It was lovely weather and the view sometimes of Blue Mountains and forest was most lovely.

We passed through a forest of gum trees and eucalyptus, sometimes the air was heavily scented with eucalyptus. We again went up & down hill & arrived at our highest point about 1.30, 4,365 ft. above the sea. The last 6 miles was all down hill and this hotel is quite close to the Fish River Caves.

I have forgotten to mention that yesterday we passed through some very clever engineering pieces of railroad, the zig-zag is very great and twice we had zig-zags coming over the Blue Mountains.

We had luncheon here, rather better than our very uncomfortable breakfast at Oberon where they brought us five big dishes, a beefsteak the size of a bath sponge, a sea of curry and a huge ham and bacon. We could get no milk to our coffee except condensed milk; there was one cow in Oberon and she was drying, the girl said.

We sent off telegrams to Mrs Newton and Mr Carington from here to tell them the weather was good, but accommodation rough.

After our luncheon, which was really dinner, we went off to the caves and had two hours good climbing. We had our candles lit and the guide had a magnesium light, which helped to show us the wonderful stalactites. The walking was a little difficult for me, and we had several hard climbs but I got over it all right.

The different caves, or rather I should [say] the different chambers of the cave, had all a character of their own. One was called the "Sculptor's Studio" and it had different groups of stalactites like figures. The walls looked sometimes as if they were carved like a Chinese Ball with inside carving, & then again like great pieces of coral.

We came out of the caves and sat opposite a great arch, and then we scrambled up the rocks and came quite close to a little rock wallaby, which sat quite still and watched us for a minute or two. Then we walked across the arch and had a very muddy scramble down hill home.

This hotel is a temperance hotel, but J.B. has brought whisky & sherry with him. We had tea muddle, but alas no eggs, eggs being out of season I fear! But anyhow there is fresh milk to be had and a fire place in our room so that I shall go to bed by a fire.

4TH JULY.
Cave Hotel, Jenolan.

We had a most terrible sort of breakfast this morning; the arrangements in this hotel are simply vile, no tubs, a great scarcity of hot water and a great scarcity of any sort of comfort.

We went to the caves at 11 o'clock this morning and walked & climbed continuously for 2 ½ hours. We saw a great many chambers, especially the Wilson and Katie's Bower and endless others with odd names; but they all resemble each other very much. The stalactites are very, very, lovely and assume all sorts of different shapes. There was one place called the Diamond Cave & another that was particularly good was called the Architect's Studio. The stalactites some times were quite thin, and looked like shawls or curtains draped against the wall; when the light was placed behind them they looked quite red and yellow and they had sometimes regular borders of a different shade.

In one place there were figures, or what looked like figures, especially the Madonna & Child; another room was called after Lady Carrington.

We returned to luncheon, or dinner rather, which was almost uneatable. A terrible turkey at least 20 years old, and the consistency of India rubber, J.B. had to carve the beast too! And a huge piece of raw beef and some uneatable mutton, so we ate gravy and potato & tried to be thankful.

We started off to the caves at 3 o'clock and were in them till nearly 6 o'clock; we saw quite the most beautiful caves this afternoon. The young people went down the rope ladder to see the Fish River, but we did not attempt it; and afterwards Miss Carver told me she did not think it in the least worth the trouble.

We did climb on our tummies down an awful sort of place called the Fairies' Retreat, which I question whether that was really worth the trouble. It was a little sparkling cave, the floor dancing with diamonds apparently, and I got my leg pulled by the guide, literally, as he caught hold of it and hauled me in. J.B. and I had hardly room to sit up even to see it. Once a lady who was rather stout got stuck in this place, lost her head and began to cry, she had to be pulled out anyhow.

We saw a lovely stalactite, which looked like alabaster, called "Lot's Wife", and some of the most beautiful chambers were called "the Crystal Palace" and "the Queen's Garden". The "Queen's Jewels" was another place to which we had to crawl. Yesterday we saw the Nettle Cave and the Devil's Coach-house; today we saw the Imperial Cave, and both morning and evening we spent in the latter; there is a great sameness in the caves of course. We saw several "Mysteries" for instance, and diamond reefs and pieces of shawl like drapery; the electric light is a great boon.

We had two laymen and an old clergyman and his brother with us for the afternoon's expedition. The brother, called Richard, was lost almost immediately after our entrance into the cave but was found again after much shouting and anxiety. The prettiest bit of the caves was called "the Gem of the West".

When we returned we were all very tired & Miss Carver got a bad fall, which gave her a headache. One feels at last quite bewildered with all one has seen; and the "Fairies Garden", the studios, and all the other chambers get irretrievably mixed in one's brain. I had to change all my clothes when I returned to the hotel, everything being covered in mud.

These caves were discovered nearly 50 years ago by an escaped convict who took refuge in them; he again was found out by a gentleman who was shooting in the neighbourhood and found a cabbage garden to his surprise, and then, in poking about, found out the convict & his caves; the gentleman was a Bushranger I believe.

In the caves today we saw a few remains of bones of dogs and other animals. Some of the caves were called Selena & Nellies Bower's after ladies who had seen them 25 years ago.

5ᵀᴴ JULY, THURSDAY.
Imperial Hotel, Mt. Victoria.

We left Jenolan this morning at a quarter to 10 a.m. in a big sort of charabanc with four horses and did the 35 miles by ½ past 4 o'clock, never changing horses. We had some tremendous hills; indeed it was collar work most of the way and the horses did their work well. About ½ past 2 o'clock we stopped at a roadside shanty for an hour's rest and a most disgusting luncheon was cooked, which J.B. and I did not touch. Everywhere in these parts they put before you a beefsteak large enough for a regiment and most vilely cooked. This morning at the Cave hotel we had no fresh milk for breakfast as the cows had wandered away and in consequence there was nothing but tinned milk.

We had a most glorious day for our drive, which was really a very beautiful one as we passed through big forests of gum trees with views of the blue hills and sometimes very fine valleys. The gum trees do weary one at last, and the endless forest becomes monotonous, but one never tires of the mountains; and certainly they are blue here, a glorious ultra marine & cobalt blended. We saw one lyrebird, some jackdaws and several red & blue parrots; but very few human beings on the road. We passed a sheep farm belonging to Lord Wolseley's brother and two villages, Great Hartley & Little Hartley; they had two churches and a school and a post office. Also we passed one or two lovely farms.

We were delighted to find a fairly comfortable hotel here with clean rooms, a fire in our sitting room, and real cow's milk for tea, and dinner at 6.30 instead of tea muddle. We cannot forget the India-rubber turkey of yesterday at the Cave hotel, and the old clergyman's joke of it being a centenarian, or the turkey that was discovered by Captain Cook. Indeed the centenarian turkey was thought such a delicious joke by the old parson that he repeated it to Miss Carver before breakfast this morning. I can never forget the discomforts of the Cave hotel, the fearful dirt, the chickens, pigs & children all over the place. I couldn't get any body even to empty my wash hand basin after I had washed my hands, so I had to throw the water out of the window. This morning no water, or rather no hot water was to be had as the maid said the fountain had been allowed to run all night long; and the wringing machine for washing was kept in the dining room. The cooking was unspeakably bad, and everything was rough and horrid.

6TH JULY, FRIDAY.
Government House.

We left Mt. Victoria at a quarter or half past 10 o'clock and drove to Govett's Leap, where there is a very beautiful view. The plains being seen beyond the mountains and it is a very extensive and fine view altogether. We then drove to Katoomba, making a drive of 14 miles I suppose, and we put up at the Carrington Hotel for a short time having luncheon there. The view of the Blue Mountains from the garden of this hotel is really exquisite.

We took the 2.50 train to Sydney and arrived at Govt. House about a quarter to 7. Everything most delightfully comfortable, tea in my bedroom and all sorts of kind care for us.

7TH JULY.
Govt. House, Sydney.

Shopped all the morning till luncheon time; afterwards went out driving on the North Shore with Lady C., J.B., Rupert Carington & Lord C. rode.

We had dinner early and went to the French play & saw "La Joie de la Maison" and "L'Étincelle", the first was a very pretty little piece, "La Joie de la Maison" made us roar, it was very well acted and we enjoyed it extremely and there was a capital house.

8TH JULY, SUNDAY.
Govt. House.

Went to call on Sir Alfred Stephen & daughters with the Carringtons after luncheon [*Sir Alfred Stephen, 1802–1894, judge and member of the Upper House*].

The day has been quite hot. Read in the English papers that Charlie Adeane is engaged to marry Miss Wyndham [*Charles Adeane, J.B.'s step-nephew, who had stayed with the Biddulphs in India, married Madeline Pamela Constance Blanche Wyndham in 1888*].

11TH JULY, WEDNESDAY.
Government House, Melbourne.

We left Sydney on Monday at 5.15. I cannot say how very, very kind both Lord & Lady Carrington were to us. They started us off with a hamper of good things, which made us quite independent of the indifferent refreshment room en route. The train is very tiring and bumpy. We had sleeping berths and a carriage reserved, but we could not sleep, and I, and my bedding were once tossed right out on the floor.

We forgot to get up early and at a quarter to 6 we had to change our carriage; for the narrow gauge ended on the frontier of Victoria & the broad commenced. It was such a hurry and confusion getting into one's clothes, rushing off for a cup of coffee, for it was bitterly cold, and settling all one's hundred and one things into another carriage. We got here at a quarter to 12 on Tuesday morning and were very kindly treated by the Custom House people.

We found Lady Loch interviewing Mr Fisher the musician, & after luncheon we all went to a loan collection of pictures, the works of a deceased artist all of Australian scenery, several of them very pretty, but as a whole, monotonous. Colonel & Mrs Brownrigg dined here. We had a delightful stroll through the Botanical gardens with Lady Loch too.

LADY LOCH'S COLD CHEESE SOUFFLÉ.

Make a custard of the yolks of 4 eggs, half a pint of milk, when made add two table spoonfuls of parmesan to it, a little salt & pepper, a table spoon of gelatine; it must not be stiff or it will spoil, set it to cool & just when setting add half a pint of whipped cream, mix altogether lightly & put in a mould but take care it is not too stiff, but just stiff enough to stand, & that is all.

11TH JULY, WEDNESDAY.
Govt. House, Melbourne.

I drove with Lady Loch in the morning and did all my shopping. John went with Sir Henry to a coursing match starting at 9.30 a.m. and did not return till 4.30. It was rather fun for a time, but they all got bored with the cold and the long day, and only revived a little over a Boar's head at luncheon.

When J.B. returned he & I went off to the Elwells and had tea with them, didn't get back till 6.30 and dinner at a quarter past 7 as Lady Loch went off to Church. I had a charming stroll in the gardens with Lady Loch and the children after luncheon.

15th JULY, SUNDAY.
The Briars, Adelaide.

We left Melbourne on Friday at one o'clock and got on board the "Victoria". I went to bed in the afternoon and only left it this morning to dress for breakfast and come on here.

The evening before we left the Lochs, young Robinson & the Elwells dined there. Lady Loch had an immense reception all the afternoon, which was rather tiring.

The Elwells came to see us off on Friday and brought me a huge bouquet of violets, which scented our cabin. I felt dreadfully sorry to say goodbye to the Lochs who had been ever so good to us and one had felt so thoroughly at home in their delightful house.

We had the most horrid rough passage between Melbourne & this, the Victoria rolls so much & is not at all comfortable, and the food is horrid.

This afternoon we drove to the Barr-Smiths; they have a beautiful place, the violet garden is a sight, and the orangery too, & the house is very nice. But as Mr Barr-Smith has quite £60,000 a year it is not very surprising. They have 12 women servants and not a man in the house. Six of these servants go out from Saturday to Monday in turn. The establishment is worked by a German housekeeper. Torren's Park is the name of Mr Barr-Smith's place.

21ST JULY, SATURDAY.

S.S. Victoria.

We left the Hawkers on Monday after luncheon; the whole family came with us to the station to see us off, and our last morning in Adelaide was spent driving about the town looking for newspapers, & in seeing Mr Minchin [*Richard Ernest Minchin, 1831–1893, zoo director*] at the Zoo and getting 2 Emu's eggs from him, and buying materials for a dirty clothes bag on board ship!

Then we had an excellent luncheon at the Briars off wild turkey and said goodbye to our kind friends with the greatest regret. Rosie Hawker gave me a bouquet of violets, Parma violets, tea roses & mignonette. We also carried off a bag of oranges & lemons, and ever so many green backs in the way of literature.

Mr Hawker told us he had lost 16,000 lambs on one of his stations from the drought, but it did not seem to affect him much now they have had good rain nearly everywhere.

We had a rough night on Monday the 16th after a most perfect day. Starting, the sea was like a lake. We had horrid wet, rough, boisterous weather till Friday the 20th so that from the night of the 16th to the morning of the 20th I spent my time in bed. On the 20th we got to King George's Sound and had some peace.

We left King George's Sound at about 10 o'clock p.m. and have since had fair weather and are making good progress. I have began to play draughts with J.B. and take a little more interest in board ship life, but the cuisine is so bad that one's meals are a sore trial, and so long – dinner tonight taking one hour and a quarter.

25TH JULY, WEDNESDAY.

S.S. Victoria. We have got into warm weather now and everybody has come out in summer clothing this morning. The ship has rolled ever since we have been on board, and last night it was dreadful. Today we are within 60 miles of the Cocos Islands [*Cocos (Keeling) Islands*]. The rain began last night at 12 o'clock and rained all the night and till about 11 o'clock this morning.

The other evening a flying fish came on to the hurricane deck, attracted by the lights I suppose, as it was the evening. It had such lovely wings, like an exaggerated dragonfly. One of the passengers bought it for 2 shillings and had it cooked for dinner; they are said to be very good eating.

The cooking here continues as bad as ever; the meat, fish & butter are all very bad. Mr Lang, one of the passengers, said the fish for dinner was not good enough for pantomime fish & would not even make a good stage property, and that the puddings ought to be photographed and the photos sent to the Directors.

The only things that have occurred on the Victoria are the fainting fits of three young ladies in the baths, owing to the stewardess putting them into hot water after 4 days of sickness in bed, and a gentleman getting an attack of D.T. during which he walked in very light attire (the Captain called it Bacchanalian) with a loaded revolver in his hand; however he was put under a guard, his weapons removed, and he is all right again.

I sit next to the "heiress" at dinner, Miss Cruikshanks. She tells me many little things about Station life in Australia that is interesting, but her account of the Mad Houses is very sad; all so full, and so many of them. The great toil for wealth seems to tell on the men and they go mad from anxiety & over work. Then the anxieties of sheep farming, the great droughts & the impossibility of getting labour at times when most wanted; and bad seasons, often add inmates to the Lunatic Asylums. There has been a dreadful tragedy in Queensland when a young squatter of the name of Wyndham going mad, killed his young wife and then children; he went religiously mad & said he gave his best to God.

We hope to get to Colombo on Sunday afternoon, but we have had so many head winds that we have not made any great runs up till now.

Miss Cruikshanks told me on Saturday that three women servants did the entire work of their Station home, there are 4 in the family & these women wash, bake, clean the house, do all the sewing for everybody and are not considered at all hard worked.

30ᵀᴴ JULY, MONDAY.
Colombo, Grand Oriental Hotel [*Ceylon*].

We have had a most disagreeable voyage and all the passengers came off the ship this morning in rages. We never came into the harbour till 12 o'clock last night, then the heat was quite intense. They began the coaling at daylight, all night there were noises, the anchor being put down and people running about & chattering, so nobody slept one wink. Then this morning the ship was so filthy with the coaling that we all came away as black as sweeps.

We had a disgusting day on Saturday, coming in for a heavy gale and the ship pitched and rolled and made us all very ill indeed. There were the theatricals in the evening, which never came off, the dance on Friday night was a dismal failure as the ship rolled so that nobody could dance except with the greatest discomfort. The stewardess was always so ill she could hardly attend on any of us, and it was impossible to get anything that one could eat at times.

31ˢᵀ JULY, TUESDAY.
G.O. Hotel, Colombo.

We shopped this morning & bought tortoiseshell things and stones. I got some sapphires for a buckle and J.B. bought two boxes. We drove in the afternoon all about Slave Island and all about Colombo and had a charming drive indeed.

In the evening after dinner, we talked to a Major & Mrs Provost who are staying in the Hotel, she is an extremely pretty woman; she told me a good deal about the Mcleods and said Dora was very much liked. The governor here, Sir Arthur Gordon, seems very unpopular [*Sir Arthur Hamilton-Gordon, 1829–1912, Governor of Ceylon, 1883–1890*].

1ST AUGUST, WEDNESDAY.
G.O. Hotel, Colombo.

Finished our shopping after breakfast; having heard the Brindisi had come in we packed everything up to go on board and then took the 12 o'clock train to Mt. Lavinia where we had luncheon and returned by the 4 o'clock to Colombo. We met Capt. & Mrs Martin at the Hotel. Capt. Martin is in the 21st Hussars and was at Canterbury with J.B. They had come over from Bangalore where they had lost their only child.

J.B. took all the luggage on board the "Brindisi" at 5 p.m. and Capt. Sherborne turned up for dinner, after which we went on board. There was such a very splendid breeze all day at Mt. Lavinia that we had not felt the least heat, and the luncheon was very nice, everything very clean. I have enjoyed these days in Colombo very much.

2ND AUGUST, THURSDAY.
S.S. Brindisi.

Weather very fair, but I was ill all the same.

3RD AUGUST, FRIDAY.
Weather muggy & hot, felt bad all day.

4TH AUGUST, SATURDAY.
S.S. Brindisi.

Got into the monsoon and have not made a very good run. I can do nothing but lie down flat feeling decidedly "chippy".

5TH AUGUST, SUNDAY.
S.S. Brindisi.

We slept on deck last night as we did the night before, but had to make a run for it in the early morning as we had a storm. Very stormy today with tremendous rain, hardly any dry cover on deck. The passengers on board number 6 in all, among them a Mr Saunders, the proprietor of the Englishman.

7TH AUGUST, TUESDAY.
S.S. Brindisi.

We had a squall on Sunday night of a cyclonic nature and the Captain turned the boat round, put on half steam, and ran away from it. So the consequence was we were behind time on Monday and only got the pilot on board at 5 p.m. We stopped all night in Diamond Harbour and shall not be in Calcutta till this afternoon. We have had terrific heat for the last three days, the nights have been fearful and the breeze seems to die quite away at times. Yesterday the ship rolled so when the pilot came aboard, that everything went flying about. The store-room had just been opened and a keg of vinegar smashed, a barrel of butter and bars of soap etc., all got mixed up together and flew all over the store-room. The whist party too broke up in confusion on deck, and my long chair turned completely over, fortunately I was out of it. J.B. has had whist every day and has come out the winner by 200 points.

I am very thankful this voyage is over and my sea troubles at an end. We are to catch the evening express (9.30) for Allahabad [*Uttar Pradesh*] this evening.

10TH AUGUST, FRIDAY.

Ajmer. We had only a few hours to spend in Calcutta, and after hunting all over the Gt. Eastern Hotel for rooms, all of which were filthy; we went to Bousard's "Hotel de Paris" and made the best of it. We had a most capital dinner, quite the best I have had in India! Mr Lambert dined with us and went to the station with us and we drank quite unlimited champagne, which set us all up immensely!

Mr Lambert's Police Inspector helped us immensely in Calcutta; he met us with the steam launch in the river and then after dinner took all our luggage to the railway station, booking it in and all; so we had great comfort. Mr Bousard was very good & kind, but oh so dirty and unkempt, and Mrs B was very ill.

Mr Driscoll is the name of the Inspector of Police in Calcutta.

Chapter X

India

The Biddulphs arrived back at Deoli, Rajasthan on Sunday, 12th August 1888 and by the beginning of October the camping season had begun again; the same routine as the last three years. This, though, was to be Julia's last winter in camp; by early February 1889, they were back at Deoli and at the end of March, they sailed from Bombay to begin their long journey home.

The Biddulphs returned to Deoli on Monday 4th February 1889 just in time to receive their friends, Mr and Mrs Hawker and their daughter Rosie, from Australia; the Hawkers had been very kind to the Biddulphs when they had been travelling in Australia the year before, and Julia and J.B. were keen to repay their kindness.

9TH FEBRUARY 1889, SATURDAY.
Deoli.

The Hawkers arrived at 6.30 and John went down to the river to meet them.

11TH FEBRUARY, MONDAY.
Deoli.

There was tent-pegging in the afternoon. Mrs Sutton Jones looked so very pretty in a white jacket & a red silk waistcoat; the whole thing was capitally got up and amused the Hawkers very much indeed. Capt. Bell had arranged it all for their entertainment.

13TH FEBRUARY, WEDNESDAY.
Bundi.

We came in here this morning, driving all the way. The Rajah's eldest son met us [*HH Maharao Raja Ram Singhji Sahib Bahadur, 21st Maharo of Bundi 1821–1889, born 1811*] and there was a grand Peshwai – a very picturesque scene [*a peshwai is a royal procession*]. In the crowd were all sorts of strange figures and the young Princes were most beautifully dressed; the horses very grandly got up too. In the afternoon there was a Durbar to which Mr Hawker and John went, and it was all very fine, the young Princes with all their jewels on, and a silver chain for Mr Hawker. Mrs Hawker, Miss Rose and I went on an elephant through the town.

14TH FEBRUARY, THURSDAY.
Bundi.

We went up to the Palace this morning and were received by the old Chief and his sons. The old man wore a white dress and a very handsome dark green mantle, and beautiful emeralds and diamonds in his turban, which was white. He threw a scarlet shawl over his head when he went from one room to another. The eldest son was in dark blue & white, the second son's dress I have forgotten, the third was in black and the grandson in mauve; but all had the most beautiful jewels on, such lovely emeralds and pearls and rubies and diamonds.

We were shown a most exquisitely painted room, really the family portrait gallery as all the ancestors were represented on the walls, riding and hunting. Every corner of the room and ceiling was delicately painted, but with such an enormous mass of figures that it was difficult to grasp the scenes. We went out onto the little balconies and looked all over the City; there are most magnificent views from all the windows of the Palace. In the corridors there were men with armour, beautiful chain armour.

Afterwards we were shown all the jewels belonging to the family; magnificent emeralds and diamonds and pearls, one necklace was made of emerald drops almost as large as pigeon's eggs – quite as large I think, and even larger diamonds. We had a great display of silver ornaments for the Hawkers to see and they bought 80 Rupees' worth.

I forgot to mention that in the Raja's painted room there was a beautiful little French picture let into the wall & covered with glass, the Rajah said it had been there before his time and he could not tell us anything about it, but as he is in his 80th year, it must be pretty old.

In the afternoon the Rajah, his sons & grandson, and a very large gathering came down to call on John and Mr Hawker, and they afterwards showed off their horses and had a sort of little tournament, which was immensely appreciated by the Hawkers. It was all very pretty, the two young Princes were dressed in yellow and gold with no end of jewels, and they rode very well and looked most picturesque. The eldest son rode about 5 horses in succession, the last was covered with ornaments, gold and silver and every sort of ribbon hung from its mane, made of beautiful rich silk of the softest shades of pink, green, yellow and mauve. When the old man left he made his horse prance too; he was entirely dressed in white and had his emeralds on.

15TH FEBRUARY, FRIDAY.
Bundi.

We went this morning to the Mausoleums and had a good look at all the carvings, and then on to the other Palace beyond the Mausoleums.

16TH FEBRUARY, SATURDAY.
Bundi.

This morning we went to the Jail and the Hawkers were much pleased with the gardens. It turned very cold and wet in the evening.

17TH FEBRUARY, SUNDAY.
Deoli.

We drove nearly all the way here this morning, only using the elephants for a little bit of the road – about 5 miles on the road from Hindoli, to the new Serai [*Inn*]. It was so very cold and poor old Hawker got perfectly chilled. We got in about 12.30 and were not warm till we had some hot coffee.

At dinner John got a telegram from King & Co., Calcutta to say George Hawker had died of blood poisoning in Australia, and asking him to break it gently to the poor old man.

18TH FEBRUARY, MONDAY.
Deoli.

John had to tell Rosie the dreadful news first, and I took her up to my room where he told her. She was so brave, but she turned so white I thought she would faint. We afterwards told her mother and then her father, their grief was very great of course and all their plans are so upset. After dinner they got a long letter from poor George full of the birth of his son Bobby, and of Betty's good health, and his own and his wife's great happiness.

[*I have no idea how long the Hawkers had intended to stay with the Biddulphs at Deoli, but this tragic news clearly altered all their plans; how shocking to have received a letter from George Hawker on the same night as the telegram announcing his death. The Biddulphs would have been very unhappy at this news; the Hawkers had been so kind to them in Australia just nine months earlier.*]

20TH FEBRUARY, WEDNESDAY.
Deoli.

The Hawkers left us this morning, the poor old man was much more composed but Mrs Hawker had bad neuralgia and looked very wan and tired. Rose had recovered her colour and was looking forward to going home.

[*The remainder of March 1889 was spent settling their affairs and preparing for their long journey home to England.*]

4TH MARCH, MONDAY.
Deoli.

We leave this for Tonk tomorrow morning and have been saying goodbye all today. We have sold everything but my saddle and have packed a quantity of things. John has been very seedy all this week with fever; he had one frightful night and looks very much pulled down. He has finished his Shahpura case, written out the report and has that off his mind.

5TH MARCH, TUESDAY.
Tonk.

J.B. and I drove over here this morning, a very cool day and we got on very well indeed. All day long visitors of course, and J.B. went to see the Nawab in the evening.

8TH MARCH, FRIDAY.
Tonk.

J.B. had a most terrible day yesterday, visitors all day long. Fortunately when the Nawab came late in the evening he was so hungry he only stayed a few minutes. The Naib, Obeidullah Khan was so affected he burst into tears and left the room sobbing, and today has taken to his bed [*a naib is a deputy governor or deputy to a high-ranking official*].

Today will be even worse as the doggies have to leave me for Alwar [*Rajasthan*], where they go to reside with Miss Esther Smith.

9TH MARCH, SATURDAY.
Deoli.

We drove here this morning; at starting the horses were so fresh and kicked so badly that they broke the harness and carriage – this was before we got into it, so another carriage and harness had to be provided; we got into Deoli though without any mishap. The dogs left yesterday in a covered cart with the sweeper and a guard for Jeypore [*Jaipur*] and then for Alwar. These long drives are now nearly over.

[*Julia was very sad to part with her two dogs, Toby and Dingo, who had been her constant companions for the last three years.*]

14TH MARCH, THURSDAY.
Deoli.

We have despatched 27 cases to Nasirabad [Ajmer] and have now nearly done all our packing. The heat has become very great and the nights are now hardly cool. John has to go and see the Bundi Chief every other day; he is 5 miles off in camp, so it necessitates either a long drive before breakfast, or before dinner and the Shahpura Chief comes on the 17th. I have paid up and dismissed several of the servants and gradually we are getting through all our business. Rose Hawker has gone to England with her mother; all the others went on to Australia.

17TH MARCH, SUNDAY.

J.B. paid the Bundi Chief his last visit on Friday; today Shahpura arrives. We had a storm last evening, but it is still very cloudy and heavy.

30 boxes have gone to be sent to England for us, of which 19 are arms, horns, skins and natural history specimens.

24TH MARCH, SUNDAY.
Great Western Hotel, Bombay.

We left Deoli on Wednesday morning at 6.30 a.m. A great many people came to see us off, among them the Chief of Shahpura and his boys.

We got into our railway carriage at 11 p.m. and slept, the heat was very great on Saturday. At Baroda we got a telegram to say Mrs Bisset was so unwell Colonel Bisset could not receive us, which was a great blow to us. He had taken rooms for us in this hotel; we do not like our rooms much, but anyhow they will be cool I think, as we have a look out on the sea.

27TH MARCH, WEDNESDAY.
Gt. Western Hotel, Bombay.

Yesterday the Wyllies arrived [*William and Katherine Curzon Wyllie*] and I drove Mrs Wyllie out shopping and lunched at the Yacht Club; J.B. was made a member of the Club for a month. I did nothing yesterday afternoon, the heat was so intense; in the evening we met Capt. Webb, Mr and Mrs Davies and the Wyllies and sat out on the lawn till quite late, looking at all the lights on the harbour. It was so nice and cool, after the hot day.

Our tickets have been taken at last and everything is now settled, but our steamer does not leave Bombay till Friday after all. The heat is intense here during the day, but there is always a breeze by the sea in the evening.

Young Harold Biddulph [*J.B.'s nephew*] has turned up; he arrived in a trooper and is going to join his regiment in Burma. He is a nice little boy, but looks quite a child.

John has paid dearly for his dentist; he had one tooth stopped, which took about an hour and a half, for which he had to pay 60 Rupees.

29TH MARCH, FRIDAY.
Gt. Western Hotel, Bombay.

Yesterday we took the Ackloms to lunch at the Yacht Club; it is the only cool restful place in Bombay to us, as the Hotels are so uncomfortable & hot, and the cooking in all is very bad. We met the Wyllies there yesterday and after a good long rest, we came back to the Hotel to pack. J.B. did all his at last, discarding a great many things, quite at the last; and even now all one's portmanteaus are up to bursting point. It seems as if one never would be off somehow, and the weather is intensely disagreeable and muggy.

Chapter XI

En Route to Japan, 1889

29ᵀᴴ MARCH, FRIDAY.
We left Bombay in the evening after lunching at the Yacht Club. The Clyde is a moderately sized boat & very fairly comfortable, with only a few passengers on board [*SS Clyde, built 1881, 4,124 tons*].

2ᴺᴰ APRIL, TUESDAY.
Colombo.

We went on shore early in the morning, I having had an uncomfortable sort of sick feeling all the time on board. We breakfasted at the G.O. [*Grand Oriental*] Hotel and spent the whole day there, taking a drive in the afternoon & looking in upon the museum.

Mrs Wyllie bought some moonstones, and I bought a few more sapphires for a brooch. J.B. got another sapphire ring thrown in to make up for the fraud that was practised on him many years ago when he bought one for me. We enjoyed the day on shore immensely, but it was very hot and stuffy with perpetual showers, that only made it hotter.

The Hotel was quite crammed with people, many of them small shopkeepers from Melbourne & Sydney; they much resembled Margate in looks & manners. We might have gone off to Candy if we could have been quite sure of the Clyde's movements, as of coming home to it after dinner, the Captain said we should not leave till the evening of the 3rd as we have to wait for passengers from the "Nepaul" which has not yet come in [SS Nepaul, *built 1876, 3,536 tons; wrecked on Shagstone Rock in Plymouth Sound, 10*th *December 1890, en route from Calcutta with no loss of life*].

8TH APRIL, MONDAY.

S.S. Clyde. We expect to get to Penang today about one o'clock, and for the last two days have had most lovely calm seas. Yesterday the sunset was the most glorious one; clouds of crimson and rose colour, over a pale sort of sea green, then masses of lavender clouds sweeping up and every wave caught a crimson reflection before it rolled over, the whole sea and sky was a mass of colour. A storm was going on near the horizon and a rainbow peeped out between the clouds.

We passed Sumatra yesterday between 12 & 2 o'clock, and some dear little islands on the left, green as possible with very quaint shapes; but I missed some of the islands through carrying on a very animated conversation with Mrs Booth after service. There are few ladies on board, two Jewesses with beautiful hair, and a Miss Vincent, a girl of about 17 with a face of 30, and the dress of a 12 year old. She sings like a cat with the airs of a professional. We had a performance on Saturday evening, a magic lantern shown by Mr Beauchamp with Japanese views, and some singing. I have never seen before people get up to sing with perfectly inaudible voices, and go through the dumb show of singing with complete composure.

The Frasers on board have come from Chile and are going to Japan, he as a Minister; his wife is a sister of Marian Cranford's and looks very pleasant. Mrs Booth, a Canadians is decidedly amusing, she told us that the Miss Vernon Harcourts were on board the Nepaul. One being 70 and the young one, who was a giddy creature, was about 60. The young one said she was taking her sister about to see if she could travel, and on finding she was able to travel, she took her round the Cape! On board the Nepaul they did not like their seats at [the] table so they came and stood at breakfast time behind Mrs Booth and in front of the Captain, and said out very loud, "We are the Miss Vernon Harcourts, we do not like our seats at [the] table. We have been put just over the screw, we are good sailors and do not mind the screw, but we insist on having suitable places provided for us at this table. We have spoken to the Steward on the subject but he has not attended." The Captain who was a very nervous shy man, and had two empty places on one side of him, immediately invited them to take these places; and then explained to them that they would not permanently have these seats as a young lady who was under his charge had to sit next to him, at present she was sick, but when well would take her place by his side. But he would see that they had good places a little lower down. At dinner the ladies found themselves about four or five places down, but the Captain again had one vacant seat beside him. The young and giddy thing of 60 peeped round and on seeing the empty seat called out, "Oh Captain I see you are alone," nipped out of her seat and sat down next to him, and did so at every meal; so that when the young lady did appear at last, she had to sit where she could. But the Captain showed great determination and succeeded in ousting the Miss Vernon Harcourt.

We have heard so many accounts of cold, heat, and different routes of travelling; every one having different ideas on all subjects, that we now feel it is very little use making any plans till we get to the different places. "Kobes" is said to be the best guide for Japan and is to be had at the Grand Hotel Yokohama. Mr Beauchamp has advised us making a long overland tour from Kobe and getting across so to Yokohama; but this I think we will not do as it necessitates such very long walks of 7 to 10 miles, too much of an undertaking in the summer.

Last night the heat was suffocating, we have had it about 87° or rather lower during the days on deck, but the still heat last night was terrible in the cabins.

9TH APRIL, TUESDAY.
S.S. Clyde.

Yesterday we went on shore at Penang about 3.30, in one of the funny native boats that have an eye painted on the prow so that the boat may see (also I am told, to avert the evil eye). Not very comfortable boats, as there is only just room for two people to sit on one seat, and one is almost in the water while the boat jumps about like a cork.

Penang is one of the loveliest places I have seen, the approach to it is quite beautiful with blue hills and islands covered with verdure, and the view of the place from the harbour most charming. We drove first through an avenue of lovely acacia trees, greener I think than any trees I have ever seen before. And then we passed the bungalows where the European residents live; they were very pretty to look at with their wide verandahs [sic], trim lawns and flowering shrubs & trees, the Gold Mohur tree being conspicuously magnificent; but we were told they were very hot to live in, however in the evening, ladies and children as well as men were playing lawn tennis. We drove up to the gardens where there is a waterfall as the great attraction, but in reality the gardens are worth seeing, but the waterfall is not, there is hardly any water there and it entails a very steep climb. Some of the flowering shrubs in the garden were so beautiful and the position of the gardens is lovely, with mountains covered with trees of every description all round. The drive to the gardens took about three-quarters of an hour, but John had to take refuge in a rickshaw. He was in the same carriage as Mrs Wyllie and Colonel Collett, and their poor little tired pony was quite knocked up before reaching the gardens. The ponies are very small Burman [sic] ponies, certainly not above 12 hands high, and they draw these carriages like the dak gharries of India. There is a miserable sort of hotel near the gardens kept by a Chinaman but we didn't go into it; the best hotel in Penang is the Gt. Eastern.

We came on board about 6.30 all declaring we never had been so hot in all our lives before. The heat in Penang is a damp heat and our cabins were 92° at 6.30; but after a good sea bath and champagne dinner we were exceedingly cheerful. The Captain said one man, a Mr Gibbs arriving on board, called out for a cool drink to be brought at once, and on it arriving, plunged his hand into the tumbler and stuck the lump of ice on his head, held it on there and then proceeded to drink the tumbler's contents, being almost speechless with thirst and heat.

One story being told on board is rather a good one. Some people were being shown over a stalactite cave in America, among them a very lively English bride. A notice was put up at the entrance that if anyone broke off a stalactite the fine was 50 Dollars. The young bride said she never heard such nonsense; she anyhow would have a stalactite so she promptly broke one off, which resounded like a cannon shot through the cave and caused the guide to say she would find it an expensive amusement, & he would report it to the Boss outside. This he duly did and the Boss claimed the 50 Dollars, a silence fell on the party for a moment when a Yankee stepped forward and said, "Fifty millions of Americans live under the protection of the Stars and Stripes, and claim liberty & justice beneath its banner and liberty and justice we'll have right away here Sir, if you please. Do you consider this stalactite worth 50 Dollars?" Whereupon the Boss became so confused by the sudden attack under the Stars & Stripes, that he confounded and let the Bride off with her stalactite on paying 10 Dollars.

Today we saw a very good water spout; at first we only saw a little cloudy sort of fountain begin in the sea, then it increased in volume, and a great water spout up in the air like a very long column hung down, and in a minute or two joined the one in the sea; a most curious sight.

Sixteen new passengers came aboard last night; those that came aboard for a short time made a tremendous noise in departing, one hugely stout gentleman in white, with large inkblots all over his trousers was especially jocular. We had a very sharp storm in the night, the lightning was extraordinary and the officers on watch said that they had never seen such vivid lightning before.

11TH APRIL, THURSDAY.
S.S. Clyde.

Yesterday we came into the harbour of Singapore between 7 & 8 o'clock, but we were all so anxious not to miss the sight that we were called at 5 a.m., and were dressed before the gentlemen had left the decks in their undress of the period. We went up on the quarter deck and for some time passed lovely islands, the sea as calm as possible and a lovely pale green colour; while all the distant islands were the most delicate blue, and the morning mists helped to make the scenery perfect. There is a very narrow passage into the harbour and the P &

O steamers do not attempt it at night. We had no words for the loveliness round us, and when we did get into harbour the heat was terrible.

After breakfast we got into two small carriages of the same kind as those at Penang, and with the same sort of little pony. We drove to the Hotel De L'Europe, which is now being managed by Fischer, who formally was at the G.O. [*Grand Oriental Hotel*] Colombo. Here we found Colonel Collett and were able to post our letters. John & I drove to the Bank (Hong Kong) and to the bookshop, but the latter had nothing that attracted us. We came back to the hotel and while J.B. and Major Wyllie went to the Museum, we mounted (Mrs W & I) to a verandah [*sic*] in another part of the hotel and rested on long chairs. The heat was intense, so stifling & fatiguing. We thought Singapore very much like Penang in colouring, but not so fascinating. The Cathedral seemed a fine one and there were some handsome buildings. The Bazar was strictly Chinese; the gardens are really the chief attraction, but unfortunately they had had so little rain that the orchids were not in bloom, & all the flowers were displaced in view of an approaching flower-show. But the situation of the gardens is so good, & the flowering shrubs, trees and ferns are indeed beautiful. The flowering trees are perfectly lovely, and there was one immense tree called the Koompassia [*sic*] something or other [*Kompassia Excelsa*], which had a splendid trunk straight up for about 150 feet without a single branch, and then it had beautiful dark green foliage. We had some little difficulty in persuading our drivers to take the carriages through the gardens, but on insisting on it they did so very unwillingly. It would have been far too hot to walk.

We reached the ship about 4 o'clock & we left the harbour at 5.30 p.m. Mrs W and I made a little sketch of the boats, but it was very difficult as a storm of rain came on. We left

Singapore in a perfect glory of sunlight from the setting sun, which was abruptly blotted out by a rain cloud. A great many more passengers came on board, among them a good many foreigners, some Russians and Dutch people. Col. Collett told us today of a Calcutta Babu who had given him the Latin name for some tree, which he asked him about, on which Col. Collett said, "Oh you are a Botanist then?". The Babu replying, "No not a Botanist, a Horte-agriculturist."

16TH APRIL, TUESDAY.
Victoria Hotel, Hong Kong.

We arrived here at 2.30 yesterday and when we got into the harbour were informed that the best hotel, the Hong Kong Hotel was full, and with great difficulty we got two very bad single rooms for the Wyllies and ourselves, and Col. Collett also got a room. We only managed this by the kindness of two young men, fellow passengers, who gave up their room to the Wyllies.

17TH APRIL, WEDNESDAY.
Canton.

Yesterday we had a long day's outing. John called on the Hollidays & also on General Edwards [*Lieutenant-General Sir James Bevan Edwards KCB KCMG, 1834–1922, commander of British troops in Hong Kong and China, 1889*]. Both of them kindly asked us to stay with them. The General has arranged a field firing expedition, which he asked us to join; so we scrambled down to Port Murray and got on board the Government steam launch at 12.30. Colonel Collett also came with us. General Edwards had his A.D.C. Major Brownrigg, a very pretty lady and her husband who was on his staff, and Colonel Craster. We had a capital luncheon on board and it was very pretty indeed going round the island.

We stopped at Stanley, which was formally used as a place of change for the soldiers, a huge barracks were built there for them but it proved so unhealthy it had to be completely given up. We passed Aberdeen, a pretty quaint little fishing village on our way to Stanley. At Stanley the 91st Highlanders (Argyllshire) and some of the 58th were there. Major Chater just now commands the 91st, a very pleasant man. John accompanied the General and all the Staff up the steep hills where the field firing went on, but Mrs Yethard, Colonel Collett and I only climbed up a small hill and watched the fun from a distance.

Stanley had about an acre of fish spread out to dry and decompose; in which state the Chinamen most enjoy it.

When the firing was over we went right round the island and came in for all sorts of excitements; the Admiral coming out to cruise about Singapore & Borneo, and the Clyde also passed us on her way to Shanghai. The scenery was perfectly lovely and we were most fortunate in being able to go right round the island in this way. We only just had time to get back to the hotel and dress for dinner at the Hollidays on the Peak. We went up in chairs, 4 men carried us wonderfully well and they only rested twice, though it is immensely steep. A cable railway goes up every quarter of an hour during the day. The Hollidays have a nice little house on the Peak and they were very kind indeed to us, we are to go and stay with them on Friday. We got back to the hotel soon after 10.30 and then had to pack.

This morning we had to leave the hotel at 7.30 to get to our cabins secured on the river steamer that goes up to Canton daily; it was a raw rainy morning and quite cold. The Wyllies joined us on board and we left Hong Kong at 8 a.m. with good fish, meat, lobster, hot breads etc., and after breakfast the weather cleared and became charming, a cool fresh wind & a bright sun.

The coast scenery is charming, full of interest with the bluest hills and green fields, pagodas and queer little houses, fishing villages and the river itself full of junks and fishing boats, making a most animated scene.

Whampoa was the largest place we passed, it had a very fine pagoda and I suppose the priest's house was close to it; such a very quaint looking building. There were heaps of junks, fishing boats, war boats with guns on board, and all sorts of queer looking boats, sampans & gondolas included.

We arrived at Canton at 3 o'clock; one saw the Roman Catholic Cathedral from afar [Sacred Heart Cathedral, Guangzhou, the Notre-Dame of East Asia], and it is perfectly impossible to describe the scene of confusion on arrival. The thousands of boats all manned by women, the junks & Mandarin boats, the immense population, overflowing houses & boats and all talking as loud as possible.

Ah-Cum [sic] the guide joined us at once with his brother, and told us he could not take us over the City today as there was an immense procession going on and it would be "too great responsibility" to take us into the crowd. We therefore got into a boat and went over to the opposite side of the river, and first went to a Temple built by some son in honour of his parents, where there was some very fine carving. The approach to the Temple was so pretty, on a little plot of ground, green with moss and big shady trees, and only patches of sunlight here & there, while children and girls were very happily playing in the shade. The inside of the Temple was so cool and there were some pieces of very fine carving, tables and long pieces of furniture like sideboards, and beautiful chairs all made of ebony. On the altar were some immense pieces of pewter polished till they looked like silver, and bronzes and other curiosities, but I really could not quite understand what Ah-Cum's brother said. He then took us to the house of "little

China gentleman with big family," which was the house of a green tea merchant, and very interesting to us. We were all introduced to the grandmother whose tiny feet and hugely long fingernails very much astonished us. She had large pearls fastened in the fillets that bound her grey hair, and she had jade ornaments and was dressed in grey silk. We saw the little Altar always kept up in all hours with the little light burning (sandal wood) and its vase of flowers and ornaments.

Upstairs there were some very wonderful gold lacquer wardrobes, the whole side of the room covered with them, like a succession of tiny cupboards. And the rooms or halls had many very curious paintings, among them lovely little tables for eating on, highly polished & beautifully carved, sometimes inlaid with mother o' pearl. The rooms were strewn with pieces of silk and silk garments.

After this we had a long hot walk to see some gardens where we saw the wonderful way they dwarf trees, and train them into shapes like men & boats & animals. There were a great many lovely lilies, but no other flowers. We went on to hear the service at a Buddhist Temple. We passed some enormous figures in a sort of separate entrance chapel, and then down an avenue into the Temple where the priests were all hard at work chanting their liturgy in minor keys. The crowd outside who were never permitted to enter the Temple, consisted mostly of boys & children, they stared in at the open doors, while we sat inside in a corner on benches. The priests were dressed in yellow sort of surplices over grey silk gowns, and had to kneel frequently and touch the floor with their heads while one young priest beat a sort of red gong, and the older priest every now and then sounded another lovely gong. There were enormous figures of Buddha all round the Temple and the largest of all in front of the altar; they were made of wood & lacquer I think.

The heat was intense and the sun was rather trying us, as well as the bad smells in the Monastery.

18TH APRIL, THURSDAY.
Canton.

Yesterday after seeing the large Temple and hearing the service we returned to our steamer, the "Powan", and after dinner the Wyllies went over to the house of Jardine & Skinner where they slept, while we put up in the steamer. At 7 a.m. this morning Ah-Cum came for us and put our luggage on to this steamer, which returns to Hong Kong tonight. After that we went over to the British Settlement to meet the Wyllies; a very pretty green oasis, after the tumult of the harbour; gardens and nice houses, and a pleasant shady walk by the river. The Wyllies had been nearly devoured by mosquitos during the night, we had none, but then we had a good deal of noise; squibs & crackers being let off ad libitum, so perhaps that compensated.

We all had chairs and four coolies to each chair, except Ah-Cum who had only two. The streets were narrow past all description, simply teeming with mankind and the smells are really too fearful, especially near the butchers' shops. But the shops are beautifully clean with substantial counters and chairs, and fitted up most comfortably. We first were taken to the shop where they paint on rice paper; (no that was the 2nd shop), the 1st was a place where they were making ornaments with the feathers of kingfishers; very fine work, the tiny feathers being mixed with gum and put on gold, more curious than really beautiful, though of course the colour was lovely. At the rice paper place we bought some paintings of birds and then we went to another shop of the same kind where they painted very much better, and there we bought some paintings of insects & flowers. Then we went to an embroidery shop where Mrs W. was sorely tempted, and to an ivory shop.

Going through the streets we twice came across the procession which had been going on yesterday, children and women were painted like dolls and dressed in stiff embroidered dresses; they looked exactly like dolls as they sat in their chairs with fans in their hands, staring at everybody, and being stared at.

We passed the Roman Catholic Cathedral but did not go in, and we went to the Examination Hall where the students (hundreds at a time) have to pass their examinations, shut up for 24 hours in the most pestilential little cells. They are never allowed to leave them, each student in his separate little den till the examination is over [*the Chinese imperial examination system, abolished 1905*].

The smells very nearly did for us all here. We visited an enamel shop and a pipe shop; at the latter place we bought one in a shagreen case. Then we went up to the city walls and declined to mount up a five storey Pagoda, but we had a very fine view of the city. We had our breakfast in the Viceroy's country house, which had the most delightful chairs and tables and was a charming place to rest. The Viceroy has a large house and grounds and a summer palace too in the town, which are marked by two large standard poles at each residence.

The beautiful black wood furniture everywhere is most fascinating, all ebony and each piece made so solidly.

I did not care much for the Chinese embroidery that they showed us in one shop. Though the work was exquisite in itself, the designs were so florid; such a great quantity of everything, flowers, birds, leaves and insects all so much jumbled up together that one could not follow the artist's idea, and the colours were so metallic. The Chinese put their leaves on a piece of embroidery in the brightest possible green; really gamboge and Prussian blue, and the blues of everything are so vivid, indeed all the colours generally are so.

There was a very charming door in the Viceroy's house opening into the saloon. A round door, which had a frame of wood carved like bamboos crossing each other and draped with curtains; these round and oval doors have a particular beauty.

We visited another Buddha Temple and heard another service exactly similar to the one we heard before. The priests do not know themselves what they are repeating, and they never stop for one instant till the whole service is over. They all look exactly the same and have a countenance devoid of all expression.

We went to some more shops, and during the day visited the silk looms, the flourmills and a big china shop, which was crammed with the greatest possible rubbish. The last shop we went to was really very fascinating, an embroidery shop where they showed us the most magnificently embroidered screen I have ever seen, more than 6 ft. high in a carved ebony frame, and four panels of white silk at the back and coloured silk in front, literally covered with peacocks and birds and flowers of all descriptions, the greatest mass of needlework of the finest kind I have ever seen; the piece was 4,000 dollars. There were some lovely curtains and piano covers etc. in this shop. We ourselves bought a small piece with gold bamboos, a bird and some grasshoppers on a peacock blue green satin, for a cushion.

I cannot imagine how so many streets of shops can find custom, even with a population of 3,000,000. We seemed to pass thousands of shops of every description winding our way through the immense labyrinth of streets.

We didn't exactly see "Black Cat, hot every day" written up, but we passed so much that was horrible, that no doubt the black cat was there. We finished all our sightseeing at 2 o'clock and my head would not have been equal to more, for it ached so with the frantic noise, and I couldn't get the smells out of my system.

This steamer has no guardian with a drawn sword facing the deck, as we had on our first one. There are stories of pirates boarding these steamers, but that must have been many years ago.

My impressions of Canton are not very favourable, it has been a wonderful sight but I should never care to do it again. Though it would be nice to be able to stroll into shops and see their contents comfortably, but that one could not do as the people without being openly rude, stare at English ladies in a very impertinent way.

I forgot to mention that in the rice paper shops we saw a series of drawings of the tortures inflicted on criminals. They were most horrible, one especially revolting was a poor wretch being shut up in a cask of lime, which slowly killed him and another was about to be cut into 24 pieces.

21ST APRIL, EASTER SUNDAY.
The Peak, Hong Kong.

We came up to Mr Holliday's house on Friday morning. He very kindly came to the Victoria Hotel at breakfast that morning & arranged that we should be up here by luncheon time. We had a very pleasant walk after luncheon and tried to make out all the points of the island, and then went down to dinner at Mr Whitehead's. Mr Whitehead is a Banker; we met the Hirsts, the Holtons, Mr Norman the Pall Mall correspondent, and a very nice little German gentleman who played delightfully on the violin after dinner. We had some very good music after dinner, Mrs Hirst played quite splendidly, she is a very handsome woman and her husband, a German, also sang very well. Then a Mr Grace sang like a professional, but his voice was far too powerful for the room. Mrs Holton sang a little French song while her husband accompanied her on the guitar. She showed me all her Canton purchases in the way of embroidered petticoats.

We came up here rather tired, but it was a most beautiful moonlight night and the view of the harbour is too lovely with all the lights in the town and on the sea.

Yesterday we had a tremendous day; after 8.30 breakfast Mrs Holliday & I went out shopping and bargained in the Chinese shops for old embroideries and Canton China. We came up to 1.30 luncheon (by tram) and packed our clothes to send down to Mr Whitehead's where we were to dress for the General's dinner. Then we went down by tram again and joined John and Mr Holliday at the Polo ground. There were only 6 players, and the Chinese ponies are not much to look at and have very bad mouths so they don't turn easily, but they got some fun out of the game and we ladies had tea.

The look out across the harbour to the mountains on one side, and then on the other the hills overlooking the town, were very pretty and it was a most lovely evening. Afterwards John came with Mrs H. and myself through the Happy Valley to the Cemetery, which is the prettiest I have ever seen anywhere. It is really a most beautiful garden with trees, shrubs and flowers of all kinds; turf everywhere and the most delicious perfumes from the flowering shrubs. The monuments are very massive and lasting, not all very artistic or beautiful in shape, but being of stone or granite will last forever. There were some very large monuments to the memory of soldiers of different regiments, the Marines, the naval Brigade, Artillery etc. After this we went through the town, changing our rickshaws for chairs in the principal street up to Mr Whitehead's, and there we dressed for dinner.

The general has a charming house and an excellent cook; we had plovers' eggs & snipe etc. but the former were served hot! Only one other lady, a Mrs Champernowne was there, but she was a host in herself and talked unceasingly. Her husband a melancholy looking man, with a large long nose, was in the Engineers and is a cousin of Col. Bullen. They had been to Peking and ridden to the Great Wall, which made me rather envious. Mr Norman told me the other night he had been there also, and nearly got killed in the City. He had also ridden through Corea [*Korea*], indeed everybody nowadays seems to go to all sorts of places; nothing is new.

We went to the Church yesterday, or rather the Cathedral, which was most beautifully decorated with flowers by all the ladies; the scent was so delicious and the pulpit was a mass of lilies & ferns. The moss and ferns and flowers here are so beautiful, and the General's table was exquisitely arranged with flowers and ferns by the Chinese gardener. We didn't come away till 10.30 p.m. Colonel Collett was dining there and gave a very nice account of Macau, which seems to have a most comfortable hotel.

We met a Capt. Fletcher at the polo ground who was at Menzies Hotel, Melbourne when we were there last year.

Chapter XII

Japan

27ᵀᴴ APRIL, SATURDAY.
The Verona, Nagasaki [*SS Verona, built 1879, 3,116 tons*].

We came on board the "Verona" on Tuesday at 12 o'clock. Mr Holliday came with us, he was so very, very kind. We had people at dinner our last evening; the Mackintoshes and the doctor and his wife, the latter sang remarkably well. Mrs Mackintosh impressed us so much by saying she had had to work so hard with her own hands in China, that actually her hands had been enlarged two sizes, and were now 5 ¾!

The doctor suddenly broke out into song unaccompanied, and from his chair in the middle of the drawing room gave forth a most extraordinary Scotch ditty.

We have had the most perfectly lovely weather since we left Hong Kong, and though it has rained often and has been very cold, the sea has been most delightfully calm.

Today we got up at 5.15 a.m. and I got on deck very soon after 5.30 to see the coming into harbour.

It was rather a grey morning but very lovely; and it was lovely coming in with the islands covered with trees & cultivation, down to the edge of the sea. And all the beautiful junks and sampans and boats; the passage is very narrow and would be decidedly dangerous at night.

We engaged a guide and at 10 o'clock, went on shore and went through the town where everybody looked like pictures or figures out of the "Mikado". The shops were full of pretty things, baskets, china, pottery, bronze etc. and everywhere heaps of fish, and a quantity of little fish like whitebait. The great things that are for sale and really manufactured here, are tortoiseshell things and porcelain.

We went to a Bazaar first where we found most delicious sweetmeats or candied fruits of all kinds, and then we went to a tortoiseshell shop where we bought a very handsome paper cutter for 4 dollars. Then a very pretty china shop in the old quarter, called Desima I think [*Dejima or Desima, the ancient Dutch East India Company trading post, was Japan's only window to the outside world during the national isolation period, 1641–1859, making Nagasaki Japan's only international trading port at that time*].

After that we engaged some more men for our rickshaws, so as to have 2 men apiece, and we went out into the country to Mogi, about 9 miles from the harbour, where we found ourselves on the coast again and we had luncheon in a tea house. It was a perfectly lovely ride, the country being perfectly beautiful, very hilly and all the country cultivated in little terraces and the bamboos and pines especially luxuriant; the bamboos being the golden variety and looking like birches almost at a distance. And the wild flowers and ferns were beautiful, violets everywhere. We spent about an hour at the teahouse and then returned to the town and the Wyllies went back to the china shop, but we came on to the harbour where we met them. Then we went round the Russian Ironclad, a very fine vessel with two turrets & bristling all over with big guns.

The day was rather grey and we had a little rain once, but the air was most delicious and it was an "excursion day" or holiday, so that all the people were out in their best clothes and the young girls and children were most fascinating. The babies fed in the most unsophisticated manner, their mothers seemed not in the least bashful, but gave them their nourishment as they walked along the public road, or when sitting chatting with their friends at the teahouses.

We got home to the Verona at about 3.30 p.m. and very soon after arriving very nearly came in for a collision with another big steamer, we escaped in a marvellous manner. Soon after the Frasers came on board and then we started. We passed the island of "Takaboko" where thousands of Christian converts were thrown into the sea from the top of a tremendous cliff at the time of the great persecutions. Mrs Wyllie and I made a little sketch of it, but of course it is very difficult to draw an outline correctly when one is passing the place very rapidly. The evening was quite perfect and the view coming out of Nagasaki was as lovely as coming in, as the sunset was so beautiful.

29TH APRIL, MONDAY.
Oriental Hotel, Kobe.

Yesterday we passed through the Straits of Shimonoseki at 5.30 a.m. It was raining, bitterly cold and misty, so we were all sorry we had got up so early, but the day became lovely later on and we enjoyed the perfect beauty of the Inland Sea all day long. At 4 o'clock we entered the Northern Passage and from 4 to 6.30 we passed through the most exquisite scenery, and met perfect fleets of Japanese Junks. We must have passed many thousands during the day, they all have the loveliest sails, large square sails, puckered in lines and drawn just like the fashionable blinds of the day – window blinds.

Most of them are grey outside, shading into white in the centre and each has a distinctive mark, either one black line on a sail, or two; or a dot or several dots etc. The Govt. now have ordered the discontinuance of these lovely sails, as they are very heavy, not easily reefed & require a great number of men to manage them, so that in the frequent storms in these parts, great loss of life takes place. In future English sails are to be used for all vessels above a certain tonnage. They look like lovely nautilus shells, or things made out of mother o' pearl and we were in great luck to see so many as the weather has been so bad here lately, they haven't been able to go out to sea. Yesterday being a lovely day they all came out in shoals. We could do nothing all day but stare at the exquisite scenery, it was impossible to sit down as one wanted eyes to see everywhere. Rocky heights covered with verdure and cultivation, forests of pine trees, coves and bays and lovely strips of sand everywhere. Sweet little villages and large towns, Temples etc. all attracted one so that it was a perpetual rush from one side of the ship to the other to see everything that one could. The population must be dense from the amount of cultivation to be seen, but there are no inhabitants to be seen in the fields at all at this time of year.

We are most comfortable in this hotel, having French cooking, good fires in our rooms, hot baths and all necessary comforts. We had a long afternoon shopping on Monday and bought a few wooden netsuke but the curio shops are now immensely expensive and ask extravagant sums for anything good. The ivory netsuke, were all 8, 7 & 6 ½ dollars each.

[*Rudyard Kipling had also stayed at the Oriental Hotel, Kobe in 1889 and wrote of his experiences:*

Let me sing the praises of the excellent M. Begeux, proprietor of the Oriental Hotel, upon whom be peace. His is a house where you can dine. He does not merely feed you. His coffee is the coffee of beautiful France. For tea he gives you Peliti cakes (but better) and the vin ordinare which is compris, is good. Excellent Monsieur and Madame Begeux! If the Pioneer were a medium for puffs, I would write a leading article upon your potato salad, your beefsteaks, your fried fish, and your staff of highly trained Japanese servants in blue tights, who looked like so many small Hamlets without the velvet cloak, and who obeyed the unspoken wish. No it should be a poem – a ballad of good living. I have eaten curries of the rarest at the Oriental Penang, the turtle steaks of Raffles's at Singapore still live in my regretful memory, and they gave me chicken liver and sucking-pig in the Victoria at Hong-Kong which I will always extol. But the Oriental at Kobe was better than all three. Remember this, and so shall you who come after slide round a quarter of the world upon a sleek and contented stomach. (Victorians in Japan: In and Around the Treaty Ports, Hugh Cortazzi, Bloomsbury, 2012.) Sir Hugh Cortazzi GCMG was British Ambassador to Japan, 1980–1984.]

30ᵀᴴ APRIL, TUESDAY.

Oriental Hotel, Kobe.

Today we made a long expedition to Arima [*Arima onsen*], a little village about 15 miles out of Kobe in the hills where there are some hot mineral springs and a great basket manufactory. The day was cold but bright when we started, six of us in all including Mr Moke. We found the road terribly rough and the rickshaws jolt one painfully over rough roads. At first it was not pretty, but afterwards it was lovely scenery and the wild flowers are beautiful; azaleas, camellias, violets and clover, and many others one does not know the names of. We kept going up steep hills and the rickshaw men found it very fatiguing, so we walked a great deal of the way. Though we started at 9 a.m. we did not get into Arima till 1 o'clock. It was a charming little straggling village up a hill, and the baskets were lovely. The people were amusing themselves with a gambling game for sweets, principally for the amusement of the children. So J.B. made some of the young girls try their luck and a few pence produced most uproarious merriment among the damsels. The rain then commenced and it simply poured all the afternoon. We had our luncheon in a teahouse and got plenty of fresh milk for our tea, we took our own luncheon with us. But there are many discomforts attending these teahouses for ladies, especially the absolute want of privacy. We did not get back till 6.30 p.m. and all were tired out with aching bones.

1ST MAY, WEDNESDAY.
Osaka.

We came here by the 12 o'clock train, J.B. feeling terribly oppressed with all our luggage, and we have vowed to reduce it. It is only an hour's rail from Kobe. This is an immense town, the 3rd largest in the country and a great commercial centre.

Jutei's hotel is not exactly luxurious and it is very likely we shall go on to Nara soon. Our rooms have glass verandahs [sic] on each side and it is very like living in a conservatory, for we have two large glass doors leading into the verandahs [sic], one on each side of the room. There is a stove in every room, which is heated with charcoal, and it is really quite clean.

[Rudyard Kipling also visited Osaka in 1889 and declared that 'there was but one hotel for the Englishman in Osaka – Jutei's' (Victorians in Japan: In and Around the Treaty Ports, Hugh Cortazzi).]

This afternoon we went to the Arsenal and were shown round by a very nice little Japanese officer who talked French.

The Arsenal is a great big place very much like a young Woolwich. Guns of all descriptions being made, and one big gun can be made in a week. The Castle is close to the Arsenal and is a most quaint looking place.

After seeing all over the Arsenal we went to the City and passed through streets and streets; one old silk shop the guide said, was 1,500 years old. There is a great manufacture here of leather work, and it is the best place for Kakemonos [*a kakemono is a scroll painting intended to be hung on a wall*]. We saw endless children and girls in picturesque dress and at last John found out a sort of furniture shop where he bought two trays engraved on bamboo. A great crowd assembled round the Wyllies and J.B. while they were purchasing, and at last a policeman had to come up and disperse the crowd.

The Wyllies, Col. Collett and others all went to the Japanese theatre after dinner, but I was too knocked up with the cold and fatigue, having caught a chill somehow, so had to go to bed.

2ND MAY, THURSDAY.
Jutei's Hotel, Osaka.

Major Wyllie came out with J.B. and me this morning and we went to see the Castle. Mrs W. stayed at home to mend before starting for Nara. We first went all over Osaka docks West End, where we supposed the élite lived, and everywhere else before we found Government House where permission was obtained to see the Castle. The Castle is not particularly interesting except for the huge slabs of granite that one sees in the walls, reminding one of the Pyramids & Egyptian work, the immense rafters in the entrance gate are very fine. We were received by the General's ADC and had the usual horribly nasty Japanese tea, after which he took us up to a summerhouse where we had a magnificent view of the City.

It is a wonderful place and the Buddhist & Shinto Temples & Pagoda stood out prominently from a mass of buildings. The Mint is close to the Arsenal & Castle. We were most politely shown everything by our little friend the ADC and then after many bows and exchange of cards, we all parted. We to luncheon at the hotel and Major W. to the Mint, but by mistake he found himself in a hospital, which was more interesting I think, he found everything so beautifully clean & well arranged.

After luncheon we had a good long shopping and there we bought some lovely Kakemonos, and J.B. got one or two little oddments; we saw some really lovely curios but they asked the most fearful prices. We finished up by going to the Exhibition where they showed us some excellent woodwork; all the carpenters' work was very good and cheap. The cold all day has been very great, a bright sun & a keen wind.

3ʳᴰ MAY, FRIDAY.
Jutei's Hotel, Osaka.

The Wyllies went off to Nara this morning and Mr Moke joined us in our morning's expedition. First we went to the Buddhist Temple, a very fine one indeed, or rather I should say a group of Temples all in one enclosure. The beauty of the inside of the temple struck us very much, chambers of gold with beautiful bronze ornaments and tables, and the most lovely hanging lamps. Everything was beautiful and there were not too many objects to prevent one looking at each individual thing. The huge moneyboxes amused us, but the people seemed to prefer to chuck their coin inside the rails of the altar and the floor was strewn with copper coins. The people all came in to say their prayers and knelt here and there, muttering some form of prayer aloud. After seeing the Temple and looking in upon other shrines, we looked in upon the toyshops, which abound in the neighbourhood, and then went on to the Shinto Temples. There we found a fair all round the Temple, and two stalls full of gold fish in little glass bowls, all the gold fish with three ends to their tails (a triple fin). One gold fish in a bowl for 1 cent & so on. In some of the big bowls there were a dozen fish, & there were some beautiful little turtles in a tub. Toys and sweets of all descriptions abounded, and in one enclosure were some sacred storks walking about. There were figures of the sacred cow, much ornamented with rags of crape and bows. The Temple inside was not very interesting, all the priests wore white, and there were some bronzes and candles. We tried the gambling game for sweets and won three pieces of excellent candy.

Having done the Temples we went shopping and bought some delightful picture books, especially some artist's models for Netsuke and sword hilts etc., and a book containing pictures of the Tokaido Road. We only spent 4 yen and became the happy possessors of about 9 books and some delightful old play bills. After luncheon we went out to the Whitechapel of Osaka, which was full of vile smells and sights; skins everywhere, as it is here that boots and everything with skins is done. And the people, who are the descendants of the Korean prisoners, are the pariahs of the country. We speedily returned from this terrible quarter, and then came in for a most amusing scene. A fire was on hand, and we saw the smoke of a burning house; instantly the streets were crowded with people, a bell ringing and the people rushing frantically here and there, leaping and shouting. Some of the officers of the Fire Brigade arriving in rickshaws, and their attendants flying after them, flags being carried about, 2 flags for every company; red, white, blue, yellow, with different insignias and writing – but no one apparently putting out the fire! We stopped at a corner and all down the street were flags to be seen, the red one being waved and then the blue one, and I thought it meant at first that a square was to be formed round the burning house & no traffic allowed to enter, but it did not mean that. At last a very small engine arrived and some more Fire Brigade people; John stood in the crowd and saw the rafters being pulled down from the house. Many people were watching on the house tops, but the leaping, shouting crowd continued to rush here and there and we left them at last, quite unable to make out the game!

We spent another hour in the curio shops and saw heaps of good paintings & drawings & kakemonos.

After dinner we went to the play and saw some dancing, geisha I think it is called. The theatre was surrounded with coloured lanterns and inside, the pit and one gallery was quite full, we had one gallery to ourselves. Below the galleries the band composed of women, played. They were dressed in dark blue dressing gowns with crimson handkerchiefs inside the bosoms of their dress, and the dark blue garment was lined with brilliant orange and turned back near the knees so that it looked like an orange petticoat, but as they didn't stand up, but knelt or sat, one could not see any petticoat. On the shoulders and sleeves an orange & a crimson flower was embroidered and their obis [*sashes*] were made of dark blue lined with crimson & bound with orange, the whole effect was quite charming.

They had 7 performers on each side, the drums on one side, the string band on the other and they sang songs without melody, on three or four notes in one minor key, which was very ineffective. The dancers were all women dressed in crimson with their hair down in long tails and tied with silver & gold ribbon. They all postured and threw their hands about and were very graceless I thought. Then the curtain fell, or rather was drawn up from a trap door, and when it was withdrawn again two figures were seated in gorgeous raiment with crowns, and brilliant colours everywhere, representing the Mikado & his spouse. After they had danced (the scene representing a garden with quantities of little twinkling lights behind them), a screen was let down before them & they disappeared. Then from the sides, immediately below the band, five maidens rose up in silver crowns and long hair tied up in a tail with silver ribbons, white silk dressing gowns with enormous sleeves and long red silk trousers, so full they looked like skirts, and so long that no feet were seen, but each leg made a train. They had to kick underneath these trousers so that they could move and stamp, which they did occasionally. After more singing the 10 all joined on the stage and danced or postured; five of them were given large branches of cherry blossom, and five had green boughs. At first they all had fans, but they exchanged these for branches and then there was some more singing and dancing, and the curtain fell again and we came away. The band amused me much, the girls had two kinds of drums each and they played these alternately, of course to some system, as they all struck together quite correctly, each drum was rapped alternately. We were presented with tea and packets of sweets at the theatre on taking our places; the sweets were made like roses and leaves and had no good taste, but the little packet was most tastefully tied up.

4ᵀᴴ MAY, SATURDAY.
Yami Hotel, Kioto [*Kyoto*].

We left Osaka this morning in pouring rain and arrived here to find the weather just as bad. This hotel is most beautifully situated on the slope of a hill looking right over Kioto and the surrounding country. After luncheon we strolled round with Col. Collett and looked in at a beautiful Buddhist Temple near the hotel. The rain then began again and we met the Wyllies returning from Nara.

This seems a comfortable hotel, barring the cooking; the only good thing we have had is salmon, which is very plentiful here. The hotel is quite full, some Austrian Royalties being here and crowds of tourists.

We met a Mr De'ath in the railway carriage coming here who told us there had not been such a wet season in Japan since 1868! After which a famine followed and all the weather prophets predict rain at present, and a hot dry summer later on. Mr De'ath has been in Japan 22 years and ought to be an authority.

5ᵀᴴ MAY, SUNDAY.
Yami Hotel, Kioto.

A pouring wet day and very cold. We had our stove lighted and we wrote all day till about 4 o'clock when it cleared for a little, and we walked into the town. We went to see a bronze manufactory where they inlaid the bronze with silver and brass, but the prices were exorbitant. Rain came on again and we returned home in rickshaws.

6ᵀᴴ MAY, MONDAY.
Yami Hotel, Kioto.

This morning we went to the Mikado's Palace and had a lovely day for sight seeing. The painted screens in the Palace are charming and we saw all the private apartments where the paintings are finer than in the public ones. But I think myself I admired the geese in the public rooms more. All round the room panels of geese in various attitudes and groups attract the eye and are most life like. The Mikado's bedroom is beautifully painted, his wardrobe having fish, birds and insects painted on a gold ground. And there was a room for bears, monkeys, squirrels, cherry blossom etc. The audience chamber was very fine with peacocks and masses of gold, deep blue & vivid green; most effective where all the frame work is a reddish brown wood, ceilings, doors etc. the key holes everywhere are exquisite work, the Mikado's crest, the Chrysanthemum, on them all in gold worked into bronze with other ornaments, scrolls & flowers.

The gardens are delicious; we saw one bit which had three bridges very close together; the water, mass of foliage and bright blue sky made a perfect little heaven.

After luncheon we went out to the Mikado's garden, which is in the old part of the town. We passed some magnificent bamboos, formally plantations of bamboos were said to surround the town, which were of immense dimensions, but now a great deal of the ground is cultivated and laid out in gardens. The Mikado's gardens were very pretty, with deep soft moss under the trees, a teahouse looking over some ornamental water and a quantity of tame carp in the water, which we fed. Inside the house were some old kakemonos of celebrated artists, but the subjects were not very interesting. It took us nearly an hour to return from these gardens as on the way we stopped to see a Shinto Temple, and the guide insisted on our admiring some very gaudy crepe pictures in vile colours framed in gilt frames, which had just been presented by the town to the Temple.

We went to the theatre after dinner and saw some more Geishas, it was exactly like the Osaka performance except that they never changed their dresses, and there were more performers. The girl's dresses were a mixture of grey, green and crimson, very pretty indeed. They postured and played with fans and tambourines, and the scenic effect was a background of rolling waves with the rising sun to finish off the performance.

7ᵀᴴ MAY, TUESDAY.
Yami Hotel, Kioto.

We left the hotel at 10 a.m. for the rapids this morning and got back at 5.30 after a most charming day [*the rapids on the Hozu River*].

It was a longish ride in a rickshaw to the rapids, 3 hours I think, but it was great fun going down the rapids & the steering was splendid. The scenery was beautiful, such splendid trees, forests of pine and maple, the woods covered the hills up to the very top and wild cherry, azaleas & wisteria were out in bloom making a wonderful variety of colour. Altogether it was a delicious day and not too hot. We went to a curio shop close to the hotel just before dinner, where they offered us some wonderful rubbish for very large sums.

8ᵀᴴ MAY, WEDNESDAY.
Kioto.

This morning we all went to the Shogun's Palace [*Nijo Castle*], which is well worth seeing. It has the most splendid ceilings inside the Palace, and outside the gateways are magnificent with gilt and bronze. The paintings in the rooms are all very bold, chiefly of animals and very large tree subjects, all on gold grounds. The ceilings are painted and gilded and have lacquer beams with a quantity of gold ornaments. The keyholes & door handles and bosses everywhere are the most beautiful work, gold & bronze. Lions and tigers were represented on the walls; the stateroom had cherry blossom, ducks and geese and flowers in other rooms, and one had a freeze of fans cleverly painted. There were no mats on the floors and the upper part of the staterooms and private room, where the Shogun used to sit, had horrible English carpets instead of the beautiful matting.

Our new guide, "Fugi" arrived today from Yokohama and we are going to dismiss the "Man of War" boy that we got from Mr Playfair at Kobe, he is a capital servant, very willing and active, but does not know sufficient English to be a guide. The weather has been very fine lately, but decidedly cold.

9TH MAY, THURSDAY.
Nara.

We left Kioto this morning at 9.30 a.m., a most beautiful morning. We started in a party of 7 rickshaws for Nara, 2 guides, 2 baggage rickshaws, Mr Moke, J.B. & myself. We came through long streets and a great part of Kioto, and then got into some beautiful country, crossing a ridge of hills where one looked down on a lovely valley, across to some very fine hills from a perfect forest of bamboo.

We got into Nara about 5 o'clock and went at once to see the great Daibutsu, which is the biggest bronze figure in the world [*the Daibutsu or Great Buddha at the Todaiji Temple*]. It is covered in dust and very massive & enormous with one hand raised as if to give a blessing, and the usual calm Buddha expression.

These sorts of figures are so alike, and I have seen so many that I cannot take much interest in them. The figures all round the Temple were very interesting, the Devils especially, for they were wonderful pieces of carving with extraordinary malign countenances. There were also a great many curios exhibited, old lacquer, bronze, arms and furniture, and besides this, a mass of modern rubbish.

We went up to the teahouse after seeing this Temple; it is most charmingly situated and has a lovely view right over the country. The big cryptomerias all round [*Cryptomeria Japonica, a genus of conifer otherwise known as Japanese cedar*], and the Temples with their hundreds of stone lanterns and red gateways, make a very striking picture.

10TH MAY, FRIDAY.
Nara.

This morning after a rainy night, the country was lovelier than ever. We climbed up the hill behind the teahouse after breakfast and saw the country for miles and miles. Then we fed the deer and wandered up to the big Temple, which has the most lovely entrance possible, an avenue of large cryptomerias in a park like country dotted over with deer, and hundreds & hundreds of stone lanterns of all sizes and shapes, with bronze lanterns all hung round the Temple itself; in all, thousands of lanterns. A number of pilgrims in red & white shirts and staffs in their hands came to worship and they threw pence and rice into the Temple, but in this particular Temple I could see no bell or looking glass. We wandered about in the lovely grounds looking at the old white pony, a sacred animal with light blue eyes and pink nose, and execrable temper. And the people every few minutes offering us food to feed deer, monkeys, goats & pony for a few cents; this is a roaring trade.

After luncheon we got Mr Moke to come out and we went to the Temple again and saw the dancing, a very funny sight. Two old priests played, one played the lute and the other played an accompaniment by clapping 2 pieces of wood together and chanting a very monotonous prayer; while two little girls in red skirts and white over dresses covered with a pattern of wisteria blossom, wisteria and roses in their hair, and with shaven eye brows and painted faces, danced a very slow dance. One little girl was bursting with laughter all the time and had to hide her face with her fan. They had a background of geese, painted very well indeed on the wall. The Japanese seem particularly fond of painting geese, and are always successful.

After this very odd religious performance we wandered down to the Pagoda, fed the turtles and gold fish in the village pond and walked home to our teahouse. A glorious sunset lighted up the distant hills and I think altogether Nara is one of the loveliest places I have ever seen. We sleep very well on the floor, but the draughts and general discomforts of teahouse life do not endear it to us, and J.B. has caught a fearful cold.

11TH MAY, SATURDAY.
Yami Hotel.

We left Nara at 10 o'clock this morning and came back by another route getting in very early. The Wyllies are still here and I went off with Major Wyllie to Nishimura, the great embroidery shop where I bought a Fukusa [*a fukusa is a cloth or textile, usually embroidered and used to wrap or conceal a gift; the fukusa was then returned to the giver of the gift*]. They have most beautiful embroideries of all kinds, tapestry of velvet, brocades, crepes etc., and the work is the best in Kioto. We met the Dormers at dinner; Lady D has become very stout and florid.

12TH MAY, SUNDAY.
Kioto.

We went to the embroidery shop "Takashimaya", where we chose three screens. The embroidery here is beautiful. The Austrian Prince had a charming screen made for him. Bamboo worked in blacks and greys on a white ribbed silk ground with a few birds, on the other side, a gold cloudy effect with some white and black reeds.

13TH MAY, MONDAY.
Kioto.

The Wyllies & Colonel Collet left us this morning for Nagoya. We first went to the fish market where we saw heaps of fish; mackerel of kinds – some enormous ones, cuttlefish, crabs, salmon and a sort of confectionery was being made out of mashed up fish & potato.

We passed a mirror shop where we ordered some of the country mirrors, which are now going out of date; we chose some very pretty ones and had a great chat with the woman over them. Then we went to Takashimaya's again and saw some photos of the lovely Kakemonos in the Emperor's Palace, part of the Mikado's Palace which we did not see. These photos used to be sold generally till last December, when an order came out that the sale was prohibited, so we paid the photographer a fruitless visit in attempting to get some.

I forgot to say that we had a charming half hour watching the artists paint with Indian ink at Takashimaya. They did some monkeys & horses in a very bold style, and never seemed to hesitate over any stroke.

We managed to see the Nishi Honganji Temples, where the ancient Ginkgo tree stands that is supposed to vomit water whenever a conflagration takes place, a most useful tree for Kioto, which has been burnt so often. We then looked in upon the grand new Temple which is being built, and where coils of hair rope lay on the platform; human hair rope, the sacrifice of 500 heads of hair! These ropes were to be used in building the sacred edifice. After this we peeped in to see the Daibutsu and rang the biggest bell in Kioto, for which we had to pay a cent for each time we struck the bell. We also saw the Temple that contains 33,333 Buddhas, the 1,000 large idols are supporting the little ones on their head and in their hands; the Temple is very poor now as people only come to stare, without giving.

We passed the "Grave of Ears" called Mimizuka, a trophy of buried ears. Two Generals defeated a Korean army and after cutting off the prisoners' ears, buried them (the ears) in this Tomb.

The Temples are occasionally furnished with tearooms and bathrooms for honoured guests, but they are never used for entertaining now. I have forgotten to mention the earthquake of Sunday morning, it really was quite a shock for a few seconds, and I thought at first somebody was tearing about on the verandahs [sic] and making the house shake.

14TH MAY, TUESDAY.
Yami Hotel, Kioto.

We had a very wet morning and were in despair at the torrents of rain, so we telegraphed to know when the P & O boat Ancona would leave Kobe for Yokohama [SS Ancona, built 1871, 3,081 tons], but as it left at 12 a.m. we had no chance of it.

15TH MAY, WEDNESDAY.
Kioto.

This morning we left at 9.30 to see the procession of Nobles come out of the Gosho Palace to worship at the Kamo Temples [Kamo Shrine on the banks of the Kamo River]. It was an extraordinary sight. They were all dressed in their old Japanese dresses and wore wonderful colours; red, purple, blue green and orange. The attendants all in the most brilliant colours, with false whiskers fastened on each side of the face. The Nobles were all riding small ill-tempered animals in the way of ponies, and had attendants walking by their sides. Occasionally a huge umbrella of artificial flowers was carried, one of camellias and another of some other flower, like a creeper. Then a huge van with lacquered wheels and a great deal of ornament was drawn by one black bullock; inside was the chief priest, but he didn't show. The procession took a long time, passing us very slowly. Little dancing girls from the Temples were among the Nobles and other people; they wore wigs and scarlet dresses with coloured rosettes and were very much painted. After the procession had gone we went on to the Temples, arriving long before the performers arrived. These Shinto Temples are most beautifully situated in groves of big trees, with bamboos near, and the whole place is alive with people. Thousands making holiday under the trees, every party or family occupying a mat to themselves on which they had the inevitable tea tray. The racecourse was lined with people and sweetmeat booths, and the races were to come off after the procession had left.

Inside the Shinto Gates were several buildings; the Governor of Kioto occupied one with the Austrian Prince, a sort of "box at the opera" business. Just opposite was a building with the usual Temple roof raised from the ground about 6 feet, and opposite this was the real Temple. Two large boxes of presents were brought in and placed in front of the Temple. The Chief Nobles were seated on campstools covered with tiger skins; they came in one by one with their followers behind them. It took an immense time to seat them properly and pull out their trains. Then one of them had to go and bless the boxes of presents, and all the re-seating and pulling out of trains took place again. Then in came the Chief swell, dressed in black (the others were in red with purple trains), he mounted up into the building in the centre of the square, and did no end of devotions. Then he came down and some ponies were brought in, led by many men holding brilliant ribbons, and these went round the square several times. Then the Chief swell got up and the band struck up dismal wails and more prayers. Finally 6 Nobles in red crepe over blue satin dresses ascended the steps of the building in a slow majestic manner and danced for about a quarter of an hour, a very tedious but curious dance. Three on one side of the building, & 3 facing them on the other, they had immense red trains and sleeves and did all sorts of gestures with their arms. They all came down at last and we thought it was all over; the Austrian Prince departed from the Governor's box, then we saw that 6 dancers had thrown back their red sleeves and drawn back a good deal of their trains, showing the pale blue satin beneath, and up they all went and began dancing again as blue figures. We came away as there seemed to be no prospect of an end to the entertainment, and we had been sitting on a parapet of a small bridge near the Governor's box for more than an hour and a half. The boots of the Nobles amused me so – huge things of black lacquer, more like small coal scuttles than shoes, they had most curious headdresses and they walked exactly like the Mikado in the play. They all had leaves in their headdresses, and the Chief priest presented the Chief Noble with a great bunch of leaves. The old priest was a perfect picture with a long white beard and a lovely dress of apricot satin; he sat in the sun watching the show, near him were two apple green figures and a group in pale blue.

16TH MAY.
Shinachu Hotel, Nagoya.

We woke up this morning to find it raining hard, and left Kioto in a deluge. Our train left a few minutes before 9 and at 10 a.m. we were leaving Otsu on Lake Biwa in a small steamer. Rain continued nearly all the 4 hours we were crossing the lake, but the latter part was very pretty and it cleared up for a short time as we reached Nagahama about 1.30. There we went to a teahouse for a few minutes and then had three hours of train to Nagoya. For the first time in Japan we met with rudeness, a tiresome boy would come and stare at us on the steamer, took John's chair and was very intrusive. Fugi [*the guide*] got rid of him at last, but again he followed us into the teahouse at Nagahama and John had to turn him out of the room. After this he came to this hotel and sat in the sitting room while we were out strolling in the streets. We think he is half-witted as he persists in talking and asks if we are French.

17TH MAY, FRIDAY.
Shizuoka.

We spent our morning in Nagoya going over the Castle. J.B. had a long interview with the Governor first, who received him in European style and the house was furnished with chairs, carpets and curtains. He was very civil and said he would have showed him everything in Nagoya if he had remained longer in the place. The Castle is a magnificent specimen of an old Castle, being in perfect repair and having massive walls and huge moats, which can be filled with water in one hour. The inside of the Castle is much the same as the Palaces at Kioto; large rooms with paintings of tigers, birds, landscapes and flowers. The ceilings [are] very handsome with a great deal of lacquer and beautiful brass fittings. There is also some very fine carving in some of the rooms, the pheasants stand out wonderfully, cocks, hens & chicks, peonies and other decorations all in one piece of carving. We mounted up the tower and had a very magnificent view of the surrounding country. Then we went to a bronze manufactory where bronze on porcelain is done, very ugly when it is done and only, I am sure made for the European market; the china was a rough sort and rather pretty, I bought a small teapot as a specimen.

At the hotel we met the Australian traveller who travelled from Otsu with us, and who remarked that he saw we were "'ard at it" when we offered him some luncheon on board the steamer!

We didn't get to Shizuoka till 7.30 and then it was pouring with rain. We passed through some most lovely country, wooded mountains, lakes & bays and the most wonderful cultivation everywhere. Snug villages with the most charming neat appearance, yew hedges and lovely azaleas & wisteria everywhere.

We walked to our hotel and found our host, the maids and the waiter all in a wild state of excitement over 99 newly arrived travellers! This hotel (Teitoku) [*sic*] is very nice and clean and has only just been started; we had any amount of bedrooms at our disposal, and a dining room to ourselves. Our dinner was really not bad; soup, fish, game and a very good beefsteak – the fish was fried lobster! The waiter, a very active little man was tattooed in a striking manner, he showed J.B. all the beauties of his decoration, but I saw his back, which was a mass of flowers and figures etc. really a work of art. It cost him 15 dollars and was done at Tokio [*Tokyo*].

18TH MAY, SATURDAY.
Miyanoshita.

We had our first view of the great Fujiyama [*Mount Fuji*] this morning from the balcony of the Teitoku hotel, Shizuoka, it was a splendid morning and we saw the mountain beautifully. Clouds covered the top, but later on they went off and we saw the mountain at its best. We left at 10.40 and got to the end of our railway journey at 3 o'clock. We had an hour and a half of train travelling and then a 3 mile walk, which took me 90 minutes to walk!

20TH MAY, MONDAY.
Miyanoshita.

We went down to a village below Miyanoshita, the prettiest little place possible with waterfalls and cascades all round it. The views from all points this afternoon were most beautiful. We finished by going to see the Elephant tree, a tree trained in that shape in a very clever manner.

21ST MAY, TUESDAY.
Miyanoshita.

This morning was perfectly lovely, the Huttons, Mr Hirst & ourselves started at 9.30 for Hakone. The Libertys from

Regent St. started about the same time and we met Mr Liberty in rather a distressed condition half way up [*Arthur Lasenby Liberty, 1843–1917, founder of Liberty Regent Street, London, 1875*], coat off and pocket handkerchief used as a mop very frequently – we didn't see him again. It was a very steep climb for about 3 ½ hours.

We passed through Ashinoyu where we looked at the sulphur baths; the bathing establishment was kept beautifully clean, like everything else in Japan.

The Twin Mountains were passed on our left, and the "Blood Pond", where some furious battle was fought, on our right. There is a monument here to the general, whoever he may have been, in the shape of a Buddha, carved into the rock. We lunched in a teahouse situated on the shores of the lake; the Emperor has a summer Palace just above it. About 2 o'clock we took boats across the lake and on landing at the other end, we found that we had about 7 miles to go to reach Miyanoshita, crossing the sulphur mountain.

We had a very slippery walk, the sulphur springs bursting through the ground on all sides of the path, and the smell was very strong. There is a crater some little distance from the path, but as several people lost their lives there a few years ago, one is not allowed to go and see it; and I doubt if one could very well, as the ground is so thinly caked over, the hot sulphur coming out from every crack. We had a very pretty walk through woods in which wild pear, azaleas, and other trees were covered with blossom, and got to Miyanoshita before 6 o'clock, the whole expedition having been most successful. I forgot to say that before we got to the sulphur mountain we passed through a village where there were sulphur springs & baths, and the place was full of individuals & sick people suffering from skin diseases and bad eyes. They were all hard at bathing, men and women tubbing together and the male population walking about from one bath to another, or house to house perfectly naked. Near this village there is an immense quantity of tall, white, reed like grass, which is used for thatching and Fugi told me it was very valuable property, as 10 shillings is given for as much as one man can carry.

22ND MAY
The Club Hotel, Yokohama.

We left Miyanoshita at 2 o'clock and had a very comfortable journey here, reaching this soon after 6 o'clock. This hotel is being painted and is otherwise not comfortable. We had two rather dreadful people to dine at our table for dinner, which was not nice and we mean to move into the Grand tomorrow. Mr and Mrs Hartland were very kind and Mr H. at once took John to the Club and made him an Hon. member.

25TH MAY, SATURDAY.
Grand Hotel, Yokohama.

J.B., Mr Moke and I left this hotel at 9 a.m. and did the Kamakura Daibutsu and Enoshima trip [*the Great Buddha in Kamakura and Enoshima Island*].

We had a most lovely day and enjoyed ourselves immensely. We admired the Shinto Temple at Kamakura very much and had a good look at all the curios there; then enjoyed our luncheon at the foot of the hill. The Daibutsu is far more imposing than the Nara one being in the open air; and it is beautifully situated with a fine garden all round. We got inside the Daibutsu and found it terribly hot.

Enoshima is a charming place, we enjoyed it so much; the beauty of the place is very great and one looks over a lovely bay from a dear little teahouse on the top of the hill, where we got some very good European tea. We lounged there some time, then went down & up many stairs – finally down a great many to the caves, which were worth seeing. The divers too were amusing; they brought up the most curious shells from the depths.

The evening was exquisite, Enoshima is full of little shops & stalls crammed with sponges and shells and seaweeds. The village goes up a steep hill and on each side are shops full of sea curiosities, with many cheerful ladies calling on one to buy. I bargained at the teahouse for a tea tray and three cups, which I carried off as a souvenir of Enoshima. We caught the 7 o'clock train at Fujisawa.

On the sands we watched the fishermen emptying their nets, which were full of odd fish, sea toads and queer little things; we passed a boy with a bucketful of still more curious fish, which a gentleman had caught with a rod from the rocks.

26TH MAY, SUNDAY.
Grand Hotel.

J.B. and I went to Tokio [*Tokyo*] this morning at 12 by train. We saw the most elaborate Shinto Temples I have yet seen; their decorations are wonderful, gold lacquer, red lacquer, carvings and paintings, everything that could be imagined in the way of gorgeous colouring. We also saw the graves of the forty-seven Ronin; the Shengakuji Temple is near these graves, which are very interesting. These forty-seven brave men lost their lives after having avenged the death of their lord; they were allowed to perform hari-kari, which was considered a very honourable death. The well is shown where they washed the head of their victim – the man who had caused the death of their lord. They seem to have washed the head then said some prayers in the adjoining Temple, then sent the head to the murdered man's relations – so they showed much consideration to everybody!

27ᵀᴴ MAY, MONDAY.
Grand Hotel, Yokohama.

We started off to the fish market immediately after breakfast where we saw some monster mackerel and all sorts of curious fish; frogs, sea slugs, cuttlefish, shell fish of all kinds and many horrible looking things that Fugi said were excellent eating. Then we ordered John's smoking coat at Shima's.

I returned to the hotel to get my cards etc. and Mrs Hutton & I caught the 12 o'clock train to Tokio [sic]. We went to the High School where we found Miss Parker in a sort of student's gown and rather dishevelled, looking pale and flabby. She seemed to dislike Japan immensely and gave one a very unfavourable account of the Japanese want of principle & morals. The house is a very large Japanese house, very cool in summer but terribly cold in the winter. The girls in the school were very young, about 9 to 13 as a rule. The chief promoter of the school seemed to be Count Ito whose daughter was there, and one of the Imperial Princesses. The princess's room was full of dolls, Japanese and European; the favourite was a French one. She had photos of all the Jap Royalties in her room and knick-knacks of no value. The working class was going on and there were some girls and ladies doing embroidery etc. The cooking classes are the favourite ones and there is a special room for cookery. We called on Mrs Fraser who told me that the Empress of Japan was very attractive, a little tiny creature, but full of dignity and very well dressed in European style. The new Palace is said to be beautiful & full of lovely things.

30ᵀᴴ MAY, THURSDAY.

This morning J.B. and I went over to Tokio and having dropped our luggage at the hotel, went straight to Ueno. There are some beautiful grounds at Ueno; the Daibutsu is the third biggest in Japan. We also saw the zoo, I pitied the poor deer having to live in such damp dirty places and I didn't think any of the animals were well cared for. At Asakusa there is a very popular Temple containing a sacred image that effects great cures when touched. One old woman was rubbing the leg of the image, and her own afterwards, with great vigour. All the features of the image are rubbed away and the body quite smooth & greasy. There is a large fair round this Temple and some very curious figures made by a man in the neighbourhood, 500 figures all with different expressions and attitudes, really very clever.

At the hotel we dressed and went off to the Legation for dinner; Mr Fraser was shy but pleasant and Mrs Fraser very nice indeed, she made a charming hostess, had a very pretty table and the dinner was excellent. [*Hugh Fraser, 1837–1894, was head of the British Legation in Tokyo from 1888 till his sudden death in 1894. His wife, Mary Crawford Fraser, 1851–1922, was American and the author of several books, including* Palladia *in 1896,* The Looms of Time *in 1898 and* The Stolen Emperor *in 1904. Fraser is buried at Aoyama in Tokyo.*]

1ST JUNE, SATURDAY.
Gd. Hotel, Yokohama.

John and I had the most uncomfortable headaches today. He really was quite ill, could remember no names and seemed in quite a dream. We can only imagine that we were poisoned, for it looked just as if J.B. had been drugged. He did not quite recover himself till the evening.

4TH JUNE, TUESDAY.
Nikko.

We left Yokohama at 10.30 and changed our carriages twice on the railway. A good-natured Englishman, who was taking care of a young Japanese lady, helped us with useful information and we accomplished our journey most successfully without a guide. It was a lovely day till quite late when it clouded over and we had small showers. We got into rickshaws at Utsunomiya and arrived here at 8.30 p.m. We only stopped at two teahouses on the way, just to rest the coolies.

5TH JUNE, WEDNESDAY.
Nikko.

A perfectly lovely morning with brilliant sunshine; we spent the morning in the Temples, which are quite indescribably beautiful. The quantity of lovely ornamentation and the most beautiful trees to throw them out, make such a perfect scene of beauty that one does not wonder at Nikko being described as one of the sights of the world. The carvings, bronze lanterns, gold lacquer, painted ceilings and beautiful buildings are all exquisite.

We walked down to see the famous red lacquered bridge, which is only painted apparently, but the effect is very good next to the mass of green everywhere. After a lovely stroll, it being a charming evening, we returned to the hotel very much in love with Nikko. It is quite useless to describe, or rather attempt to describe all the wonders of the Temples. The carvings of birds alone deserve volumes of description; the paintings of 32 phoenixes, all different in position and colouring, fill me with admiration.

8TH JUNE, SATURDAY.
Nikko.

I spent all the morning sitting near the entrance of the big Temple and Pagoda sketching; it was so very hot. J.B. came and helped me and got rid of a large and embarrassing audience, one man rather the worse for Saki, was quite troublesome.

10th JUNE, MONDAY.
Nikko.

Today we accomplished our visit to Chuzenji; we have had the most beautiful day possible for the excursion. Mr Moke and Capt. Steele joined us and J.B. walked with them all day. I had a chair, but the road was so steep I walked a good deal too. We passed several very fine waterfalls, but the great one was within half a mile of Chuzenji, the "Kegon no Taki", this was a splendid fall of water 350ft high. We stopped at several pretty teahouses on the road, but I enjoyed the torrents most of all, beautiful foaming water rushing down over rocks, and wishing pools bridged over by little rustic bridges – poles of wood with twigs & branches laid across. The water was lovely with its blue green depths, and the mountains were covered with trees, azaleas of several colours, white, scarlet, pink and a sort of mauve. We had some fresh trout, taken out of the lake alive, killed and cooked in little more than a quarter of an hour. The teahouse charged exorbitantly which enraged Mr Moke and Capt. Steele, but apparently the extra charge was made to cover the guide's usual fee, Mr Moke's tutor was offered a dollar by the teahouse people, they mistook him for a guide.

15th JUNE, SATURDAY.
Gd. Hotel.

We left the English Hatoba [*wharf or quay*] at 10.30 a.m. with the Wyllies and our steam launch took an hour & a half reaching Yokosuka. Then we had a very steep ride and walk up to William Adams's tomb, where there is a perfectly beautiful view. [*William Adams, 1564–1620, English sailor and navigator, the first Briton to reach Japan. Known in Japan as Miura Anjin, he is often referred to as the first foreign samurai.*]

We returned to Yokosuka and took a sampan and had a delightful sail to Kanazawa, and from there we had rickshaws to Yokohama. This was a long ride as we had to mount up at Nokendo; Kanazawa is really 10 miles from Yokohama and we did not get back till nearly 7 o'clock.

18TH JUNE, TUESDAY
Gd. Hotel.

Waterloo Day. The Wyllies dined with us and we drank good luck to our country in silence, for fear of offending the foreigners! The heat is exhausting; one is always in a vapour bath.

19TH JUNE, WEDNESDAY.
Gd. Hotel.

We had a most tremendous day in Tokio today; we must have gone 20 miles in rickshaws, which ended with another immense ride to the Legation; Mrs Fraser was very charming and her house delicious. We met Major Wyllie there and we all headed back by the 5 o'clock train. Katie [*Mrs Wyllie*] came on with him afterwards to see Fujiyama again but it was too cloudy.

20TH JUNE, THURSDAY.
Gd. Hotel.

The Wyllies, John and I left Yokohama at 8.45 in the morning and were met by the Japanese officer who was travelling in India two years ago, at Shimbashi Station, Tokio. He marched us all into the waiting room and there introduced us to his friends, an A.D.C. and a gentleman in a tall hat and frock coat, who was some relation. We then were taken in three carriages to the barracks. John, Major W. with the A.D.C. and I with the Tall Hat. The heat was intense and we drove a very long way. At the barracks we were introduced to countless officers and given coffee and cake. Then we saw the

Regt. paraded and some soldiers doing gymnastics, then all the barracks, the cook-room and the soldiers' dinners. After all this we drove off to the Sandhurst of Tokio. There we saw all the young soldiers, the hospital and the lecture rooms etc., the riding school and some young soldiers who rode up and down hill with musket and sword without stirrups. They jumped fences and rushed up and down hill, many came off, but the horses seemed none the worse for the violent exercise, or the young men. On our way to the arsenal gardens the heat was intense and the dust fearful; my friend (tall hat) and I watched a man's hat carried off into a moat, whereupon he remarked, "t'is an ill wind that blows nobody not any good!". The arsenal gardens were lovely and there was a charming house in the grounds where we had luncheon. Several more officers joined us and we were introduced to heaps of people and had to drink tea, coffee or champagne. The irises in the garden were a lovely sight, dark blue, purple & white. We ladies rested while the others went to see the Arsenal. On the luncheon table were large baskets of flowers, which were presented to us on leaving. Altogether we spent a most interesting but fatiguing day.

21ST JUNE, FRIDAY.
Gd. Hotel.

Packed all morning and went for a lovely drive. The Gaelic has not yet come in and we hope not to start very early on Sunday after all.

22ND JUNE, SATURDAY.
Gd. Hotel.

We spent all morning packing after running round the shops paying bills and getting our last oddments. The weather changed very much and became quite cold before evening.

Agustuma [sic] our boy, was very sad at parting with us, or rather at hearing he would have to part with us tomorrow, he burst into tears to my great discomfort.

We took a stroll in the evening and then had the usual dance after dinner. Two ladies appeared in low evening gowns expecting a great dance, I am afraid they were a good deal disappointed.

23ʳᴰ JUNE, SUNDAY.
Gd. Hotel.

The Gaelic only came in this morning so we shall not leave now till tomorrow morning. There have been a good many gales about; a typhoon at Kobe, rough weather everywhere and the weather is much colder.

Chapter XIII

Return to England via the USA and Canada

30ᵀᴴ JUNE 1889 (EXTRA DAY).
The Gaelic [*RMS Gaelic, built 1885, 4,206 tons*].

We left Yokohama on the morning of 24th, Monday. It was a pouring wet day; the rain coming down in sheets and of course our last hope of seeing Fujiyama again from the harbour was a vain one.

Monday & Tuesday were wretched wet days; I spent most of them in my berth feeling wretchedly ill and seasick. We have a cabin just opposite the Wyllies, a very good one; the ship is wonderfully steady and free from bad smells, altogether very comfortable with electric light everywhere. The sea has been so calm too and we have been very fortunate, but the cold is great, the day before yesterday being 38°. Today is a sort of "no day"; yesterday, Sunday was the real 30th of June but today has to be called the 30th to make up for Greenwich time.

The food on board is very American and consequently not at all to my taste. Pies are the chief thing and all sorts of messes of green corn and clam soup.

The O'Connors are on board and we see a great deal of them; the rest of the passengers are mostly American, Australians, Germans and American missionaries and their families. The cold has been too much for Major Wyllie; he has caught a bad cold and looks really ill. We shall all be very glad to arrive at Frisco on the 8th July.

My last walk in Yokohama was with Mrs O'Connor; we went on the Bluff and then through the Cemetery, which was beautifully kept and full of lovely flowers. Lovely wreaths and bouquets were placed on nearly all the graves.

2ND JULY, TUESDAY.
The Gaelic.

We are having the calmest seas possible and now the thermometer is 46° so it is not so cold on deck. We have only seen a few birds and have not passed another living thing since we left Yokohama on 24th June.

One of the passengers on board was talking to John about his early days in Australia; J.B. asked him if they had had much trouble with the natives in those days, to which he replied, "indeed we'd not sir, they came into our camp and we gave them tobacco, whisky and brandy and they became quite civilised."

8TH JULY, MONDAY.
Occidental Hotel, San Francisco [*Occidental Hotel on the corner of Bush Street and Montgomery Street San, Francisco, destroyed after the earthquake of 1906*].

We arrived here this morning at an early hour; the last two days on board ship were very disagreeable, rough stormy weather. The 4th July was duly kept by the Americans, the saloon covered with flags etc., and the health of America proposed by the Captain. The Doctor answered it in a ridiculous speech in which he said America was now "a big girl" and in time he hoped would develop into a "noble woman, that best of God's creations." After dinner the children asked for games and many of the men enjoyed musical chairs as much as the children. The widow, Mrs McLeod Smith was particularly lively.

This morning we were routed up very early on account of the health officer and had a very tiresome time, the morning so wet, cold and miserable. The Custom House gave us no trouble, our boxes being passed through very quickly.

San Francisco is a large commercial town, very busy & noisy with distracting trams everywhere.

We have very nice rooms here and are likely to be most comfortable; the Proprietor, or rather Manager of the Hotel sent us some lovely flowers and fruit, peaches, figs & apricots; we are thankful for a fire in our sitting room.

9TH JULY.
Occidental Hotel, San Francisco.

I stayed at home all morning. Last night after dinner we went over to the Palace Hotel with the O'Connors and heard a very good band, which plays every Monday evening in the Palace courtyard [*the Palace Hotel on the corner of Market Street and New Montgomery Street, San Francisco, demolished after the earthquake of 1906*].

This afternoon we all went out to see the Golden Gates and the Harbour and the Sea lions. The Sea lions were very curious great big creatures, massed on some rocks, all roaring continuously and smelling extremely strong. One enormous fellow was perched on the top of the rock and seemed to lord it over all the others. We had a long journey to & fro in railway cars & trams and the day was very raw with cold with a misty rain at intervals. We saw a good deal of the town though and passed a number of big houses with pretty gardens looking over the bay. The hills of S. Francisco are wonderful; everything is up one hill, down another, no two yards on the flat.

We have arranged to go to the Yosemite Valley tomorrow evening.

10TH JULY.

Occidental Hotel, S. Francisco.

This morning we went to see the Fire Brigade drill at 12 o'clock. It was the most rapid thing I ever saw and took exactly 7 seconds. The horses ran into their harness, which was suspended from above; the men slid down poles from a good height and fire engine, horses and men were ready to drive out of the building in exactly 7 seconds.

We then had to pack and make ready for our Yosemite journey, as we had to leave by 7.30 in the evening.

13TH JULY, SATURDAY.

Stoneman House, Yosemite [*Stoneman House Hotel, Yosemite, built 1886/7, destroyed by fire 1896*].

We left San Francisco on Wednesday night (July 10th) crossing the harbour in a huge ferry steamer. Then getting into a Pullman car where we passed the night. Katie [*Mrs Wyllie*] and I had a parlour car to our own selves, so we undressed and had as good a night as we possibly could, but the jolting was terrible. In one frightful jolt the coupling broke so that the jars were stupendous ever after. We arrived at Raymond Station at 6.30 a.m. and had breakfast. Our breakfast cost us 2 dollars each, 9 shillings for some coffee, bread and butter.

We started at about 8 o'clock in a wagonette, J.B. & Major Wyllie in front, Katie, Col. Collett & I behind. The vehicle was too small for such a large party, the dust and heat very great and we were all dreadfully tired & dirty before we arrived at our luncheon place at 12.30. Grant Springs was a charming little hotel, very clean and comfortable. An old couple waited on us and gave us a capital luncheon; good soup, vegetables, meat and such excellent raspberries and ice cream. A large party conducted by Cook arrived a few minutes after us, mostly women of a very noisy kind. They swanned into the ladies' dressing room where we were trying to wash ourselves and get a little of the dust off our dress; they showed no shyness in making themselves thoroughly comfortable.

We had a still hotter drive after luncheon, even more dusty and fatiguing, arriving at Wawona quite deadbeat. The hotel was so full we could only get the rooms occupied by the landlord and his wife; all their clothes, boxes, boots, brushes etc., left in the rooms and everything intensely uncomfortable. We went to bed weary and disgruntled. A fiddle was played after dinner and the Cooks etc., danced about on the verandahs [sic]; I fell asleep in spite of the noise.

We left Wawona next morning at 7 a.m. and had a better conveyance (one of the big cars), with a delicious cool breeze and a great deal of shade all the way. The drive was really charming, the views splendid and we had far less dust. Behind us, three very talkative men sat; a Mr Anderson from Mysore, an old Yankee and a terrible man from Birmingham of the name of Yates. They were making notes, writing diaries, relating personal adventures and introducing politics all the time; their views rang in our ears for hours afterwards. We stopped at various points of view to see the famous mountains, the Three Brothers, the Cathedral Spires, El Capitan and Sentinel Rock and the waterfalls, the Bridal Veil and the

Yosemite Falls, but the falls were not at their best on account of the dry weather. We stopped at Inspiration Point and had a very fine view, we all felt quite rewarded for our fatigues. The driving on the Yosemite road is first rate; the road though good, being narrow, with the sharpest turns and up and down hill to any extent. The drivers manage their teams splendidly, having often to pass other cars on the road.

We got into this Hotel about one o'clock and found everything very comfortable; the Hotel has good bathrooms and keeps a very fair table, all the waiters etc., are very civil, and we have a very decent room. We did nothing but sit in the verandah [sic] & sketch yesterday afternoon, and after dinner we walked down past the bridge and along the river Merced to watch the sunset effect on the mountains. It was so beautiful, the rocks turned a lovely pale pink and all the shadows were violet & lilac. Afterwards they looked very lovely by moonlight. Soon after 9 o'clock we all thankfully went to bed.

We got up at 6 a.m. this morning to see the sun rise on the Mirror Lake; we had a very early breakfast and started at 7 a.m. After a short drive we found ourselves at the lake, which is really only a good large pond or pool. The mountains are reflected in it beautifully, and at this early hour the water is perfectly still and quiet so that it earns its name of Mirror very truly. On our return, one of the party of ladies who were riding was thrown on her head & dreadfully frightened. The ponies seemed very quiet, but the saddle turned round so that the girl could not help herself. We took her into our carriage and she was found to be more frightened than hurt.

14TH JULY, SUNDAY.
Stoneman House, Yosemite Valley.

We had a very long drive down the valley yesterday afternoon; we went to the Yosemite waterfall and then on to El

Capitan and the "Bridal Veil" fall etc., ending up in an Indian camp. The dust was very great, but otherwise one enjoyed the drive very much as most of it was in the shade. I saw one of the red headed woodpeckers on a tree and some large squirrels, and the most beautiful butterflies. The rainbow on the Bridal Veil Fall was very beautiful.

Our great disappointment was the Indian camp; three or four Indians in Billycock hats with a dirty looking woman in a dirty dress sitting over a fire eating a pie, or anyhow their dinner – no scalps about and a little hut held all the family.

Today we went up to the Vernal Fall and the Nevada Falls. We started at 7.30 a.m., did half a mile in a car, then rode mules for about 1 ½ miles and then walked; this was as far as the Vernal Fall, which is really a very splendid one. We walked up to the top and then got on our mules again till we reached the foot of the Nevada, here we had to dismount again and cross over a horrid little shaky plank bridge. Mrs Wyllie and I were rather done, and sat on a log while the others, J.B., Col. Collett & Major Wyllie went right up under the fall. We had to walk down again to the place where we first left our mules and got back to the hotel about 12.30. It was a very beautiful expedition, the gorges were so wild and the iris, or rainbow in the Vernal Fall was lovely.

A poor little boy was lost in the Valley the day before yesterday; he belonged to one of the party of visitors here. They found him yesterday afternoon, he had fallen down a precipice and is so much hurt, poor little fellow, they hardly think he can recover. Our guide was nearly bitten by a rattlesnake this morning.

The thermometer was 88° in the shade of the verandah [sic] to day and tomorrow we are to return to Wawona. The great beauty of the Valley is the shape of the large silver-white rocks, and the firs and cedars throw them out in such relief;

the air is delicious too, but at this time of year it really is too hot to be out except early mornings and evenings.

[*And this comes from a lady who has just spent over three years in Rajasthan.*]

18TH JULY, THURSDAY.
The Golden Eagle Hotel, Sacramento.

We left the Yosemite Valley on Monday morning at 6 a.m. and had a very cool drive, and a very pretty one. The Valley looked most lovely in the early morning, especially from Artist Point. We reached Wawona at 12 o'clock and after luncheon I rested all afternoon, then went for a stroll with Katie. J.B. went out fishing and got a dozen and a half nice trout. He borrowed his fishing tackle from Mr Hill the artist, who has a studio close to the hotel [*Thomas Hill, 1829–1908, artist whose studio was at the Wawona Hotel*].

On Sunday evening J.B. and I sat by the riverbank watching a boy fishing, John took the rod for a few minutes and caught two trout. They are called Rainbow trout I believe and are very pretty; different in colouring from other trout and very tasteless to eat, but this may be from bad cooking.

On Tuesday we went to see the big trees, we left the hotel at ½ past 8 a.m. and had the most beautiful shady drive through the forest. The trees are splendid; we drove through one tree, it is quite impossible to describe the size of these giants. The stems are a beautiful bright golden red, but all of them have been touched by forest fires. They have different names, "the Telescope" being quite hollow; one looks right up through the tree. The big trees are called Sequoias. The trees of Mariposa, which we saw, are the biggest of all; they grow in groups nearly forty miles apart from the first group to the last, and generally in sheltered hollows. Their age is very great, many of them are said to be from three thousand six hundred years to four thousand years old. The Grizzly Giant struck us all as a very splendid tree and the Wawona is the name of the immense tree one drives through. Then there are the Washington, the Ohio, U.S. Grant and many others. The forest is a world of beauty in itself, the bright yellow lichen that grows on the firs and the cedars lights up the darkest bits, and all sorts of flowers and ferns grow. We had to be careful where we trod for rattlesnakes are very common.

After luncheon, Katie and I tried to sketch and returned to the hotel about 5 o'clock having spent a delightful day. In the little cabin there are some specimens of the wood, which we bought, in the shape of paper cutters. The dust was beyond all description, never have we been so dirty.

We left Wawona yesterday at 8 a.m. and lunched again at Grant Springs, waited on by Judge Grant, the wealthy proprietor of the place. The dust and heat in the afternoon were very great, and the car was so full; in the back seat, Colonel Collett had two women, one girl and a baby – and the poor people had to pay 22 dollars for this accommodation! [*The cars that Julia refers to were a type of stagecoach or horse-drawn wagon with four rows of seats, including the driver's, with a roof but no sides; these were drawn by four horses or mules.*]

We reached Raymond at 5 p.m. and had a little wash and some supper before getting into our Pullman. We spent a very quiet and peaceful night and reached Sacramento at 9.30 this morning.

Last night at Berenda, we had a most delightful chat with a Yankee who gave us his experience of Jubilee Day in 1887 in London. His account of their guide in Edinburgh who tried to take them from house to house, and told them the history of everybody who had lived in the houses for the last 1,000 years made us scream!

21ST JULY, SUNDAY.
Tacoma Hotel, Tacoma [*Washington*].

We left Sacramento on Thursday night at 11 o'clock. We went to see the Senate House and the Cathedral there; the former had two rather handsome halls for the meetings of Senators and officials, Upper & Lower Houses of sorts. In the lower hall or vestibule there was rather a fine group in marble; the Queen of Portugal assisting Columbus with means to prosecute his voyage of discovery [*Columbus's last appeal to Queen Isabella by Larkin Goldsmith Mead, 1835–1910*].

We had a very good rest during the night and passed through some very fine mountain scenery on Friday; California is certainly a very fine county.

In Oregon the hills are covered with pine & cedar trees, the valleys full of corn & orchards. The heat was tremendous between 12 & 4 o'clock, the thermometer was 98° but it felt very much hotter. The engine driver very nearly broke our necks & more nearly succeeded in killing the conductor with bad driving, but happily we all escaped alive and reached Portland at 10.45 on Saturday morning. We had to check our luggage through to Tacoma and go across the river on a ferryboat, finding our train on the other side. We passed through beautiful country in Oregon and in Washington Territory; the Columbia is a lovely river and the valley quite delightful, so very fertile with fine trees everywhere; farmhouses here and there and very fine cattle with large stretches of corn land. We had our train put on a ferryboat to cross the river Columbia; it was very cleverly done, the train being made into three sections and so taken over. We didn't get to Tacoma till 7.45 and found the place very full indeed; no place to be had in this hotel so we had to pass the night in a sort of public house where there was neither food or baths to be had. We really slept well and came over here to breakfast; none of us got a bath of course.

There is a thick white fog so that we cannot see Mt. Tacoma [*Mount Rainier*] and the town is most miserable looking. No one ever attends to you in these hotels Far West, J.B. had to fetch hot water for me, carry down the bags and go out to have his shoes blacked.

We had a much cooler day yesterday and though it is close and stuffy here, it is not nearly so hot as in California.

23RD JULY, TUESDAY.
Driard House, Victoria, Vancouver.

We arrived here yesterday at 5.30 p.m. after 10 hours of disagreeable shaking in a steamer. The last night in Tacoma was a very tiresome one; a fire broke out in the town during the night near the hotel and at 2 o'clock it was raging within one street of us so that our rooms were lighted up with the red glare. We all got up and dressed ready to fly if necessary but fortunately the firemen got the fire under, and the hotel was not touched. About twenty men were on the roof though, throwing off cinders, sleep was impossible & at 6.15 we had to make a start for the steamer.

26TH JULY.
Driard House, Victoria.

Yesterday was John's 49th Birthday. We have parted with the Wyllies; they left us on the night of the 24th for their journey towards Montreal, Major Wyllie looking very seedy alas. We took two charming drives with them; the first day going to Esquimalt [*on the southern tip of Vancouver Island*], where there is a large dry-dock and a good harbour. There were very few ships in, I think only two men of war – an American and an English one.

We drove next day to the Beacon Hill Park where on a clear day there is a good view of the Olympian Mountains, but we only saw the outline of them, there being a haze over the sea and of course Mt. Baker has been invisible all the time we've been here.

The houses and gardens here are so pretty, clean and bright and the climate continues to be perfect. Yesterday we went out shopping and were not tempted by the Indian curios! After luncheon we went to the Gorge with the O'Connors, J.B. & Mr O'Connor rowing. I made a small sketch from the grounds of a public house and we enjoyed ourselves immensely.

After dinner we went to the play and saw a ridiculous piece called "the Twelve Temptations" which, if it had been better would not have amused us half so much, but we failed to discover what the 12 temptations were – or even one of them! The clowns were really very good indeed.

27TH JULY, SATURDAY.
Driard House, Victoria.

This morning we went by train to the Shawnigan Lake; it is a most beautiful place and the scenery all along the line is lovely. We left at 8.30 and reached Shawnigan in about an hour & a half. The O'Connors were with us and we all went across the lake and sat on a fallen tree in the beautiful pinewoods till luncheon time. I made a little sketch there and we had an excellent plain luncheon in the little Inn, the old landlord was a delightful fellow.

After luncheon we all went up to the huge barn, which is the dancing hall of the Victorians on occasions; J.B. fell asleep in some hay and we had some tea before starting homewards by the 5.30 train. The scenery was even lovelier than in the morning; great purple shadows thrown by the mountains over the water. The railway passes over some trestle bridges, which look very insecure and one looks down an immense height from these bridges. The wild flowers and ferns were very pretty; we also saw some grouse or partridges in several places. J.B. made the acquaintance of an old gentleman who had passed 32 years in this place and was invited to luncheon on Sunday.

28ᵀᴴ JULY, SUNDAY.
Driard House.

J.B. and I went to the Cathedral this morning; the congregation was very much composed of women and children. J.B. spent a very pleasant afternoon with old Mr Crease and came home with lovely flowers and in the evening a box of fruit was sent to us for our journey.

29ᵀᴴ JULY, MONDAY.
Driard House.

We have been packing all this afternoon and leave tonight for Vancouver.

I took a walk with the O'Connors yesterday afternoon and in the evening when J.B. and I strolled out the mountains were quite clear, with patches of snow on them. This morning Mrs O'Connor and I did some shopping and now our pleasant week in Victoria is over.

The Parisian & another are the only good boats that leave Quebec for England and our plans are still uncertain.

2ᴺᴰ AUGUST 1889, FRIDAY.
Banff Hotel, Alberta.

We left Victoria on Monday night and had a good shaking all night in a horrible little steamer, the dirtiest boat John said he had ever seen. Our boat was late in arriving at Vancouver but we drove up to a very comfortable hotel, the C.P. Hotel [*Canadian Pacific Railway*]. We left at one o'clock and had the parlour car to travel in so we were very comfortable. We dined at North Bend [*Fraser Canyon, British Columbia*] where the waiters were insufficient for the company but the food was good. After North Bend we saw a magnificent forest fire, the trees like pillars of fire against the sky. Unfortunately the forest fires are so plentiful that the whole country is covered with smoke and mist and one sees little of the beautiful scenery.

We arrived at Glacier House at 2 o'clock on Wednesday 31st [*a CPR hotel built in 1886 near the Illecillewaet Glacier, then known as the Great Glacier*], the hotel is on the railway. The glacier is a very fine sight from the hotel; we were charmed by the cleanliness and comfort of the hotel and we enjoyed our stay there very much. J.B. bought the skeleton of a mountain goat for the British Museum; shooting and fishing are to be had from Glacier House.

We walked up to the Glacier on Wednesday afternoon, it was a lovely walk; there were many artists taking the Glacier. On Thursday morning I tried to sketch, but the blue flies devoured one.

We left at 2.30 on Thursday afternoon and arrived here at 12 o'clock; the train was late rather, but as an omnibus meets the trains we soon found ourselves in the hotel. This morning we tried a walk, but the heat and the mosquitos are bad and the mist prevents one seeing or enjoying the very lovely scenery. The hotel is delightfully placed and the country round is very beautiful but owing to the forest fires, there is really nothing but smoke & fog everywhere. There is a fine lake about 9 miles off and an excursion to be made up the river for 8 miles, but today it is useless to attempt either.

8TH AUGUST, THURSDAY.
Queen's Hotel, Toronto.

We arrived here very early this morning after 5 nights & 4 days in the train, we left Banff on Saturday night at 12 o'clock.

We spent our second day at Banff very pleasantly going up the creek and the Bow River in a little steam launch. The river is very pretty indeed, but we never saw the mountains properly as the fog and smoke never cleared off. We had the band of the Mounted Police at the Hotel one evening, the men were very fine strong looking fellows & they played very well.

We were fortunate in getting the parlour car reserved all the way from Banff to North Bay [*North Bay, Lake Nipissing, Ontario*] where we changed trains last evening at 6.30 p.m. We had dining cars on the train, which were very good.

A very nice old lady was travelling with us, Mrs Keefer from Rockcliffe, Ottawa; she told us a great deal about Canada, having lived in the country all her life, and her father before her.

Lord Stanley seems to have made a great sensation by allowing himself to be tossed in a blanket at the Ice Carnival at Montreal last winter and from all accounts is too anxious to be popular at the risk of being undignified. When he first gave a dinner at Govt. House and all the ladies rose when he came in, he begged them to be seated saying, "he was not accustomed to that sort of thing".

[*Frederick Arthur Stanley, Lord Stanley of Preston, 1841–1908, later 16th Earl of Derby KG GCB CCVO PC, Governor-General of Canada, 1888–1893, was in fact a very popular governor-general of Canada. He saw his first game of ice hockey at Montreal's Winter Carnival in 1889. Lord Stanley donated the Stanley Cup, the oldest professional sports trophy in North America (icehockey.fandom.com, hhof.com).*]

The only large place we stopped in was Winnipeg, which is a flourishing city; as the train stopped there for an hour, we took a carriage and drove round the place. There was one very wide handsome street full of shops and some very pretty wooden houses with bright flower gardens, and an air of well to do inhabitants.

We saw a good many Indians at Medicine Hat [*Medicine Hat, Alberta*], all painted and wrapped up in blankets, and some women with papooses; they offered us buffalo horns for sale but we did not buy any. The heaps of buffalo bones all along the line in the prairie districts show what a tremendous slaughter of the animals took place a few years ago, now there are none.

We passed through nothing but prairies all Sunday, but I never saw any little prairie dogs. Tuesday we came into more interesting country and on leaving Port Arthur [*Port Arthur, now Thunder Bay, Lake Superior, Ontario*] the Lake District was very beautiful. Lake Superior was the first, but all Wednesday we passed lakes and fine scenery and lovely trout rivers. We saw Jackfish Bay by moonlight and it was particularly beautiful [*Jackfish Bay, Lake Superior, was abandoned in the early 1960s and is now a ghost town*].

The weather has been very pleasant, the evenings cool and the mornings most delightfully fresh. We hear the Wyllies have gone on to Niagara.

9TH AUGUST, FRIDAY.
Queen's Hotel, Toronto.

Yesterday John was very seedy with a regular attack of Indian fever. We took two walks about Toronto but did nothing beyond that, as he really was not up to it. Today the Wyllies and Col. Collett turned up to luncheon and went on by the 2 o'clock steamer to Montreal; Major Wyllie is looking so much better. John is not well today & after the Wyllies had gone we went for a drive and I am afraid stayed out a little too long. We visited the Museum where there are some most interesting old prints of Canada, and then we drove all over Toronto. It is a charming city, the houses are so pretty and the Park and Public gardens very pretty. All the churches and

Colleges etc. are handsome and the streets have trees on each side, at least the streets of private residences; we thought it all very attractive.

We visited the Cook's agent and have engaged our berths on the "Parisian" on the 29th of this month. We have decided to go to Niagara tomorrow & stay till Tuesday, Monday being a civic holiday here.

11TH AUGUST, SUNDAY.
Clifton House, Niagara.

We left Toronto at 2 o'clock yesterday afternoon and had the rather amusing experience of a Saturday excursion party in the steamer. I never saw so many extraordinary get ups in my life before; the boat was crammed with women, babies & children making the "all round trip". Babies in arms, babies in buggies, children eating sweets and everybody moving restlessly about eating horrible compounds of stickiness. The young women were dressed in the brightest colours and wore the strangest headgear, bandsmen's caps, Duchess of Devonshire hats, smoking caps, sailors' hats, bonnets and stalking caps, with every variety of dress.

When we got to Niagara we found that our train did not start for an hour and a half, so we took a drive for an hour and enjoyed the beautiful country, with splendid orchards and very pretty cottages and flower gardens very much. Then we got the train and got up to the falls about 6.30. We saw the falls from the train, but directly we arrived at this hotel, we were opposite to them. They are very grand and beautiful and quite exceed the great expectations that I had. The falls by moonlight were beautiful and we could not resist getting up several times during the night to look at them.

This morning after breakfast we took a carriage and drove first to the rapids on the Canadian side where poor Captain

Webb was killed. We then drove over to the American side and saw the splendid whirlpool at the end of the rapids, where the river makes a great bend and then goes racing on.

[Captain Matthew Webb, 1848–1883, was a merchant navy captain and the first man to swim unaided across the English Channel on 24th August 1875. On 24th July 1883, he was drowned during his attempt to be the first person to swim through the Niagara River Whirlpool rapids. It is uncertain whether he made it across the rapids before he drowned or whether he was drowned in the rapids. His body was recovered four days later at Queenston. Captain Webb is buried at Oakwood Cemetery, Niagara Falls.]

We visited all the most beautiful places, Goat Island, The Three Sisters and the Horseshoe Fall from the American side and spent more than three hours in seeing all we could; then we drove home over the new suspension bridge.

At 5 o'clock we started for a walk and walked up the Park to the Horseshoe Fall where one can have a most beautiful view of the falls; the rainbows were splendid and the day has been simply perfect in every way.

We walked on nearly to the Dufferin Islands; the rapids above the falls are even grander than those below, they are such a mass of dancing water. With the sun on the water and all the beautiful trees and turf, one feels that the whole thing is beautiful beyond description, and words seem very poor and inadequate – it is so difficult not to gush. John and I thoroughly enjoyed it all, we strolled along and sat down here and there to watch the water and did not get back till past 7 o'clock.

This is a very comfortable hotel and we have a most charming confidential old waiter, who passes various cakes etc. on me and takes quite a fatherly interest in us. He offers me a dish of cakes saying, "you may have any one you like", and the home made ginger bread he assured me was unlike anything I had ever tasted before – so it was I think, in that it was very unlike ginger bread.

14TH AUGUST, WEDNESDAY.
Queen's Hotel, Toronto.

We had another beautiful day at Niagara Falls on Monday; in the morning we walked up the Canadian side and I tried to finish my little sketch. After luncheon we went in the little steamer, "The Maid of The Mist" and went past the falls, we had to be covered with tarpaulin hats and coats, as the mist was rain, as far as drenching went. It was at first difficult to see anything but spray, but we did have a fine view of the falls from the deck of the steamer. Then we took a carriage and drove right up to the top of the Park and, dismissing the carriage, walked back through the Dufferin Islands; it was a beautiful evening and we enjoyed our walk most thoroughly.

Yesterday we left Clifton House for the 9.30 train, we had to wait a very long time at Niagara for the boat but fortunately when it did come, it was not so crowded as the Saturday one.

We got here in time for luncheon and afterwards went over to Cook and found that our passage had been secured for the 29th in the Parisian. The Wyllies found that their expedition down the St. Lawrence was most thoroughly uncomfortable and they strongly advised our taking the train as far as Kingston. We have decided to go by train tonight and have taken the parlour car.

Today we went to the Museum again and had a good look at the old prints drawn, "on the spot" by Richard Short 1761. They are prints of Quebec; there are many very valuable old prints, and pictures of Indians at games etc.

Our bill at Niagara was very heavy, 10£s [sic] for 2 ½ days and we only had two carriages, one for about 20 minutes.

Everything is charged exorbitantly, nothing under a dollar, and our baths were a dollar a day.

16TH AUGUST, FRIDAY.
Windsor Hotel, Montreal [*closed 1981*].

We arrived here yesterday morning and found Major Wyllie in the hall, Katie had been ill at Quebec with a bilious headache and it had worried him so much that he looked quite ill.

Katie and I went to see the Decorative Art & Needlework shop, where we saw some really exquisite work of all kinds and we felt very tempted to go in for several things.

The Wyllies left at 4 o'clock for the lakes George and Champlain, en route for New York.

We had a delightfully comfortable sleeping car from Toronto to Montreal, the best we have had anywhere and a most civil conductor, our old friend from the C.P.R.

Last night there was music in the corridor, piano and fiddle – very fair music so we went to bed rather early.

We went to the Bonsecours Market & Church, and the Cathedral of Notre Dame, the latter is in excellent taste and very handsomely decorated. The market was full of buyers and sellers; I heard a great deal of French spoken and saw a great quantity of fruit, cheese & poultry.

It has been a lovely day, with a shower in the afternoon. Montreal is a most charming City, full of good streets and quaint little squares and pieces of green, with trees everywhere.

18TH AUGUST, SUNDAY.
Windsor Hotel.

This afternoon we went to see the game of Lacrosse; it was a champion match between Ottawa & Montreal. The grounds and the grandstand were crowded, men sat on the top of walls and palings and anywhere they could get any sort of holding. We stood for an hour watching, it was quite impossible to get a seat. Montreal won; the game is a particularly pretty, graceful one to watch, quite a young man's game. The captains apparently don't play, but direct the game.

We drove up to the Mount and had a most lovely drive, there is a splendid view of the City from there; then we visited the Cemetery, which is the largest I have ever seen. It is charmingly situated and full of trees and shrubs and flowers and the place is kept most carefully. I noticed one rather touching little grave, a headstone with some flowers carved on it and "José" written on it, nothing more, no date or age. The French part is quite distinct, one drives through it, but this is not allowed in the English part. There are Stations of the Cross all the way up the drive to the French Cemetery and the gateway is very fine with lovely flowers and turf in front of it. A great many people had arrived with baskets of provisions and were picnicking in the grounds; I noticed one man with a little child having his luncheon by the side of a grave, I thought it must be his wife's.

19TH AUGUST, MONDAY.
Russell Hotel, Ottawa [demolished 1928].

We left Montreal at 8.50 in the morning and reached Ottawa somewhere about 1 o'clock. The country between Montreal & Ottawa is very pretty, but the fields are small and there is rather a look of poverty about the houses, which are nearly all built of wood. Ottawa itself is not a large place, but the buildings are handsome. Government having made it its headquarters, of course the place is rapidly improving.

We went over the Parliament buildings, they are most beautifully situated on the bank of the Ottawa and the view from the terrace over the river, the lumberyards and the surrounding country is very extensive and beautiful. The Parliament houses and Government buildings form a square and are built of grey stone; the grounds are very charmingly laid out and the whole thing is very imposing. Inside there is a most delightful free library filled with valuable & interesting books of all kinds, newspapers and periodicals etc. all available to the public from 10 till 4 p.m.

The Senate House and House of Commons are fine rooms and the stained glass windows & decorations are in good taste. There are 76 Senators I think, and 250 MPs.

After this we took a tram and went out to Rockcliffe to see the Keefers. [*Julia had met old Mrs Keefer travelling on the train between Banff and Toronto.*]

Mr & Mrs Keefer both came out to meet us at the entrance of their pretty place and they were very anxious we should see all the pretty views of the Ottawa River. They have very extensive grounds and a very pretty place. After rambling about with them we all went back by tram to Ottawa and on to the Chaudière Falls and the Saw Mills. Young Mr Keefer showed me his new photographic apparatus before we left. Young Mrs Keefer was a very pretty childish looking little creature though the mother of 4 children, one of 11 years old and as big as herself.

We found the people leaving off work at the Saw Mills so we went all over one, and found it very interesting. The Falls were very fine; the spray drenched one like a young Niagara. We didn't get back to the Hotel till quite late and found dinner over and supper reigning!

20TH AUGUST, TUESDAY.
Windsor Hotel, Montreal.

We arrived here at 8.30 p.m. having spent all day at Ottawa. We went to the Natural History Museum in the morning where they have a very good collection of birds and fossils, and curiosities belonging to the Indians. The birds are very interesting; there was a duck called the wood duck I was particularly delighted with. The animals were few but very good – all Canadian animals – a tiny skunk was very fascinating. The wild goat was a good specimen, and the reindeer. The pieces of carved ivory done by the Indians were very curious and all their masks and barbarous ornaments.

21ST AUGUST, WEDNESDAY.
St. Louis Hotel, Quebec.

We had to get up at 5.30 this morning to catch the 8.10 a.m. train for Quebec. We left Montreal in a grey gloom but found it much worse here. The C.P.R. Station is a long way from the Windsor Hotel. We had a most luxurious parlour car and got to Quebec at 2.30 p.m.; a bride and bridegroom travelled with us in honeymoon attire & looks. We find the Birmingham gentleman & Mysore tea planter are here; our friends from the Yosemite Valley!

After luncheon we strolled round and had a look at the place but the day was not a good one to enjoy Quebec, it was so grey and dull and the streets so muddy. We saw a great number of old guns and had a sort of general impression of the place. This hotel has no bathrooms attached to the rooms.

22ND AUGUST, THURSDAY.
St. Louis Hotel Quebec.

This morning we had rather a skirmish to get up; the one bath available was an ancient tub of great discomfort.

We sallied forth after breakfast and walked up to the Houses of Parliament and then to the Citadel, where we wrote our names in the Governor's book and had a great opportunity of seeing the town from the battlements or ramparts.

It was rather like entering a house from the back door there was so little formality about the Governor's residence. We strolled about Lord Dufferin Terrace and then drove to the Plains of Abraham and saw the monument erected to Wolfe's memory on the spot where he died, we also saw the joint monument to Wolfe and Montcalm in the morning.

[*The Battle of the Plains of Abraham, or Battle of Quebec, was fought on 13th September 1759. The British invasion force under General James Wolfe, 1727–1759, defeated the French under the Marquis de Montcalm; both died of wounds received during the battle.*]

It has been a very fine day except for an hour or two in the afternoon. Quebec has been so constantly burnt that the old buildings are few and it is not at all a bustling, flourishing place, but a pretty, quaint, rather out at the elbows French town. French is most generally spoken though the inhabitants seem to speak English and French equally well.

We do not find this hotel comfortable, indeed the Windsor at Montreal & the Clifton at Niagara Falls have been by far the best hotels we have been in in Canada, though at the latter one we had to pay ½ a dollar for a bath every day. Here there are no baths except the ancient tub and a bath in the barber's shop below! The hotel at Toronto was very dark, the people very, very civil, but it was always very muggy and close and the dining room so hot.

24TH AUGUST, SATURDAY.
St. Louis Hotel, Quebec.

We have had quite a day of sight seeing; it was such a splendid morning that we started off immediately after breakfast for the Montmorency Falls; a long but very pretty drive, cottages all along the road and everything showing French inhabitants. The Falls are very fine, but the chief attraction is the view of Quebec & the Citadel. We were pointed out the ruins of Montcalm's residence in Beauport and we didn't get back till nearly 2 o'clock.

After luncheon we drove to the Lacrosse ground; two clubs were playing very roughly, and having seen one man very severely hit on the head & so injured he couldn't go on playing, we came away rather disgusted. This rough sort of play quite destroys the pleasure of watching the game. We went on to the cricket match where all the Government House party were. Soon afterwards, Sir Henry Loch arrived with his son; we had a long chat with Sir Henry and find that they are on their way to Victoria, Australia, and then going to the Cape.

[*Sir Henry Loch and his family were on their way to Melbourne, Australia where he had been governor since 1884; the Biddulphs had stayed with the Lochs at Government House, Melbourne during their visit to Australia in 1888. This was Sir Henry's last visit to Melbourne before taking up his post as High Commissioner for South Africa and Governor of Cape Colony where he was to remain until 1895. On his return to England in 1895, Sir Henry was created 1st Baron Loch; he died in 1900.*]

Sir Henry introduced Lord Stanley to us, and then Lady Stanley drove off to see Lady Loch. After some chat with Lord Stanley we came back to the hotel where I found a letter waiting for me from Lady Loch and we are going there tomorrow morning.

Barnum's show has met with a terrible railway accident in which 24 horses and 2 elephants have been killed besides other loss, so now it is doubtful if they will arrive here on Monday.

[*The train carrying Barnum & Bailey's Circus had crashed at Potsdam, NY on 22nd August 1889.*]

25TH AUGUST, SUNDAY.
St. Louis Hotel, Quebec.

We went over to the Lochs after breakfast and found them comfortably located at the Florence, clean rooms, good cooking & great civility. We all went to Church together in the same street, a very nice service, and after Church came back to the hotel and chatted for an hour.

We got back at 6.30 o'clock and found the hotel full of Barnum's Circus people.

27TH AUGUST, TUESDAY.
St. Louis Hotel.

Yesterday Lady Loch came over to see us in the morning, and in the afternoon we went to Barnum's Show where I stopped with John till ½ past 4 – it began at 2 o'clock. We thought it very amusing, the dogs especially and the number of things that went on; the great quantity of animals and performers of every kind are astonishing; the crowd was immense and the heat very great. The dog race and the monkeys racing on ponies amused me much. Tightrope dancers, Japanese jugglers, performing sheep, goats, elephants and zebras, all going on rapidly with their tricks, kept the ball rolling.

After dinner we went to the Citadel Ball. It was a very pretty sight, the terrace is too lovely and the Ballroom is a good one. The Stanleys kept on their dais or platform the whole time and did not mix with their guests at all. Lady Stanley looks delightful and he is very popular, but nobody looked as charming as Lady Loch. Miss Lister was a pretty girl in a pretty grey tulle gown with broad pale pink sash & ribbons. Lady Alice Stanley had on a pretty frock too and there were many nice fresh pretty dresses among the quite young ladies. The supper was very nicely arranged and the whole thing went off with a great deal of spirit. We came away at ½ past 12.

We have had so many invitations to gaieties that we are quite unable to accept, picnics, garden parties, dances etc.; tonight we are to attend a dance at the Lt. Governor's, Mons. Angers [Sir August-Réal Angers, 1837–1919, Lieutenant-Governor of Quebec, 1887–1892].

I was much amused at hearing that the proprietor of the Florence Hotel had amassed thousands of dollars by robbing Govt. Contracts & bribing the Municipal Council to keep quiet. He said of himself that he was a robber, but not a white-livered liar and that he would say in Court that he had taken 60,000 dollars out of this, and 40,000 dollars out of that contract, and spent another 20,000 dollars in bribes. He prided himself immensely on his truthfulness and thought his dishonesty not worth discussing!

The newspapers have taken John up and are very patronising to the first officer from India who has registered in Canada, or really Quebec, on his way home.

This afternoon we accomplished a good deal, we went to the C.P. Railway Station and saw the Lochs start for Montreal. Then we met the Forsyths and Mr Forsyth drove us to the Confectioner to get some luncheon, but as there was nothing to drink on the premises and only cakes to eat, we devoured 2 cents worth of cakes and went on to Laliberté [Laliberté, furriers founded 1867]. We spent an hour looking at furs and I ordered a set of mink; cape, hat & muff.

After that we took the ferry and went over to Point Lévis and drove about for an hour. It is an exceedingly picturesque quarter, we passed some delightfully pretty cottages and the view of Quebec is very fine.

John spent a very happy morning at the Cavalry School and in the Parliament Buildings. We have invested in another deck chair, a very expensive business!

28TH AUGUST, WEDNESDAY.
St. Louis Hotel.

We went to Mons. Angers's dance at Spencer Wood last night and did not come home till one o'clock. The dance was very pretty, there were five dancing rooms and as many little rooms for sitting out; the long verandah [sic] was always crowded and the grounds were lighted up and people walked about despite the chilly air.

[Spencer Wood, now known as Parc du Bois-de-Coulonge, was the residence of the Lieutenant-Governor of Quebec until 1966.]

6TH SEPTEMBER, FRIDAY.
S.S. Parisian [SS Parisian, *built by Robert Napier & Sons, Glasgow, 1880, 5,395 tons*].

Our last day in Quebec was a very quiet one for John had such a violent cold he was obliged to go to bed at 3 o'clock in the afternoon. I dined with the Forsyths alone; I had a very pleasant evening, though I did hate so going alone. The Forsyths gave an excellent dinner and the party of 10 were all very sociable.

I got home at 10.30 and had to do all my packing, which kept me up rather late. We got up very early on Thursday 29th and went on board at 8 o'clock, the boat being advertised to start at 9 a.m. However our luggage didn't arrive till a quarter to 9, and many others arrived after that; then we had to wait some time for the Montreal boat as the fog on the river had detained it. We didn't really start till 10 o'clock down the river, and didn't get to Rimouski till 10.30 p.m.

We had a very good time on Friday and Saturday, but on Sunday we were tossed about a little & I was ill all day long. On Saturday afternoon we saw some icebergs, they were small ones and some distance off – one was said to be 100ft high.

We had splendid weather for coming through the St. Lawrence Gulf, which is a difficult piece of navigation and often very foggy. I had the satisfaction of seeing the shores of Newfoundland and since that, we have seen nothing till we arrived at Moville [*County Donegal*] on the Irish coast this morning. We have had head winds and bouts of foggy weather, so that our passage has not been a quick one.

We had a concert yesterday in aid of the Seaman's Home in Liverpool, which brought in a sum of a little under 8£s [*sic*]; the talent of the performers was not overwhelming. A clergyman read Mark Twain in a lugubrious tone and the usual vulgar comic songs and recitations took place – one lady was a good pianist.

This boat is a remarkably steady one and the cooking is very fair, plain and wholesome; but the cabins are too small and badly lighted. The Captain (Captain Ritchie) never appeared at meals till Sunday evening, and has not appeared again since yesterday's dinner. These fogs make some anxiety; last voyage the Parisian was detained 4 days & nights in one.

Epilogue

The Biddulphs landed at Liverpool on 7th September 1889; since leaving England by the 8 o'clock train from Victoria on 15th July 1885 they had spent over four years in India, travelled to Australia, Japan, the United States and Canada, passing many other places en route. How many miles they had travelled in those four years is impossible to guess, but this would not be the end of Julia's travels. In 1892 she returned to India with her husband, where they remained until J.B. retired in 1895. His last two appointments had been as Resident of Gwalior and then Baroda.

For the next ten years or so the Biddulphs would make regular forays to Norway for the salmon fishing. Between November 1902 and March 1903, they would tour the West Indies and in early 1906 they travelled for three months to Portugal via Tenerife.

Julia Biddulph really was a daughter of the empire; Queen Victoria had been on the throne for seven years when Julia was born and she was fifty-six years old when the queen died.

Julia writes in her 1901 journal:

On the 22nd January Queen Victoria died, I can hardly believe it now. She was not long ill, but the rumours from the very beginning of her illness were most disquieting. That evening we were dining with the Masters at Montrose House [Petersham]; Mrs Master would not believe that the Queen was dying but before we left her house we knew for a fact that the Queen was dead, it was dreadfully sad. [John Henry Master JP, 1831–1919, who the Biddulphs had known since India. JH Master had been in the Indian civil service.]

She writes again on 16th April 1901:

Today the public mourning is over and I suppose we are all getting reconciled to King Edward & Queen Alexandra, but hardly.

Julia Biddulph had, I am sure, met her husband during her first visit to India in 1864 and although they did not marry until 1882, it was then that they fell in love. From the day that they married until J.B.'s death on 31st December 1921 they had hardly been apart. On the day that J.B. died, Julia wrote: *My dear John died about 8.30 this evening, he had no suffering. It seems impossible. The separation is so awful.*

Julia Biddulph died on 19th May 1933 aged eighty-nine and is buried beside her husband.

References.

The plates in this book are taken from a Laurie family album, Julia Biddulph's Journals and family papers.

OTHER REFERENCES:
Sir Ranald Martin by Sir Joseph Fayrer, A D Innes & Co London 1897.
Biddulph: Tribes of The Hindoo Koosh.
Biddulph: The Nineteenth and Their Times.
The India List and India Office List.
The Oxford Companion to British History, Professor John Cannon, Oxford University Press 1997.
Australian Dictionary of Biography.
The Dreadnaught Project www.dreadnaughtproject.org
Legion, Canada's Military History Magazine www.legionmagazine.com
The National Army Museum www.nam.ac.uk
British Battles www.britishbattles.com
The Ships List www.theshipslist.com
History by The Yard www.historybytheyard.co.uk
Liverpool Hidden History www.liverpoolhiddenhistory.co.uk
Ancient History Encyclopedia Joshua J Mark 2012 www.ancient.eu
Victoria Cross www.vconline.org.uk
Great Irish People www.greatirishpeople.com
Deogarh Mahal www.deogarhmahal.com
Rajput Provinces of India www.indianrajputs.com
Eternal Mewar www.eternalmewar.in